MEN AND MASCULINITIES

MEN AND MASCULINITIES

Theoretical Foundations and Promising Practices for Supporting College Men's Development

Edited by

Daniel Tillapaugh and Brian L. McGowan

Foreword by Ryan P. Barone

Afterword by Tracy Davis

Routledge
Taylor & Francis Group

NEW YORK AND LONDON

First published 2019 by Stylus Publishing, LLC

First Edition, 2019

Published 2023 by Routledge
605 Third Avenue, New York, NY 10017
4 Park Square, Milton Park, Abingdon, Oxon OX14 4RN

*Routledge is an imprint of the Taylor & Francis Group,
an informa business*

Library of Congress Cataloging-in-Publication Data
Names: Tillapaugh, Daniel, 1979- editor. | McGowan, Brian Lamont, editor.
Title: Men and masculinities : theoretical foundations and promising
    practices for supporting college mens development / edited by Daniel
    Tillapaugh and Brian McGowan ; foreword by Ryan P. Barone ; afterword
    by Tracy L. Davis.
Description: First edition. | Sterling, Virginia : Stylus Publishing, [2019] |
    Includes bibliographical references and index.
Identifiers: LCCN 2018051053 |
    | ISBN 9781620369302 (cloth) |
    ISBN 9781620369319 (paperback) |
Subjects: LCSH: Men--Education, Higher--United States. | Male college
    students--Services for--United States. | Masculinity--Social aspects--
    United States. | Sex differences in education--United States. | Academic
    achievement--United States. | College dropouts--United States--Prevention.
    LCC LC1397 .M44 2019 | DDC 378.1/98--dc23

LC record available at https://lccn.loc.gov/2018051053

ISBN 13: 978-1-62036-931-9 (pbk)
ISBN 13: 978-1-62036-930-2 (hbk)
ISBN 13: 978-1-00-344598-2 (ebk)

DOI: 10.4324/9781003445982

For my parents, Allan and Nancy,
who model what it means to be of service to others
and have given me the love needed to march
to the beat of a different drum.

—DWT

To my parents, Hill and Arlene,
you have been my greatest source of inspiration
and strength. Rest in heaven.

—BLM

CONTENTS

FOREWORD

*Learning to wear a mask (that word already embedded in the term "masculinity")
is the first lesson in patriarchal masculinity that a boy learns. He learns that his core
feelings cannot be expressed if they do not conform to the acceptable behaviors sexism
defines as male. Asked to give up the true self in order to realize the patriarchal ideal,
boys learn self-betrayal early and are rewarded for these acts of soul murder.*

(hooks, 2004, p. 153)

I have been committing small acts of soul murder since I first realized I was a boy, learning not to cry, to fabricate confidence, and to view every social interaction as a competition. I still commit these acts at work and at home, when my insecurity motivates me to be inappropriately assertive in a meeting, or when my tendency to make some family decisions without consulting others arises. Higher education leaders are searching to better understand the theoretical and epistemological underpinnings that inform destructive hegemonic masculinity. We see the negative impact of hegemonic masculinity on people of any gender identity across colleges and universities, inside and outside classrooms. Although we need not seek formulaic best practices (Nicolazzo, 2017), strategies for how to engage thoughtfully in our unique institutional contexts are needed as we design educational experiences intended to unravel the destructive impacts of hegemonic masculinity and other toxic masculinities on individual, group, and institutional levels. Building on important and diverse related scholarship, this book helps higher education and society writ large engage in reflection and subsequently informed design for interventions, programs, and the narrative and culture shifting needed for all students to realize their fullest potential.

In 2004 I led my first workshop for a group of men in a historically White fraternity about gender socialization and interpersonal violence. In the dark fraternity house basement with 60 men, I ironically performed hegemonic masculinity as I attempted to engage these men in critical reflection about privilege, power, and oppression. I was stoic, assertive, and aggressive, shutting down men who offered trite rape myths and immature jokes about women. I did harm in that workshop and may have undermined any educational value because of the mask I used. The body of literature I used in 2004 to inform my programming concerned with masculinities was mostly from second-wave feminist writers. My work was not intersectional; it was myopic and relied on a limited body of knowledge related to social psychology and bystander intervention in higher education. Today, we have a stronger theoretical and practical knowledge base for grounding programming and activities, and I hope our efforts as a field have evolved. This book brings together thoughtful scholars in this evolving field of masculinities studies in higher education and is beautifully timed to inform student affairs practitioners about assumptions, constructs, and practices for programs like the one I conducted in 2004, which will help predict productive outcomes.

Although this book is timely, it is also overdue, as the daily impacts of violent masculinity are felt on our college campuses and beyond. On individual campuses as a conduct officer, academic adviser, residence hall director, and campus activities professional, I have seen scores of examples of harmful behavior committed by men rooted in insecurity and the performance of hegemonic masculinity. On the national level, Elliot Rodger, the 22-year-old man and former University of California, Santa Barbara, student who killed 6 students near the campus and sent 7 to the hospital, gave us a valuable and tragic insight into the danger of hegemonic masculinity and misogyny when he wrote,

> You forced me to suffer all my life, now I will make you all suffer. I waited a long time for this. I'll give you exactly what you deserve, all of you. All you girls who rejected me, looked down upon me, you know, treated me like scum while you gave yourselves to other men. (Valenti, 2014, para. 8)

The intersections of hegemonic masculinity, racism, and White supremacy were front and center when Dylann Roof killed nine Black parishioners at Emanuel African Methodist Episcopal Church in South Carolina in 2015 after spending an hour praying with them. Roof has since said, "I would like to make it crystal clear, I do not regret what I did. I am not sorry. I have not shed a tear for the innocent people I killed" (Zapotosky, 2017, para. 2). The impacts of remorseless acts of violence stemming from gender socialization and a larger oppression-based social milieu are felt across U.S. college campuses. The theory and strategies needed for interrupting and unlearning hegemonic masculinity, which are provided in this volume, are desperately needed.

For years, women, people of color, queer people, trans* people, and people with disabilities have organized to resist the impacts of violent hegemonic masculinity, typically as performed by White heterosexual men. Most recently, the #MeToo movement has brought sexism, misogyny, and interpersonal violence by men to the mainstream media at a level previously unseen. The national and international #MeToo movement, introduced in 2006 by Tarana Burke, an African American activist from the Bronx in New York, and popularized by mostly White women, including many well-known celebrities (Guerra, 2017), has created an expanded platform to help motivate cultural change. Notably, many men with privileged identities have profited from speaking, consulting, and writing on the topics related to #MeToo and men and masculinities. I have been a campus host and signed several generous speaking contracts without intentionally thinking about a more equitable allocation of institutional resources to people with less identity-based privilege. Critical analysis of institution resource allocations related to work on broader social justice efforts of men and masculinities is essential for realizing congruent and sustained cultural change.

The work of culture change surrounding men and masculinities must happen pervasively, consistently, and at all levels of an institution. Museus and Jayakumar (2012) remind us that culture, unlike environments or climate, which are static and decontextualized, must directly address assumptions hindering institutional transformation. These cultural assumptions include the following:

1. The natural occurrence assumption: It's the way we do things around here.
2. The displaced responsibility assumption: If we offer it, they will come.
3. The out-of-sight-out-of-mind assumption: Everything must be ok.
4. The specialization assumption: I have my job to do, and you have yours.
5. The incompatibility assumption: If we do this, it compromises excellence. (Museus & Jayakumar, 2012, pp. 17–20)

If higher education is to take advantage of the contributions in this book to help inform sustainable cultural change related to toxic and violent masculinities, we must be prepared to respond to each of these short-sighted assumptions that impede our change efforts. The status quo is powerful, as we are reminded by Pasque (2010):

> Higher education leaders need to pay more attention to the ways in which we are perpetuating or interrupting the status quo that is not functioning effectively. Intention is not enough; higher education leaders need to speak dangerous truths as these discourses have the potential to impact policy, procedures, and—in turn—people's daily lives. (p. 176)

With the insights and guidance provided in this text, higher education leaders are equipped to move beyond good intentions to shift oppressive institutional cultures.

The text you are about to read does several things particularly well. As a practitioner scholar who has been involved in program design, implementation, and assessment for two decades, my analysis is that this book does a brilliant job of providing context along with practical ideas and strategies to be adapted and implemented regardless of institutional type. The contributors present a case for passion, commitment, and high standards for a cultural shift to occur immediately and do not fall prey to incrementalism. This book represents high standards from all the contributors, with appropriate impatience and the wisdom of experience, knowing that efforts in shifting oppressive cultures are complex and must be viewed as a process and a goal. The intentional selection of the contributors and chapters also reflects the evolving nature of the national work related to men and masculinities and the increasing recognition that these efforts must be intersectional. It is not acceptable, as it has never been, to have programs, samples, authors, or practitioners with homogenous identities. We need to acknowledge the limitations of the many men and masculinities authors who themselves are heterosexual cis White men like myself. The text is a great model for these intentional perspectives, offering as compulsory to our analysis and work embracing and engaging identities intersecting with gender.

Daniel Tillapaugh and Brian L. McGowan, along with the other contributors to this book, have provided an exceptional resource for higher education practitioners. They have perfectly balanced breadth and depth as they constructed this book, serving as a foundation and a blueprint, in a manner accessible to staff at all levels of a higher education institution, spanning every sector and institution type. I hope readers will digest this content with the same sense of immediacy and passion shown by the contributors. This struggle is not only essential for us as we aim to construct the most welcoming and inclusive campus experiences for students in the twenty-first century but also an effort required for the figurative and literal survival for the souls of boys, men, and all who are in our community of learners.

Ryan P. Barone
Assistant Vice President for Student Success
Colorado State University

References

Guerra, C. (2017, 17 October). Where'd the "Me Too" come from? Activist Tarana Burke, long before hashtags. *Boston Globe*. Retrieved from https://www.bostonglobe.com/lifestyle/2017/10/17/alyssa-milano-credits-activist-tarana-burke-with-founding-metoo-movement-years-ago/o2Jv29v6ljObkKPTPB9KGP/story.html hooks, b. (2004). *The will to change: Men, masculinity, and love.* New York, NY: Washington Square Press.

Museus, S. D., & Jayakumar, U. M. (Eds.). (2012). *Creating campus cultures: Fostering success among racially diverse student populations.* New York, NY: Routledge.

Nicolazzo, Z. (2017). *Trans* in college: Transgender students' strategies for navigating campus life and the institutional politics of inclusion.* Sterling, VA: Stylus.

Pasque, P. A. (2010). *American higher education, leadership, and policy: Critical issues and the public good.* New York, NY: Palgrave Macmillan.

Valenti, J. (2014, 24 May). Elliot Roger's California shooting spree: Further proof that misogyny kills. *The Guardian.* Retrieved from https://www.theguardian.com/commentisfree/2014/may/24/elliot-rodgers-california-shooting-mental-health-misogyny

Zapotosky, M. (2017, 4 January). Charleston church shooter: "I would like to make it crystal clear, I do not regret what I did." *Washington Post.* Retrieved from https://www.washingtonpost.com/world/national-security/charleston-church-shooter-i-would-like-to-make-it-crystal-clear-i-do-not-regret-what-i-did/2017/01/04/05b0061e-d1da-11e6-a783-cd3fa950f2fd_story.html?noredirect=on&utm_term=.e177cebed485

ACKNOWLEDGMENTS

First of all, as coeditors of this volume, we want to express our gratitude to you, the reader. We hope you picked up this book because you have a genuine interest in making a difference in the lives of college men. This work is critical and vital. We hope the information contained in this text provides you with greater clarity and insights into what we know about college men and their development and that you will take direct action, using these theories, to effect positive change in our higher education communities.

We are incredibly lucky to have such talented contributors without whom this book would not be possible. Our contributing authors share their expertise and know-how, and we are grateful for their efforts as we moved from outlines to drafts to final manuscripts. We were intentional about our desire to have a scholar practitioner who has spent a great deal of his career caring deeply about the issues of college men and masculinities begin this text; we are thankful that Ryan P. Barone agreed to take this on for us. Likewise, we wanted the final word of this book to be from someone who has been a model of genuine curiosity and personal growth through his own scholarship on college men and masculinities to so many of us who are beginning this work. Tracy Davis has been an incredible resource and sounding board for both of us, and we are indebted to him for his contribution here.

Whether through our scholarship or our practice, we have benefited greatly from the conversations and resources shared by our colleagues associated with American College Personnel Association's (ACPA) Coalition on Men and Masculinities and NASPA–Student Affairs Professionals in Higher Education's Men and Masculinities Knowledge Community. We continue to be thankful for these affinity groups, which make space for critical conversations about the development of college men.

In particular, Dan wishes to thank his students at the University of Maine and California Lutheran University, who continue to help him keep thinking about the complexities of college men and their lived experiences. Additionally, he thanks Yesenia Ibarra, his departmental graduate research assistant, for her help in checking references, finding citations, and helping whenever needed. He acknowledges his dear friends Z Nicolazzo, Edlyn Vallejo Peña, Paige Haber-Curran, Rachel Wagner, and D. Chase J. Catalano for being his brain trust, providing support and frankness throughout this process. Dan also is eternally grateful to his coeditor, Brian L. McGowan, for being willing to come on board with this idea of coediting a book and being a partner in making that happen. Finally, he expresses his love and appreciation to his husband, Martin Fernandez, for being his companion on this adventure, encouraging him when needed, and putting up with the stress and anxieties that come along with life.

Brian wishes to thank Dan Tillapaugh for extending the invitation to serve as his coeditor. Brian is forever grateful for Dan's leadership and support as he lost his parents during this book project. Brian also appreciates the overwhelming support from some of the contributing authors, colleagues, and friends. Brian appreciates his colleague Reginald Blockett for being an amazing thought partner throughout this process as well. Brian would like to express his gratitude to the countless number of educators across the country who are actively working to create campus environments that are inclusive of all masculinities and gender expressions. Your commitment served as inspiration for this book.

Finally, a sincere thank-you to John von Knorring and the entire Stylus Publishing team for their support and belief in this work. Special thanks are extended to Alexandra Hartnett for her gracious help throughout the production process. We are indebted to everyone at Stylus for your efforts in making this text come to fruition.

Advancing Men and Masculinities Work

Daniel Tillapaugh and Brian L. McGowan

D avis and Laker (2004) issued a clarion call for college student educators working in student and academic affairs to learn how to better support the men attending their colleges and universities. They argued that individuals working with college men needed to keep 3 foundational questions in mind for their professional practice: "Are they consistent with what we know about developmental theory and the socially constructed contours that shape men's development? Do they recognize important differences among men and masculinities? Do they balance challenge and support?" (p. 49). In the 15 years since their work was published, these questions remain essential. You may be wondering why we think these questions are still relevant. Well, much of that can be answered merely by doing a quick scan of higher education and our larger global society.

The National Center for Education Statistics (2018) reported that between 2000 and 2016, college student enrollment increased from 13.2 to 16.9 million students, a jump of 28%. Of that number, in the fall semester of 2016, 44% (or 7.4 million) were identified as male students (National Center for Education Statistics, 2018). Yet, there has been a great deal of concern about the retention and persistence of college men, particularly Black, Latinx, and Native American Indian men at 2-year and 4-year institutions as these populations are at greater risk for stopping out of college (Musu-Gillette, de Brey, McFarland, Hussar, Sonnenberg, & Wilkinson-Flicker, 2017; Shapiro et al., 2017). Of the students starting college in the fall semester of 2008, only 35% of Black men, 39% of American Indian and Alaska Native men, and 49% of Hispanic men graduated with a degree from their institution within 6 years (Musu-Gillette et al., 2017). Additionally, for those students who do persist, we know that men are overrepresented in student conduct cases (Harper, Harris, & Mmeje, 2005), particularly because of negative behaviors associated with drugs and alcohol (Kimmel, 2008; Wechsler & Wuethrich, 2002). With the #MeToo and #ItsOnUs movements and statistics of sexual violence on college campuses and off, we continue to have an epidemic of assault, rape, and other forms of violence perpetrated most often by men (Carr & VanDeusen, 2004; Harris & Linder, 2017; Young, Desmarais, Baldwin, & Chandler, 2017). These wide array of issues, often formulated and grounded through the adherence to hegemonic masculine gender role socialization, or more commonly discussed as toxic masculinity, are alarming and troubling.

Given this information, research and practice have shifted in the past two decades to focus on college men and their development. Scholars have continued to explore aspects of college men's development across a variety of domains (see chapters 1 and 2 for a richer discussion of this). This research has been useful in helping college student educators obtain a clearer understanding of not only how young men are socialized prior to their arrival to campus but also, and perhaps more important, how the collegiate environment becomes a training ground for the socialization of masculinities by students, their peers, the media, and their educational institutions. Harper and Harris (2010a) argued that individuals working in higher education have a moral responsibility to help young men understand not only why and how they have been socialized to their gender identity but also what their gender identity and sense of masculinity means for their future. That is exactly why we wanted to publish this book. In this introduction, we introduce the ways men's programming work on campus has become professionalized and discuss what that means for practitioners working to support college men and their development. Additionally, we discuss aspects of how this professionalization has provided helpful and promising practices for college men. Last, we discuss the ways we envisioned you, the reader, using this text and introduce you to the content that remains in the pages ahead.

College Men and Their Development

As we have already alluded to, there has been a significant increase in attention to the developmental needs and issues college men are experiencing during their time in higher education. To be sure, there is a direct need for higher education professionals, faculty, staff, and administrators, to be cognizant of the ways men are grappling with the socialization of masculinities in their lives and the often confusing and sometimes conflicting messages about what it means to be a man in today's world. In this section, we address some of the common myths and assumptions about college men, the need for intersectional perspectives of understanding gender alongside college men's other social and personal identities, and a brief discussion of the terminology we use for this book and our rationale.

Is It Really All Doom and Gloom?

A quick Internet search for news stories on college men results in head-lines such as "Why Men Are the New College Minority" (Marcus, 2017), "Men Pay a Steep Price When It Comes to Masculinity" (Destagir, 2017), and "The End of Men" (Rosin, 2010). Todd Starnes (2017), a commenta-tor with Fox News, published an opinion piece titled "'Toxic Masculinity'? Dude, Now America's Universities Are Turning Men Into Women." Within, Starnes discusses some of the programs that are specifically designed to involve college men in engaging with and talking about issues of hegem-onic, toxic, or unhealthy aspects of masculinity and how they can make other choices that may be healthier. Starnes said, "In today's reengineered version of manhood, guys no longer have friends—they have bromances and they settle disputes by hugging it out" (para. 10). We ask, is it really that horrible to actually hug it out after a dispute? Is it so hideous for indi-viduals to imagine a world where men could actually engage in some sort of intimate physical act? Of course, Starnes is clear; he rejects the notion of having men in college think critically about masculinity, but his discussion of college programs and services involving masculinity does not provide the proper context of their intent or outcomes, nor is his description of these programs accurate.

As individuals who study men and masculinities in higher education, we have very real concerns about the ways men are socialized in our soci-ety and the pressure cooker that institutions of higher education can be in that process. Watching the nightly news, we hear and see news stories of groups of men (and women) marching in Charlottesville, Virginia, as part of a White nationalist movement (Spencer & Stolberg, 2017). Young men, par-ticularly those who are White, perpetrate violence on their college campuses, sometimes with guns and other weapons, because of revenge or perceived slights, such as Elliot Rodger at the University of California, Santa Barbara, who had ties to the men's rights movement and who murdered six people and seriously wounded seven others (Valenti, 2014). Additionally, there are legitimate causes for us to be concerned considering the number of young men who experience hazing from other men in their student organizations, fraternities, or athletic teams and who often do not deem such acts as vio-lence because these rituals or rites are considered important mile markers of being inducted into a group or as a real member of the group (Allan & Madden, 2008).

As Kimmel (2008) stated in his groundbreaking book, *Guyland*:

> College becomes the arena in which young men so relentlessly seem to act out, seem to take the greatest risks, and do some of the stupidest things.

Directionless and often clueless, they rely increasingly on their peers to usher them into adulthood and validate their masculinity. And their peers often have some interesting plans for what they will have to endure to prove that they are real men. (p. 43)

Kimmel's comments may truly reflect the patterns of the narratives of the hundreds of men he interviewed as a part of his study. Yet, we seemingly have a different take on college men. The men we work and engage with do not seem to be the bumbling, clueless people Kimmel makes them out to be. Instead, we see many of the men on our campuses posturing, acting out what they've been told to do, or more often emulating the men in their lives and what they do. Many of these men are craving conversations and true, genuine connection with other people in their lives, yet they are not always equipped with the tools necessary to build those relationships or even act authentically because upholding restrictive masculine norms can impede one's ability to be genuine and open with others.

To return to the question we pose at the start of this section, Is it all doom and gloom for college men? Certainly, challenges exist for men entering colleges and universities today. We cannot deny that. However, we also know that many men are finding connections, getting involved, and participating fully in campus life. Although we maintain there are challenges for college men, not all of these men face challenges that disrupt their ability to be successful. We also acknowledge that much of our understanding of college men and masculinities has historically centered White men (Harper & Harris, 2010b; Kimmel, 2008; Laker & Davis, 2011), and there is a great need for more intersectional perspectives on men in higher education.

The Need for Intersectional Perspectives on College Men

Given the past scholarship and attention paid to masculinity that upholds White dominant views, it is essential for college student educators to understand how identity convergence plays a significant role in college men's holistic sense of self. As Tarrant and Katz (2008) stated, "Masculinity comes in many forms and packages and these multiple masculinities are informed, limited, and modified by race, ethnicity, class background, sexual orientation, and personal predilections" (p. 10). As a result, college student educators need to understand the ways one's social and personal identities play a role in shaping college men's perspectives and worldviews on masculinity. For example, a queer Filipino 18-year-old man attending his local community college may have a very different notion of what masculinity means to him compared to his peer who is a middle-aged adult learner, father of 3, and returning to college after a 20-year military career. The various agents of socialization, including peers, family members, religion, educational institutions, and the media, often inform these perspectives on masculinity. Therefore, it is essential to know that men attending colleges and universities are also affected by the institutional types and environments where they live, work, and study.

We believe there is an imperative need to examine and understand college men as multifaceted individuals with unique multiple social and personal identities rather than one monolithic group. Our thinking is informed by Crenshaw's (1991) concept of intersectionality; focused on looking at the issues and concerns of Black women, Crenshaw argued that "the intersection of racism and sexism factors into Black women's lives in ways that cannot be captured wholly by looking at the race or dimensions of those experiences separately" (p. 1244). As a result, intersectionality offers a nuanced understanding of how various interlocking forms of power systemically create conditions of power, privilege, and oppression that affect individuals and their understanding of their multiple social identities (Bowleg, 2008; Crenshaw, 1991; Mitchell, Simmons, & Greyerbiehl, 2014). Therefore, sexism, genderism, heterosexism, ableism, and other forms of oppression contribute to tensions experienced and felt by individuals who hold multiple dominant and subordinate identities (Bowleg, 2008; Mitchell et al., 2014). Therefore, it is not surprising that many gender scholars have used intersectionality as a lens and conceptual framework for their work as Robbins and McGowan (2016) noted. They gave three reasons intersectionality has been a popular and useful tool to examine gender and gender identity with college students: the interconnections between gender and other forms of identity; the fact that social systems and structures shape gender and other forms of identity; and the rationale that gender is a socially constructed concept shaped and constructed by peoples' performance of gender. These concepts are discussed in greater depth in chapters 2 and 4.

A Word About Terminology

As we have stated, this text is deliberate about focusing on the gender identity development of college men and the ways these students grapple with the concepts of masculinity. As a result, we have asked our contributors to be conscious about the language in these pages. In particular, the terms *male* and *males* are understood as identifiers of sex, and *man* and *men* are gender markers (Lev, 2004). Likewise, the terms *masculine* and *feminine* are connected to one's gender role socialization (Lev, 2004). Patton, Renn, Guido, and Quaye (2016) stated, "When working with college students it is important to recognize that sex and gender, while very closely related, are not synonymous, and students' gender cannot be assumed in all cases to match what is expected based on their sex" (p. 176).

We are purposeful in using the term *men* throughout this book because we are asking readers to consider their professional practice with college men through the lens of gender rather than the lens of sex. In fact, we argue that if we use the term *males*, we are doing a disservice because ultimately by focusing on sex we are essentializing masculinity and manhood in the body or a biologically determined idea rather than understanding gender (and thus being a man) as a socially constructed idea that is performed (Connell, 2005; Jourian, 2017). In particular, when we use the term *men* we include all students who identify as men, whereas the previous literature on college men and masculinities has often equated an incorrect fallacy of "male (assigned at birth) equals (cisgender) man equals masculine" (Jourian, 2017, p. 247). This connects to the viewpoints of Wagner, Catalano, and Tillapaugh (2018) who state, "Failure to consider who fits the category of men, and constructing research that precludes inclusion of all possible men and masculinities, actively harms existent community members through erasure and invisibility and prevents the flourishing of emancipatory gendered futures" (p. 65). We find this type of marginalization extremely problematic and instead argue for a more gender-expansive view of who is included in the aggregate use of *men*. These concepts are discussed in more depth in chapter 1. One small caveat: Throughout the following chapters, if the contributors use the word *male*, they are referring to past scholarship that used that term specifically.

Professionalization of Programs and Services for College Men on Campus

Since the early 2000s, increased attention has been paid to the experiences of men in college and interest has been building among college student educators on how to begin to create programs, initiatives, and services geared to this population. During this period, the scholarship examining college men and their development has been increasing, which has informed and shaped the aforementioned programs and services. Additionally, key professional development opportunities in the form of professional associations or affinity groups as well as conferences are focusing on college men. In this chapter, we provide some background on each of these points when framing the professionalization of programs and services for college men in higher education.

Campus-Based Work and Programming

In the 1990s there seemed to be a growing dichotomy in understanding and making meaning of masculinity. The men's rights movements, including organizations such as the Promise Keepers, were acting out and espousing particular messages rooted in hegemonic masculine norms and beliefs, particularly evangelical views of masculinity informed by the Bible (Levant, 1997). Another faction—the mythopoetic men's movement—was formed as a call to reclaim masculinity by men who had felt diminished by modern society. Driven by self-help–based retreats and workshops, the mythopoetic men's movement was ultimately asking men to engage in masculinity through storytelling and spiritual endeavors (Kimmel & Kaufman, 1994; Levant, 1997). A third group tended to be men who were interested in engaging in pro-feminist work or as allies with women in making positive social change concerning gender and masculinity (Canon, 2004). This movement has historically informed much of the men's studies work happening in colleges and universities, particularly in campus-based programming and services geared to college men and masculinities.

In the early 1990s, a number of programs geared to engage college men in sexual violence prevention began to form. For example, Alan Berkowitz (1994), a well-known scholar and practitioner on sexual violence prevention, began to examine and advocate for training on sexual violence prevention with all-men audiences. He gave the following rationale for such experiences, saying that these training sessions

> allow men to speak openly without fear of judgment or criticism by women, make it less likely that men will be passive or quiet, and avoid the gender-based polarization that may reinforce men's rape-prone attitudes. In addition, a diversity of opinions and viewpoints can be expressed, reflecting men's variety of attitudes and beliefs about appropriate sexual relationships and allowing participants to deconstruct the monolithic image of masculinity the media have presented to them. (p. 36)

This type of program then influenced others about such practices, including the Mentors in Violence Prevention Program (Katz, 1995; Kilmartin & Berkowitz, 2005). Today many men's-only prevention programs on college campuses focus on the eradication of rape culture and sexual violence, such as the California State University, Northridge's (CSUN, n.d.) MenCARE (Creating Attitudes for Rape-Free Environments) or Northwestern University's (NU, n.d.) Men Against Rape and Sexual Assault (MARS). These programs are all similar in concept to the Men's Project, a bystander intervention program geared to college men on sexual violence prevention (Stewart, 2014). Yet, as Harris and Linder (2017) argued, the statistics on sexual violence on campus have stayed relatively consistent for a number of years; this fact inevitably raises the questions of whether these types of programs are truly having a campuswide impact on eradicating sexual violence. This is not to minimize the good work and outcomes that can come from the learning of the men who participate in such programs, but ultimately one knows that many of the college men who might most need this type of programming are the very ones who do not seek it.

In addition to programs focused on sexual violence prevention, some colleges and universities have expanded their work to support men and their development. Dialogue-based programs are commonly held on campus to help men make sense of masculinity and the ways it can create healthy and unhealthy outcomes in their lives. Some campuses have student organizations designed for college men to do self-work on their gender identity. For instance, Trinity College, in Hartford, Connecticut, has a student organization called the Masculinity Group, which brings together college men to engage in healthier and more inclusive aspects of masculinity (Trinity College, n.d.). At some colleges and universities, men's retreats are a way of creating community for men to reflect on their gender identity and masculinity and form bonds with each other as they unpack and unlearn hegemonic masculine norms in their lives. Colleges and universities today provide a host of various services and programs that are crafted specifically to help their students who identify as men think critically about their gender and the ways masculinity can be detrimental and also very helpful to them. In part three of this book, the contributing authors expand further on some of the particular delivery methods you might choose to implement on your own campus.

The Evolution of Scholarship

In conjunction with the proliferation of campus programming for college men and masculinities, research and scholarship on college men and masculinities has increased. The late 1990s and early years of the twenty-first century brought about emergent research looking at college men through the lens of gender and masculinity, contextualizing the ways the college environment socialized young men (e.g., see Davis, 2002). Cuyjet (1997) explored pertinent issues and concerns on the development and success of African American college men in higher education. Seven years later, Kellom (2004) published a monograph on supporting the development of college men. Focused on addressing men's behaviors and development in college, this monograph offered key implications and recommendations to college student educators on how to connect men to their academic curriculum and address behavioral issues among college men (Kellom, 2004). Kimmel's (2008) large-scale study on the experiences of (mostly White) college men was an important contribution illuminating some of the critical challenges and obstacles men between the ages of 18 and 26 face in contemporary U.S. society. This was followed closely thereafter by Harper and Harris (2010b) and Laker and Davis (2011). Both of these works not only expanded on the central ideas in Kimmel's study but also forwarded a more intersectional perspective particularly in light of the ways that other forms of identities (i.e., race, disability, social class) affect college men's lived experiences in higher education.

A plethora of scholarship in the form of peer-reviewed journal articles has explored various dimensions of college men's development. Much of this scholarship is expanded on throughout this book, given the theory-to-practice philosophy shared by all of the contributing authors. In particular, we encourage you to read chapters 1 and 2 closely to understand the ways the scholarship of men and masculinities is particularly positioned through an epistemological viewpoint and how that affects your own professional practice and our collective understanding of how college men develop during their time in their educational institutions. The scholarship of our field also is promoted and shared through professional development opportunities, particularly in our associations and their conferences. In the next sections, we discuss particular associations or affinity groups and their conferences that center issues and concerns pertaining to college men.

Association History

Several professional associations and affinity groups are dedicated to the advancement of research and practice on men and masculinities, and a couple are directly focused on issues pertaining to college men. In the period of second-wave feminism that began in the 1960s, there was an incredible amount of attention to advancing gender equity and parity along with a parallel movement of men interested in being allies to women and their movement for equal rights (Digby, 1998). The ripple effect of this movement was also experienced in higher education professional associations. In the late 1970s, a workshop at Northern Illinois University brought together a group of higher education administrators to discuss commonly held issues experienced across genders. Led by Cynthia Johnson and Murray Scher, the workshop space was the impetus for what would ultimately become the Standing Committee for Men, associated with American College Personnel Association (ACPA) (Canon, 2004). In the short time after this workshop, members of ACPA, which was still a subsidiary of the American Personnel and Guidance Association at that time, began to advocate for programming on "what it means to be a male, how to explore being male, and how that experience impacts women and other groups" (Canon, 2004, p. 2). From there, the Standing Committee for Men, now known as the Coalition on Men and Masculinities, was established in 1984, although this caused contention among some ACPA members who were distrustful of the purpose of such a group. On the twentieth anniversary of the group, Canon said,

> It is important to note here that the males involved in working to establish the Standing Committee for Men in these early years were strongly committed to the feminist movement, and were very much inclined to view androgyny as a positive and useful model for male development. (p. 2)

This mission allowed the Standing Committee for Men to garner support from other identity-based entity groups within ACPA's organizational structure, including the previously established Standing Committee for Women (Canon, 2004).

Since that time, higher education professional associations have focused on college men and masculinities issues. In the summer of 2005 NASPA–Student Affairs Professionals in Higher Education formally approved the Men and Masculinities Knowledge Community (MMKC) as an affinity group focused on the dissemination of information pertaining to men's development in college. In his materials to NASPA discussing the rationale for the MMKC's existence, Laker (2005) wrote:

> In order to make any progress with male student development, we must prepare CSP [college student personnel] staff to understand the theoretical basis of this standard, and we must provide training and support in training and supervisory relationships so that this knowledge informs practice. It is my view that the foremost task to be accomplished in order to facilitate male student development is the capacity of these students to relate authentically to one another. (p. 9)

This emphasis on working to educate student affairs professionals on the specific and unique needs of college men continues to be a central theme of the MMKC's goals and vision.

Although ACPA's Coalition on Men and Masculinities and NASPA's MMKC have had a long-standing tradition of centering college men and their development, other professional association groups also have had a keen interest in men and masculinities issues. Founded in 1991, the American Men's Studies Association brought together scholars focused on men and masculinities to share insights from their research and implications for professional practice (Doyle & Femiano, 1999). Likewise, the Society for the Psychological Study of Men and Masculinities (also known as Division 51), an affinity group of the American Psychological Association, began in 1995 (Berkowitz, 2005). Division 51 brings together scholars and practitioners in psychology who want to identify the ways toxic masculinity is detrimental to boys and men and help them live healthier lives (Berkowitz, 2005). Both of these professional groups often provide scholarship and programming that are informed by and address issues pertaining to college men and their gender development, particularly through professional development opportunities.

Conferences

In addition to professional associations geared toward college men and masculinities, conferences have been instituted across the country to help provide tools and resources to college student educators interested in supporting men and their development on campus. Jason Laker, the founding chair of NASPA's MMKC, helped found the inaugural Institute on College Males in May 2007 (NASPA, 2017). Now called the Conference on College Men, this biennial conference, hosted jointly by ACPA and NASPA, brings together individuals across the country for a two and a half days to "challenge attendees to critically reflect upon how their own identification and expression of gender influences their work with college and university students while also treating them to the most recent scholarship and services in the field" (NASPA, 2017, para. 1).

In addition to the Conference on College Men, many campuses have established masculinity conferences for their students. For example, Oregon State University's (2017) Diversity and Cultural Engagement Office has hosted an annual Examining Masculinities Conference for the past six years. Likewise, some conferences intersect multiple perspectives and topics, such as the Texas Male Student Leadership Summit, a two-day conference geared toward men of color from high schools, community colleges, and four-year colleges and universities across the state (Texas Education Consortium for Male Students of Color, 2017). Similarly, some regional associations or affinity groups also conduct professional development workshops, such as NASPA's MMKC, which has often hosted drive-in (or one-day) conferences for members of its regional network groups. Professional organizations, such as the American's Men Studies Association and the American Psychological Association, do not specifically focus on college men but often have practice-based or research sessions that address aspects of college men's development and understanding masculinity and its socialization in higher education. The impetus of this book originated with our attendance and participation at these conferences and programs.

Overview of This Book

As colleagues, we met and connected through ACPA's Coalition on Men and Masculinities. Daniel Tillapaugh served as the chair of this affinity group from 2012 to 2016, and Brian L. McGowan served as the group's scholar in residence. The coalition serves as a space for individuals who are engaged in supporting the development of college men and their masculinities to come together, share insights, and exchange ideas and information on how to best support college men. Throughout Tillapaugh's tenure as chair of this group, he received e-mails or phone calls from colleagues across the country (and even internationally) who would often ask him where they should start with this work. Similarly, as a scholar and consultant, McGowan would often be asked a similar question by campus colleagues. Ultimately, we both suggest starting with the literature.

Indeed, incredibly helpful texts exist, written by esteemed colleagues, about college men and masculinities. For instance, we often direct colleagues interested in professional development through readings to review the following:

- Connell (2005)
- Dancy (2012)
- Harper and Harris (2010b)
- Kimmel (2008)
- Kimmel and Messner (2007)
- Laker and Davis (2011)
- Pascoe (2011)

All these texts are wonderful contributions to the knowledge base on men and masculinities, particularly the ways young men are socialized over the course of their lives. If you have not read them or do not have them for your bookshelves yet, we encourage you to acquire them even though they do not directly answer the earlier question we are often asked.

The content of those books may shape and inform how professionals in higher education understand the socialization of young boys and men, but they never directly give helpful direction or guidance to professionals on where to start in their work. As a result of those conversations,

Tillapaugh started to believe in the need for this book, a how-to manual of sorts for individuals in higher education—students, staff, faculty, or administrators—who want to figure out ways to support college men and their development. Our hope as coeditors is that the information in this book provides readers with options to consider how to best develop programs, services, and initiatives that may meaningfully meet the needs of your specific students. There is no one-size-fits-all approach to men and masculinities work and no magic wand for getting college men to show up for campus programs or find their niche. We cannot promise that, unfortunately. What we can promise, however, is that the contributing authors offer their insights from their professional experiences that may be beneficial for you and your colleagues to consider as you move forward with your own work in this area. Our goal was to bring together a group of incredibly insightful collaborators to share the ways they are doing critically informed *praxis*, defined by Freire (1993) as the practice and use of theory in liberatory education. If our work is to be informed by theory, as it so often is in higher education, we want to ensure that it is done so with the intent of creating better, more inclusive, and more life-expanding outcomes for our students, in this case, college men.

Using This Text

We aim to highlight the ways theory can be put into practice for powerful, transformative learning to support college men and their development. We discuss ways that student development and student learning inform our work with college men and further examine how programs and services can be shaped to engage college men. This book is meant to inform professional practice and equip college student educators with the tools necessary to help college men make meaning of their gender and the concept of masculinities. Although we have chosen to present the chapters in a particular sequence, we urge readers to think about their own specific needs and take their own routes through the content provided. We suggest using this text as a handbook, and we hope over time you can add to the knowledge herein to expand your campus's efforts to support the development of college men.

This book has three parts: Theoretical Foundations for College Men and Masculinities, Program Design, and Specific Program Content and Delivery. The chapters in part one focus on the theoretical foundations for college men and masculinities work. In chapter 1, Daniel Tillapaugh, D. Chase J. Catalano, and Tracy Davis frame a discussion about the ways theoretical epistemologies play a role in college student educators' professional practice. Expanding on this discussion in the context of student development theory among college men, Brian L. McGowan, Daniel Tillapaugh, and Frank Harris III in chapter 2 interrogate the ways Harper and Harris's (2010a) notion of the model gender majority myth has been embedded in the work of college student educators. We wholeheartedly believe in the importance of the role of theory and its use in professional practice. Therefore, we begin this volume from this vantage point to set the stage for how we see these theories and theoretical perspectives informing the ways we can engage college men in higher education.

Part two then moves into discussions of program design. In chapter 3, Keith E. Edwards, Zak Foste, and Chris Taylor share insights from their professional practice on how to effectively build a campus coalition invested in working on men and masculinities efforts. In chapter 4, Kyle C. Ashlee and Rachel Wagner present an intersectional model of college men and masculinities programming that takes into account the ways race, social class, sexuality, and other identities inform and shape professionals' understanding of college men. In chapter 5, Lucas Schalewski, Brian Lackman, and Jamie Utt provide a rich overview of how assessment and evaluation of programs and services for college men can provide meaningful data and create a culture of data-driven decision-making. We see these chapters as a bridge between theory and practice, and we hope readers will think critically about using the content of these chapters to situate decision-making and preparation work in developing their programs and services for college men.

Finally, in part three we move to content that is specifically geared to the contexts and the actual delivery of programs, initiatives, and services. In chapter 6 Peter Paquette and Vernon A. Wall detail aspects of implementing retreat-based programs, including recommendations on curriculum development. In chapter 7 Wilson Kwamogi Okello and Stephen John Quaye reimagine dialogue-based praxis and how college student educators can help college men engage in critical self-reflection through intergroup dialogue as well as dialogical storytelling. Taj Smith, Vern Klobassa, and Cristobal Salinas Jr. offer key insights in chapter 8 on peer education and mentoring programs, which can be transformative in the development of college men. In chapter 9 Jason Laker discusses how college student educators can develop academic curriculum geared to college men in curricular or cocurricular formats and offers strategies on building these curricula. Cameron C. Beatty, Jonathan A. McElderry, and Jason J. Dorsette call on their professional experiences in discussing comprehensive initiatives and programs for college men in chapter 10. They mention specific comprehensive programs, many of which focus on the support of historically marginalized subpopulations of college men. In the final chapter, Z Nicolazzo offers eight key considerations for college student educators to consider regarding their gender-based educational work to help men and their understanding of masculinities. We feel these chapters focus on the nitty-gritty of this work through discussing how and why these various types of programs may be useful for specific campus populations.

Concluding Thoughts

The eminent gender studies scholar R.W. Connell (2005) wrote, "Sciences of masculinity may be emancipatory or they may be controlling. They may even be both at once" (p. 7). Our intention for this book is to help college men understand that the socialization of masculinity is not all inherently bad or all inherently good. Instead of being an either-or issue, we subscribe to Connell's suggestion that it is a both-and issue. As college student educators, we play a vital role in helping college men begin to examine, problematize, and resolve the ways masculinity plays a role in their daily lives. Our hope is that when done well the programs, services, and initiatives we build and implement for college men will be emancipatory and a true liberatory praxis; however, this can be tricky. As our dear friend Rachel Wagner (2011) wrote, "*Patriarchy can exist even without men in the room*" [emphasis in original] (p. 221). We all are affected by systems of sexism and patriarchy.

We want to contribute to a cultural shift to change the narrative of college men. As college student educators reading this text, we expect that you want to be a part of that shift too. But be forewarned that this work can be challenging, taxing, and sometimes very life affirming. To engage in the type of liberatory praxis we are aiming for, we implore you to engage in your own self work on these issues. Our understandings of our own gender identities are informed by our daily practices (i.e., what we wear, how we speak) but also on how we also may restrict ourselves based on our internalized sexism and genderism. To help our students, we must also help ourselves. Beatty and Tillapaugh (2017) stress the need for college student educators supporting men to engage in critical self-work: "In order to facilitate liberatory pedagogy, educators must be able to acknowledge the role toxic masculinity plays in all aspects of their own lives" (p. 54). This echoes Wagner's (2011) thinking of the multiple layers and contexts of power in our relationships with our students:

> More often than not individuals are more conscious of the identities they have that are marginalized by the dominant culture. Young men in my office may have access to power through their membership in the category men, but still may feel powerless when faced with the institutional power I wield. Being conscious of how my identities surface and act as

a lens through which I see and hear the world can offer insight into an interaction that has quickly deteriorated. (p. 220)

If you are a faculty member, student affairs administrator, or paraprofessional who has some type of role or authority in which you are supervising your peers, you wield power in that role. Your own multiple and social identities play into how college men may perceive you and how they also perceive themselves. As a result, we encourage you to take stock in how your identities inform your thoughts and actions. How can you build a connection with the college men you work with? In what ways can you listen to understand their thoughts and feelings? How can you look beyond the posturing or surface-level affectations these men are exhibiting and see them authentically? How do you perform some of this posturing and affectation yourself, and what can you do to model more authentic, healthier behaviors for others?

As you set out to either start or continue this work to support college men and your development, please know that we applaud you for your commitment. In an increasingly polarized, fragmented society, we hold strong to the idea that we need these types of programs on our college and university campuses even more. It is imperative that faculty and staff create spaces where college men can come together to reflect on how masculinity plays a role in their lives and understand the power and privilege they have based on their gender identity. We want to extend that awareness to action and have college men also begin to understand that they can use their privilege in powerful ways as allies and can advocate with others and eradicate power structures and systems that marginalize and subordinate others. Our work is grounded in a pro-feminist perspective. If you're expecting a men's rights-informed perspective or a mythopoetic perspective, this is not the book for you. But if you're interested in making inroads to help college men see there are other options beyond hegemonic masculinity, if you want to help men come together and be curious about their gender identity, if you want to help men navigate and problematize the ways masculinity is socialized in the world, then this is exactly the book you may need. This work is crucial. Your efforts are needed more than ever. Go forth and do good work.

References

Allan, E. J., & Madden, M. (2008). *Hazing in view: College students at risk.* Retrieved from http://www.stophazing.org/wp-content/uploads/2014/06/hazing_in_view_web1.pdf

Beatty, C., & Tillapaugh, D. (2017). Masculinity, leadership, and liberatory pedagogy: Supporting men through leadership development and education. *New Directions for Student Leadership*, 154, 47–58.

Berkowitz, A. D. (1994). A model acquaintance rape prevention program. *New Directions for Student Services*, 65, 35–42.

Berkowitz, F. (2005). *History of Division 51*. Retrieved from http://division51.net/about/governance/history-of-division-51/

Bowleg, L. (2008). When Black + lesbian + woman ≠ Black lesbian woman: The methodological challenges of qualitative and quantitative intersectionality research. *Sex Roles*, 59, 312–325.

California State University, Northridge. (n.d.) *MenCARE*. Retrieved from https://www.csun.edu/counseling/mencare

Canon, H. (2004). *Back when.* . . . Retrieved from http://www.myacpa.org/sites/default/files/SCM%20Thought%20Brief%202004%20-%20History.pdf

Carr, J. L., & VanDeusen, K. M. (2004). Risk factors for male sexual aggression on college campuses. *Journal of Family Violence, 19*, 279–289.

Connell, R. W. (2005). *Masculinities* (2nd ed.). Cambridge, UK: Polity Press.

Crenshaw, K. (1991). Mapping the margins: Intersectionality, identity politics, and violence against women of color. *Stanford Law Review, 43*, 1241–1299.

Cuyjet, M. J. (1997). African American men on campus: Their needs and perceptions. *New Directions for Student Services*, 80, 5–16.

Dancy, T. E. II. (2012). *The brother code: Manhood and masculinities among African American males in college.* Charlotte, NC: Information Age.

Davis, T. L. (2002). Voices of gender role conflict: The social construction of college men's identity. *Journal of College Student Development, 43*, 508–521.

Davis, T. L., & Laker, J. (2004). Connecting men to academic and student affairs programs and services. *New Directions for Student Services, 107,* 47–57.

Destagir, A. E. (2017, March 31). Men pay a steep price when it comes to masculinity. *USA Today.* Retrieved from https://www.usatoday.com/story/news/2017/03/31/masculinity-traditional-toxic-trump-mens-rights/99830694/

Digby, T. (1998). *Men doing feminism.* New York, NY: Routledge.

Doyle, J., & Femiano, S. (1999). *History: The early history of the American Men's Studies Association and the evolution of men's studies.* Retrieved from http://mensstudies.org/?page_id=5

Freire, P. (1993). *Pedagogy of the oppressed* (M. B. Ramos, Trans.). New York, NY: Continuum.

Harper, S. R., & Harris, F. III. (2010a). Beyond the model gender majority myth. In S. R. Harper & F. Harris III (Eds.), *College men & masculinities: Theory, research, and implications for practice* (pp. 1–16). San Francisco, CA: Jossey-Bass.

Harper, S. R., & Harris, F. III. (2010b). *College men & masculinities: Theory, research, and implications for practice.* San Francisco, CA: Jossey-Bass.

Harper, S. R., Harris, F. III, & Mmeje, K. (2005). A theoretical model to explain the overrepresentation of college men among campus judicial offenders: Implications for campus administrators. *NASPA Journal, 42*, 565–588.

Harris, J. C., & Linder, C. (2017). *Intersections of identity and sexual violence on campus: Centering minoritized students' experiences.* Sterling, VA: Stylus.

Jourian, T. J. (2017). Trans*forming college masculinities: Carving out trans*masculine pathways through the threshold of dominance. *International Journal of Qualitative Studies in Education, 30,* 245–265.

Katz, J. (2005). Reconstructing masculinity in the locker room: The Mentors in Violence Prevention Project. *Harvard Educational Review, 65,* 163–175.

Kellom, G. (2004). Developing effective programs and services for college men. *New Directions for Student Services,* 107.

Kilmartin, C. T., & Berkowitz, A. D. (2005). *Sexual assault in context: Teaching college men about gender.* Mahwah, NJ: Erlbaum.

Kimmel, M. S. (2008). *Guyland: The perilous world where boys become men.* New York, NY: HarperCollins.

Kimmel, M. S., & Kaufman, M. (1994). Weekend warriors: The new men's movement. In H. Brod & M. Kaufman (Eds.), *Theorizing masculinities* (pp. 259–288). Thousand Oaks, CA: Sage.

Kimmel, M. S., & Messner, M. A. (2007). *Men's lives* (7th ed.). Boston, MA: Allyn & Bacon.

Laker, J. A. (2005). *Rethinking our engagement of male students: Proposal for establishing a Men and Masculinities Knowledge Community within the National Association of Student Personnel Administrators.* Unpublished manuscript, Saint John's University, Collegeville, MN.

Laker, J. A., & Davis, T. (2011). *Masculinities in higher education: Theoretical and practical considerations.* New York, NY: Routledge.

Lev, A. I. (2004). *Transgender emergence: Counseling gender-variant people and their families.* Binghamton, NY: Haworth.

Levant, R. F. (1997). The masculinity crisis. *Journal of Men's Studies, 5,* 221–231.

Marcus, J. (2017, August 8). Why men are the new college minority. *The Atlantic.* Retrieved from https://www.theatlantic.com/education/archive/2017/08/why-men-are-the-new-college-minority/536103/

Mitchell, J. D., Simmons, C. Y., & Greyerbiehl, L. A. (2014). *Intersectionality & higher education.* New York, NY: Peter Lang.

Musu-Gillette, L., de Brey, C., McFarland, J., Hussar, W., Sonnenberg, W., & Wilkinson-Flicker, S. (2017). *Status and trends in the education of racial and ethnic groups 2017* (NCES 2017-051). Retrieved from http://nces.edu.org/pubsearch/

NASPA–Student Affairs Professionals in Higher Education (2017). *2017 Conference on College Men.* Retrieved from https://www.naspa.org/events/2017CCM

National Center for Education Statistics. (2018). *Undergraduate enrollment.* Retrieved from https://nces.ed.gov/programs/coe/indicator_cha.asp

Northwestern University. (n.d.). *Men Against Rape and Sexual Assault (MARS).* Retrieved from https://www.northwestern.edu/care/get-involved/student-involvement/mars/index.html

Oregon State University (2017). *Examining Masculinities Conference: Through the looking glass.* Retrieved from http://dce.oregonstate.edu/mde/hmc

Pascoe, C. J. (2011). *Dude, you're a fag: Masculinity and sexuality in high school* (2nd ed.). Berkeley: University of California Press.

Patton, L. D., Renn, K. A., Guido, F. M., & Quaye, S. J. (2016). *Student development in college: Theory, research, and practice* (3rd ed.). San Francisco, CA: Jossey-Bass.

Robbins, C. R., & McGowan, B. L. (2016). Intersectional perspectives on gender and gender identity development. *New Directions for Student Services, 154,* 71–83.

Rosin, H. (2010, July–August). The end of men. *The Atlantic.* Retrieved from https://www.theatlantic.com/magazine/archive/2010/07/the-end-of-men/308135/

Shapiro, D., Dundar, A., Huie, F., Wakhungu, P., Yuan, X., Nathan, A & Hwang, Y. A. (2017). *A national view of student attainment rates by race and ethnicity—fall 2010 cohort.* Herndon, VA: National Student Clearinghouse Research Center.

Spencer, H., & Stolberg, S. G. (2017, August 11). White Nationalists march on University of Virginia. *The New York Times.* Retrieved from https://www.nytimes.com/2017/08/11/us/white-nationalists-rally-charlottesville-virginia.html

Starnes, T. (2017, January 17). "Toxic masculinity"? Dude, now America's universities are turning men into women. *Fox and Friends.* Retrieved from https://www.foxnews.com/opinion/toxic-masculinity-dude-now-americas-universities-are-turning-men-into-women

Stewart, A. L. (2014). The men's project: A sexual assault prevention program targeting college men. *Psychology of Men & Masculinity, 15,* 481–485.

Tarrant, S., & Katz, J. (2008). *Men speak out: Views on gender, sex, and power.* New York, NY: Routledge.

Texas Education Consortium for Male Students of Color. (2017). *The 2017 Texas Male Student Leadership Summit a resounding success!* Retrieved from http://diversity.utexas.edu/txedconsortium/2017/08/the-2017-texas-male-student-leadership-summit-a-resounding-success/

Trinity College. (n.d.). *Organizations and resources.* Retrieved from http://www.trincoll.edu/StudentLife/Diversity/WGRAC/Pages/OrganizationsandResources.aspx

Valenti, J. (2014, May 24). Elliot Rodger's California shooting spree: Further proof that misogyny kills. *The Guardian.* Retrieved from https://www.theguardian.com/commentisfree/2014/may/24/elliot-rodgers-california-shooting-mental-health-misogyny

Wagner, R. (2011). Embracing liberatory practice. In J. A. Laker & T. Davis (Eds.), *Masculinities in higher education: Theoretical and practical considerations* (pp. 210–223). New York, NY: Routledge.

Wagner, R., Catalano, C., & Tillapaugh, D. (2018). Starting with men: Emancipatory possibilities for higher education praxis. In E. F. Henderson & Z Nicolazzo

(Eds.), *Starting with gender in international higher education research: Perspectives on evolving concepts and methods* (pp. 62–82). New York, NY: Routledge.

Wechsler, H., & Wuethrich, B. (2002). *Dying to drink: Confronting binge drinking on college campuses.* Emmaus, PA: Rodale.

Young, B.-R., Demarais, S. L., Baldwin, J. A., & Chandler, R. (2017). Sexual coercion practices among undergraduate male recreational athletes, intercollegiate athletes, and non-athletes. *Violence Against Women, 23,* 795–812. doi:10.1177/1077801216651339

PART ONE

THEORETICAL FOUNDATIONS FOR COLLEGE MEN AND MASCULINITIES

To create loving men, we must love males. Loving maleness is different from praising and rewarding males for living up to sexist-defined notions of male identity. Caring about men because of what they do for us is not the same as loving males for simply being. When we love maleness, we extend our love whether males are performing or not. (b. hooks, The Will to Change: Men, Masculinity, and Love, *New York, NY: Atria Books*)

I

THEORETICAL COMPLEXITIES OF COLLEGE MEN AND MASCULINITIES

Daniel Tillapaugh, D. Chase J. Catalano, and Tracy Davis

Over the past three decades the focus and attention on the development of college men has been increasing, particularly through the lens of gender and masculinity. Much of the scholarship has centered positivist or constructivist paradigms and the related assumptions that underlie such research. More recently, critical researchers have viewed college men through intersectional and critical race theory lenses (e.g., Davis & Klobassa, 2017; Harper, 2009; Harper, Wardell, & McGuire, 2011; Tillapaugh, 2015, 2016); examined masculinities through the framework of oppression, trans*ness, and liberation (Catalano, 2015a, 2015b; Jourian, 2017); and excavated what it means to start with men as a form of research (Wagner, Catalano, & Tillapaugh, 2018). These epistemological standpoints serve to not only frame our understanding of college men and their development but also influence professional practices. College student educators operate from an epistemological framework in their professional engagement with college cultures and students. We argue that many educators rarely examine the influences of their own epistemological views or the epistic filters of students, and this oversight prevents more effective educational practices and policies.

The importance of building congruence among epistemology, methodology, and methods is well documented in the qualitative research literature (Carter & Little, 2007; Denzin & Lincoln, 2011; Jones, Torres & Arminio, 2014). Although qualitative researchers need to be critically aware of the connections between their epistemological frame and data-gathering strategies, for example, we similarly believe that college student educators need to be mindful of how epistemology aligns with their practice, the interventions they design, interaction styles with individual students, and policies they construct. Without such theoretical and epistemological complexity, professionals are using practices and policies that lack necessary sophistication and precision.

In fact, this connection between theoretical and epistemological complexity and professional practice is exactly what is meant by the concept of praxis. In his work on education as a practice of freedom (a kind of liberation), Freire (1993) discussed the limitations of knowledge in assisting individuals to understand the world in which they live. Freire suggested that learning requires critical reflection and action to create change (praxis), whereas praxis toward liberation requires collective action that transforms our world, and we accomplish this mutually, by and with those oppressed and those in the position to oppress. We assert that our epistemological stances inform our collective praxis as educators, whether we are conscious of them or not. Throughout this chapter, our aim is to help educators who are working with college men understand that the ways they conduct their work (or praxis) are informed by their epistemological perspectives.

Although a formal discussion of epistemology is beyond the scope of this chapter, it is essentially a theory of knowledge or how we come to know what we know. Epistemology refers to the assumptions we make about acquiring knowledge and serves as a significant influence in how we view the world, how we determine truth, and what we accept as viable evidence (Jones, Torres, & Arminio, 2014). In this chapter, we examine how positivist, constructivist, and critical perspectives can shape professionals' work with college men and masculinities. In addition, we use a commonly used activity called the Gender Box to encourage students to think about the socialization of gender, and to illuminate different epistemological approaches. Finally, we offer a framework for developing a liberatory consciousness (Love, 2013), which offers a praxis approach to facilitations of the Gender Box activity, as well as conversations about gender. We envision liberatory consciousness as a function of self-awareness and awareness of epistemological nuances to engage with audiences that want to explore men and masculinities.

The Gender Box Activity

As people who engage in conversations about gender in collegiate settings, we tend to conduct training sessions and workshops about gender socialization. Among higher education circles, many professionals have used the Act Like a Man (more commonly referred to as the Gender Box activity), an introductory exercise created to have individuals think about the socialization of gender and masculinity with college men. Created by the Oakland Men's Project (n.d.), this activity has three main steps. The facilitator draws a box on a board. Participants brainstorm phrases, characteristics, or messages they have heard about what it means to act like a man in our society; specifically, they are asked to think about gender role expectations and norms for boys and men and write them inside the box. Next, facilitators ask participants to come up with labels and names used for men who do not conform to those gender norms and write these labels outside the box. Facilitators might also ask participants to think about the consequences faced by individuals who do not conform to the these gender norms, either physically or verbally, and place those outside the box as well. Although an Internet search of phrases like *act like a man activity* or *gender box activity* yields different variations of these steps, we are including this activity for a few main reasons.

Although it is a helpful starting point particularly for college men who have not reflectively thought about what it means to be a man or the ways masculinity plays a role in their lives, this activity may essentialize the ways individuals think about their gender and their sense of masculinity. In many cases, when doing this activity, participants might say they were told that boys don't cry, men are the breadwinners, young men need to be tough and aggressive, or boys will be boys. These descriptors, and others like them, are important beginning steps of understanding how socialization about gender roles and expectations happens throughout men's lives. However, if facilitators accept these answers without challenging them or asking how these responses may not be the case for all men, then we risk ignoring critical issues related to socially constructed notions of masculinity. This silence misses the nuances in dimensions of race, ethnicity, social class, sexuality, and gender identity. This is one example of how important it is to ground student affairs practice in an epistemological approach. Throughout this chapter, we foreground epistemological approaches used in research on college men and their masculinities and how higher education professionals might use and facilitate the Gender Box activity from positivist, constructivist, and critical approaches.

Epistemological Approaches

One way to think about the difference that epistemological perspectives make is to consider where to locate truth and the related assumptions a student affairs professional would have about understanding the students they work with. Jones and Stewart (2016) argued there are three waves of student development theories that are informed by three major epistemological perspectives (discussed in more depth in chapter 2). From a positivist perspective located in the first wave of foundational student development theories (Jones & Stewart, 2016), professionals seek empirical truths that are generalizable so that they can employ valid and reliable interventions, policies, and practices. *Truth*, from a positivist perspective, is essentially located objectively outside of the person and all subjectivities related to personal perspectives (i.e., biases) must be mitigated in order to demonstrate empirical viability. In contrast, the second wave of student development theories used a constructivist view to focus on social and holistic identity development (Jones & Stewart, 2016). In this wave, student affairs professionals can't rely on generalized external truths because they assume that human perceptions of reality can be quite different: Truth is in the mutual construction between two people or between a person and some phenomenon. The third wave involves critical theories of student development and explores issues of power dynamics, specifically the reproduction of normativity (Jones & Stewart, 2016). Moving even further away from an essentialist truth, a critical theory perspective attends to questions about the historical, political, economic, and social influences that reinforce categories, structures, and how we come to know ourselves. Reality is a reflection of hegemonic powers (the norms that push us to not question the way the world works), and the idea of self requires an exploration of context, multiple social identities and their intersections, systems of oppression and their intersectionality (Dill & Zambrana, 2009), and individual agency (Jones & Stewart, 2016).

The dramatically different assumptions about reality, truth, and understanding will influence how one practices, designs programs, and develops policy. For example, consider a team of student affairs professionals who serve on a task force and must design a new policy on gender-inclusive housing. How would a group representing the three epistemological perspectives go about gathering information differently? What would be considered valid evidence to move policy one way or another? How would student concerns be heard? How would political climates be interpreted? Would gender be seen as rooted in biological sex or as an ever shifting series of performatives with no original, as Butler (1990) suggests?

It's important to remember that one epistemological framework is not necessarily better than another. In fact, professionals need to have access to all three views because the people we work with will be operating on assumptions rooted in all three perspectives. Senge, Scharmer, Jaworski, and Flowers (2004) similarly argued,

> The problem is that most of us have spent our lives immersed in analytic knowing, with its dualistic separation of subject "I" and object "it." There's nothing wrong with analytic knowing. It's useful and appropriate for many

activities—for example, for interacting with machines. But if it's our only way of knowing, we'll tend to apply it in all situations. (p. 99)

We run the risk, for example, of dogmatically insisting that everyone should view gender the way we do. Professionals, particularly in the field of student affairs, where we work with a complex array of human beings (varying identities, personalities, learning motivations, preparations, social capital, etc.) in a variety of different environments, need to be able to draw on approaches that parallel the intricacies of our work. Being aware of our own perspective, as well as being able to develop a hypothesis related to others' assumptions, is a critical competency. As Wineburg (2001) stated,

> The narcissist sees the world—both the past and the present—in his [*sic*] own image. Mature historical knowing teaches us to do the opposite: to go beyond our own image, to go beyond our brief life, and to go beyond the fleeting moment in history into which we have been born. When we develop the skill of understanding how we know what we know, we acquire a key to lifelong learning. (p. 24)

In many respects, this is what we mean when we say we must meet others where they are. Student affairs work requires us to be self-aware, have content knowledge about epistemologies, and be thoughtful enough to seek understanding of the perspectives of others.

Positivist Approaches to College Men and Masculinities

Foubert's (1998) *The Men's Program: How to Successfully Lower Men's Likelihood of Raping* is an example of positivist approaches to working with college men and masculinities. According to Foubert, "By framing the workshop as a training workshop in which men learn how to help women recover from a rape experience, The Men's Program appeals to a 'potential helper' persona, rather than the 'potential rapist' persona" (p. 5). Framing sexual assault in this manner reflects a positivist standpoint. For example, the trope that men must take care of women feeds into the archetype of gender and supports essentialist and binary notions of gendered relationships. In addition, it is an expectation that all men and all women have common experiences, and according to this model, programmatic intervention should apply well-worn stereotyped behaviors to produce learning. Programs like this one, which do not specifically illuminate critical distinctions between gender and sex or mention sexual diversity, conflate gender and sex and participants receive no challenges to the heteronormative assumption (among potentially other dominant notions of race, class, etc.) that ignores all but heterosexual relationship violence.

The Men's Program is also based on the premise that rape is something that emerges from rapists as individuals rather than as centrally a behavior that emerges from a systematic culture of oppression.

On one level this positivist approach has benefits. It is not only geared toward raising issues of sexual coercion and assault with a group that historically has had too few developmentally focused interventions but also calls on individual men to develop compassion for survivors. This reinforces the idea of what it means to be a good man beyond being just empty words because these men are not engaged in issues of causing harm to others. Because the program fails to incorporate an understanding of constructivist, critical, and post-structural perspectives on gender and sex, however, the program actually serves to reinforce normative and hegemonic notions.

Positivist Approaches to the Gender Box Activity

The initial framing of the Gender Box activity sets up the assumptions of the truth of a gender binary as well as uniformity and rigid expectations of gender identity, role, and expression. Missing from the introduction is any transparency about assumptions about how we define *man* and whom we exclude from that category through general assumptions of biology, morphology, and social constructions. The positivist perspective assumes a truth about gender as a quantifiable, biologically essentialist, and accepted reality. For students who are new to gender explorations, the positivist approach allows a comfort of sorts (at least for cisgender men) about what they already know about themselves as men. Cultural power dynamics (e.g., patriarchy in the United States) means that most cisgender men are relieved of the responsibility to explore gender norms through socialization (Harro, 2013). The Gender Box activity, with tidy (i.e., lacks messiness) rules of engagement, has the potential to help cisgender men begin to name the characteristics of normative masculinity as well as the penalizations that exist for variations of masculinity when deviating from the norm. For example, a facilitator can use this knowledge to talk about men in the aggregate (shared beliefs) to reveal generalized assumptions about men then introduce how those ideas are troubling generalizations. From there, the facilitator can encourage participants to think more critically about themselves, who they want to be, and how they want others to perceive them. To return to Foubert (1998), the facilitator can ask the group about the benefits and limitations of men *fixing* issues of sexual violence, then follow up with how that approach further silences women's experiences of sexual violence. These techniques can accelerate conversations to question assumed or perceived truths to attain deeper reflection and critical thinking from audience members.

Constructivist Approaches to College Men and Masculinities

An example of a constructivist approach to men and masculinities is Davis's (2002) study, which was meant to "explore the impact of socially prescribed gender roles on college men's identity development" (p. 508). Using this epistemological framework moves gender into the negotiated space between individuals and the hegemonic roles delivered as societal norms. This perspective assumes there is conflict between lived experiences of self and messages from society, and one constructs a sense of identity in that space. Although gender has fluidity in a constructivist negotiation, it still adheres to an undergirding assumption of a binary gender of men and women, and a gender expression of femininity and masculinity still undergirds the assumptions of this study. In addition, although the institutional press of hegemonic masculinity has some salience, the implications of this perspective does not necessarily push practitioners to focus on patriarchal systems that extend well beyond individual reflection and self-awareness.

Like the positivist framework, the constructivist lens is not without benefits. Moving beyond the essentialist notions of immutable gender and sex, the constructivist approach invites individuals to consider choice and agency over the hegemonic messages sent. Facilitation can guide individuals to focus on what they are being sold and whether the lessons they have learned are consistent with their own values and individual beliefs. On the other hand, the patriarchal system that promotes oppressive institutional policies and practices remains unilluminated. In addition, gender remains constructed in a binary of feminine and masculine stereotypes, and gender transgression is either a violation of norms or invisible.

Constructivist Approaches to the Gender Box Activity

In a constructivist framework, the Gender Box activity has the capabilities to complicate what we mean when we say *men* and *masculinity*. In fact, through a constructivist framework we can begin to explore types of men (multiple social identities) and consider masculinities as a plural concept. For instance, facilitators can ask participants how the messages of correctly performing masculinity show up in their daily lives, and how the views of others shape their own view of self as a man. We can guide participants to delve beyond accessible popular culture and explore early childhood messages with the hope of understanding the factors that influence what they thought were personal choices. The activity still locates the knowledge mostly from the internalized messages and focuses on self-awareness; yet a constructivist approach provides nuances to generalized ideas about gender and gender performances. In these reflections, systems and structures that reinforce behaviors might surface, such as how teachers, coaches, siblings, or doctors encourage or incriminate people for their gender expressions. The facilitator who engages in a constructivist approach excavates ideas of gender certainty to encourage doubts about what might be universally true about men and what it means to be a man. Further, facilitators can induce questions about whether masculinity is the same in different cultures across nations and in subcultures of the United States, and what those differences mean. With a gentle and share-by-choice style, a facilitator can ask participants how it felt when they did masculinity wrong, so to speak, and why we should judge any-one in such a way. These explorations will allow participants to disentangle messages about masculinity that result in value judgments from others.

Critical Approaches to College Men and Masculinities

An example of a critical approach to men and masculinities is Nicolazzo (2015), who uses "queer theory and crip theory—a conceptual framework that merges queer and critical disability theory—to explore both the positive outcomes and potential harm done in the production and implementation" (p. 1) of the Walk a Mile in Her Shoes event. This event is intended to end gender-based violence through the performance of (ostensibly) cisgender men experiencing the pain of walking in high-heeled shoes for a particular distance (a mile). A critical theoretical reading of this program examines how it reinforces gender normativity through a celebration of cisgender gender transgression (i.e., it takes a real man to walk a mile in women's shoes), which actually serves to reify gender normativity, misogyny (i.e., women's shoes should make the feet hurt), compulsory able-bodiedness (i.e., those who can walk) and trans oppression (i.e., gender transgression is a perfor-mance). Instead of liberatory potential, Walk a Mile in Her Shoes replicates oppression through masculine hegemony, ableism, and reification of beauty standards. The critical perspective takes the position that hegemonic power constructs what we understand as normal (power relationships), and such disruptions of power lead to social change. The reinforcement of structural norms on masculinity and femininity, for example, have become taken for granted as normal while simultaneously inaccurately representing the range of genders and other dimensions of identity. Nicolazzo's (2015) critical approach raises questions about what wearing high heels signals when they are worn by cisgender men, who can wear high-heeled shoes (able-bodied peo-ple), and how trans oppression manifests itself when gender-nonconforming men wear those same shoes. A critical analysis of the program examines the contexts in which a pair of shoes becomes about gender performativity and the ostracization of mobility limitations. Nicolazzo's (2015) use of queer and crip theory asks how we can imagine inclusivity and liberatory values when our programmatic practices reinforce assumptions that exclude and marginalize.

The critical approach appropriately focuses on power and oppression, pointing out normativity (centering who and what) as well as how invisibility cloaks those culturally unintelligible (Butler, 2004). In a critical frame, gender is more complex and understood to include a range of lived experiences. This perspective does not rely on, and actually firmly rejects, biological essentialism of a positivist view, disrupts binaries of all types (gender, racial, ways of knowing, etc.), and focuses attention on systemic and institutional oppression in a way a constructivist approach generally overlooks. However, critical theoretical perspectives come with their own potential problems when guiding professional practice. It is our experience that using a critical approach can create significant distance between positivist and even constructivist knowledge claims. Such distances may cause severe judgments by those with critical theoretical stances about people holding positivist or constructivist perspectives, such as individual versus more expansive views of power, and result in lower levels of professional compassion and understanding. Those with different epistemological frameworks may forget that liberation requires everyone's investment for sustainable change (Love, 2013). Those using a critical perspective must remember that epistemological righteousness reflects a positivist view of truth, and a plurality of perspectives enhances our coalition building through exploring competing assumptions. The assumption that there is an essential truth that undergirds positivism, for example, can naturally and understandably lead those using a positivist perspective to think that the plurality of perspectives or multiple truths reflect confused and unanchored relativism, rather than a legitimate and competing perspective on the truth. Those with a critical theoretical stance must remember that systems of oppression (racism, sexism, etc.) are often made invisible by cultural hegemonies that serve the status quo. Therefore, it should be unsurprising to thoughtful professionals that considering various epistemological frameworks isn't intuitive but is part of a learning process, often through deep contestation, and this learning process is more effective when compassion, empathy, challenging examples, and other appropriate learning strategies are employed.

Critical Approaches to the Gender Box Activity

As we previously mentioned, critical approaches interrogate systems of power. In a critical theory approach, any point in the facilitation may lead to questions : who constructed the box, does anyone ever fit in the box, what are the consequences of the box existing, and how do we reimagine the box? These questions all relate to dynamics of power. For instance, if we think about the positivist or constructivist frames using this activity, a facilitator may not really be focused on examining the ways that power, privilege, and oppression are manifested and continue to perpetuate how individuals come to understand what it means to be a man; who is understood to be a man; and the continuous replication and reinforcement, overt and covert, of hegemonic and toxic masculinity in our daily lives. Facilitators using a critical approach may shift the discussion of the completed Gender Box to ask participants to consider the intersectional dimensions of race, sexual orientation, ability, and other identities as they relate to understanding men and masculinities. For example, do the characteristics of the man box coconstructed by participants reflect men of different religions, races, sexualities, or abilities and disabilities? Additionally, a facilitator might ask participants to engage in critical self-reflection on the distinctions among *gender identity*, *gender expression*, and *gender performance*; this serves as a way to extend the conversation and reinforce the ways that conversations about men and masculinities typically uphold these categories as aggregate terms, meaning that society often centers White, cisgender, heterosexual, upper-middle-class, able-bodied men and their lives. Yet, a critical approach can reframe this conversation and instead center historically minoritized men and the ways they perform masculinity. For example, what is the difference between a strong woman and female masculinity? Such a question requires participants to reframe their thinking as a critical reconsideration of who owns masculinity. In many ways, these notions of critical approaches are tied to liberatory consciousness and praxis, which we suggest can play a distinct transformative role in supporting college men and their development.

Framing Liberatory Possibilities

In higher education, data-driven decision-making and assessment culture in student affairs divisions construct collegiate environments where we use quantitative data to determine, say, how many students attended a program, and answer qualitative questions like, How do our programs help students develop? Neither data-driven decision-making nor assessment culture approaches are bad, as that only sets up a false binary. Instead, we offer that the liberatory potentialities of our student affairs praxis means that we must imagine different possibilities for how we use theory to guide our work. We must recognize that much of the programming in student affairs uses overly simple notions of identity. Whether because of limitations in funding, foresight, or collaboration, our programmatic interventions translate into one-off programs or month-long programming trends. Our efforts tend to rely on a singular identity approach, such as the Gender Box. As a result, who gets left out? Who gets centered? Why do we engage in programmatic endeavors that perpetuate vicious cycles of erasure and marginalization? These questions become critical considerations, particularly in our work with college men and their development.

Efforts to work with men, a socially constructed category with variations in privilege based on other intersecting and salient identities, requires us to give more than a glancing nod to social justice education. Developing a liberatory consciousness (Love, 2013) means resisting faux math approaches to social justice, such as privileged identities minus marginalized identities equals amount of oppression; instead, we approach student affairs work as liberatory workers. As a guiding framework, liberatory consciousness reminds us that socialization is a process where we learn through interpersonal, institutional, and cultural interactions about how society operates in a way that makes inequity and unfairness invisible through the mechanisms of power dynamics, that is, structures, policies, practices, and beliefs (Love, 2013). The development of a liberatory consciousness "enables humans to live their lives in oppressive systems and institutions with awareness and intentionality, rather than on the basis of the socialization to which they have been subjected" (Love, 2013, p. 601). One of the important grounding tenets of a liberatory consciousness is that "no single human can be charged with the creation of oppressive systems in operation today" (Love, 2013, p. 601). Our student affairs work must engage students in ways that require them to examine themselves and beyond themselves (e.g., institutions and cultural assumptions). The Gender Box activity allows a nuanced understanding of the self, as well as the self in relation to other people, institutions (e.g., law and medicine), and cultures (e.g., language and media; Harro, 2013).

The development of a liberatory consciousness has four elements (nonlinear components): awareness, analysis, action, and accountability (Love, 2013). We review the components as a progression for clarity but emphasize that they happen simultaneously. Awareness is about developing the capacity to notice what occurs in "our daily lives, our language, our behaviors, and even our thoughts" (Love, 2013, p. 602). Developing awareness is one of the Gender Box's major components. We ask participants to notice gender in ways that may seem obvious and push them toward deeper levels of attention.

Analysis requires an individual to make meaning of and find an explanation for what the individual notices in the world, determine if change is necessary, and consider "the range of possible activities and the results that each of them is likely to produce" (Love, 2013, p. 603). The Gender

Box requires participants to reflect on how they understand gender and whether those understandings reflect the world in which they want to live. Awareness and analysis are important, but they are not enough to create sustainable change. Love (2013) stated, "The action component of a liberatory consciousness is based on the assumption that the participation of each of us in the liberation project provides the best possibility of gaining liberation for any of us" (p. 603). Through the Gender Box activity, action could be asking questions and finding resources. Actions such as joining a student organization on ending sexual violence may lead to discussions or programs that expand rape culture understandings (awareness and analysis) and remind students that collaboration is a path toward sustainable change (accountability).

Accountability reminds us that "working in connection and collaboration with each other, across and within 'role' groups, we can make progress in ways that are not apparent when working in isolation and in separate communities" (Love, 2013, p. 604). As we are all responsible for colluding with oppression because of our multiple identities, experiences, and various levels of power (situational, institutional, educational, etc.), then we must understand how we are all responsible to each other for bringing change that is holistic. Learning more about rape culture (awareness), understanding the impact of rape and rape culture (analysis), taking steps to end sexual violence by joining an organization (action), and considering who is left out of the actions and conversations (accountability, awareness, and analysis) are ways to communicate to students how knowledge and social change are complex, never ending, and integral to our praxis.

Concluding Thoughts

As scholars who are passionate about expanding the discourse on gender in higher education, we urge professionals to continue to intentionally reflect on the epistemological stances they take in their professional praxis. When considering our own journeys in higher education, our epistemological paradigms shifted over time and through experiences, personally and from interactions with students. We believe that you may experience this same shift and may need to consider your students' epistemological stances too. As individuals working with students, either as peers, administrators, or faculty, it is essential for you to understand your assumptions of cultural expectations about who and what we mean by college men and masculinities, and our students should have these same conversations. Throughout this chapter, we use the Gender Box activity as an example of how each of the three epistemological waves—positivist, constructivist, and critical and pos-structuralist—shift the facilitation and praxis of the work of engaging college men and masculinities.

To be sure, this praxis work can be difficult, frustrating, and challenging; at the same time, it can be exhilarating, rewarding, and transformative for everyone involved. Such is the work of supporting students and their developmental needs. You are likely reading this chapter because you have an investment in supporting college men in their holistic development. We want to encourage you to take the time to consider the ways you engage in your professional praxis. How do you incorporate knowledge into action to support students' development, particularly college men? What epistemological stances inform the work you do, and are those paradigms working in the ways they should be? Critically reflect on what shapes, organizes, and operates without your conscious noticing to excavate truths that you may hold or need to examine about gender. When thinking about the possibilities that may emerge if we could be engaged in developing a liberatory consciousness and using a framework that centers and promotes equity and justice for all, ask how you can incorporate those tenets into your praxis to benefit the college men you work with. Throughout this book, you will gain insights on various methods and programmatic interventions designed to engage college men. However, as you read, we encourage you to consider the larger questions: What would these interventions look like using the various epistemological stances that exist and how can we contemplate integrating these programs or initiatives with the aim of building a liberatory consciousness among the college men who participate in these programs?

References

Butler, J. (1990). *Gender trouble: Feminism and the subversion of gender.* New York, NY: Routledge.

Butler, J. (2004). *Undoing gender.* New York, NY: Routledge.

Carter, S. M., & Little, M. (2007). Justifying knowledge, justifying method, taking action: Epistemologies, methodologies, and methods in qualitative research. *Qualitative Health Research, 17,* 1316–1328.

Catalano, D. C. J. (2015a). Beyond virtual equality: Liberatory consciousness as a path to achieve trans* inclusion in higher education. *Equity & Excellence in Education, 48,* 418–435.

Catalano, D. C. J. (2015b). "Trans enough?": The pressures trans men negotiate in higher education. *Transgender Studies Quarterly, 2,* 411–430.

Davis, T. L. (2002). Voices of gender role conflict: The social construction of college men's identity. *Journal of College Student Development, 43,* 508–521.

Davis, T., & Klobassa, V. (2017). Honoring the "face behind the mask": Interrogating masculine performatives as counter-hegemonic action. In P. Eddy, K. Ward,

& T. Khwaja (Eds.), *Critical approaches to women and gender in higher education* (pp. 299–322). New York, NY: Palgrave Macmillan.

Denzin, N. K., & Lincoln, Y. S. (2011). *The Sage handbook of qualitative research* (4th ed.). Thousand Oaks, CA: Sage.

Dill, B. T., & Zambrana, R. E. (2009). *Emerging intersections: Race, class, and gender in theory, policy, and practice.* New Brunswick, NJ: Rutgers University Press.

Foubert, J. (1998). *The men's project: How to successfully lower men's likelihood of raping.* Holmes Beach, FL: Learning.

Freire, P. (1993). *Pedagogy of the oppressed* (M. B. Ramos, Trans.). New York, NY: Continuum.

Harper, S. R. (2009). Niggers no more: A critical race counternarrative on Black male student achievement at predominantly White colleges and universities. *International Journal of Qualitative Studies in Education, 22,* 697–712.

Harper, S. R., Wardell, C. C., & McGuire, K. M. (2011). Man of multiple identities: Complex individuality and identity intersectionality among college men. In J. A. Laker & T. Davis (Eds.), *Masculinities in higher education: Theoretical and practical considerations* (pp. 81–96). New York, NY: Routledge.

Harro, B. (2013). The cycle of socialization. In M. Adams, W. J. Blumenfeld, C. Castañeda, H. W. Hackman, M. L. Peters, & X. Zúñiga (Eds.), *Readings for diversity and social justice* (3rd ed., pp. 45–52). New York, NY: Routledge.

Jones, S. R., & Stewart, D.-L. (2016). Evolution of student development theory. *New Directions for Student Services, 154,* 17–28.

Jones, S. R., Torres, V., & Arminio, J. (2014). *Negotiating the complexities of qualitative research in higher education: Fundamental elements and issues* (2nd ed.). New York, NY: Routledge.

Jourian, T. J. (2017). Trans*forming college masculinities: Carving out trans*-masculine pathways through the threshold of dominance. *International Journal of Qualitative Studies in Education, 30,* 245–265.

Love, B. J. (2013). Developing a liberatory consciousness. In M. Adams, W. J. Blumenfeld, C. Castañeda, H. W. Hackman, M. L. Peters, & X. Zúñiga (Eds.), *Readings for diversity and social justice* (3rd ed., pp. 601–605). New York, NY: Routledge.

Nicolazzo, Z. (2015). "I'm man enough; are you?": The queer (im)possibilities of Walk a Mile in Her Shoes. *Journal of Critical Scholarship on Higher Education and Student Affairs, 2*(2), 18–30.

Oakland Men's Project (n.d.). *Gender role boxes: Presentation and discussion.* Retrieved from https://www.pcc.edu/resources/illumination/documents/gender-role-boxes-glbtq-and-sexism-exercise.pdf

Senge, P. M., Scharmer, C. O., Jaworski, J., & Flowers, B. S. (2004). *Presence: Exploring profound change in people, organizations, and society.* New York, NY: Doubleday.

Tillapaugh, D. (2015). "Writing our rule book": Exploring the intersectionality of gay college men. In D. J. Davis, R. J. Brunn-Bevel, & J. L. Olive (Eds.), *Intersectionality in educational research* (pp. 172–188). Sterling, VA: Stylus.

Tillapaugh, D. (2016). Understanding sexual minority male students' meaning-making about their multiple identities: An exploratory comparative study. *Canadian Journal of Higher Education*, *46*, 91–108.

Wagner, R., Catalano, C., & Tillapaugh, D. (2018). Starting with men: Emancipatory possibilities for higher education praxis. In E. F. Henderson & Z Nicolazzo (Eds.), *Starting with gender in international higher education research: Perspectives on evolving concepts and methods* (pp. 62–82). New York, NY: Routledge.

Wineburg, S. (2001). *Historical thinking and other unnatural acts: Charting the future of teaching the past*. Philadelphia, PA: Temple University Press.

2

CONSIDERATIONS OF STUDENT DEVELOPMENT IN MEN AND MASCULINITIES WORK

Brian L. McGowan, Daniel Tillapaugh, and Frank Harris III

In the United States, the ways men perform their gender, particularly their masculinities, receive considerable attention. In the past decade, a simple Internet search revealed a host of blogs, newsletters, websites, and books on the topic of masculinities. This is particularly evident in several books about the varied ways men from differing racial and ethnic backgrounds experience masculinities (Anthony, 2013; Edley, 2017; Howes, 2017; Innes & Anderson, 2015; Keith, 2017; Kimmel, 2010; Levant & Wong, 2017; Myers, 2016; Neal, 2015; Pascoe & Bridges, 2016; Rudolph, 2012). For instance, Howes (2017) encourages men to transcend previously learned toxic and unproductive forms of masculinity and "begin the process of removing the stoic mask and opening [themselves] up to the possibilities of the world around [them]" (p. 38). Innes and Anderson's (2015) edited volume challenges us to think differently about contemporary indigenous masculine identities as some men embrace cultural foundations that point to the decolonization and healthy expression of indigenous masculine identities. Neal (2015) urges Black men to display their masculinity in ways that support Black feminism and fight homophobia. Through the lens of sports, theater, and music, Rudolph (2012) explores the cultural interrelationship of different Latino masculinities in constructing *masculatinidad*. Collectively, these works yield important insights about men from differing racial and ethnic groups and challenge readers to reframe how they think about these populations.

Similar themes can be found in the college student development literature. Throughout this chapter, we extend the contemporary conversation about masculinities at large and situate it in the context of colleges and universities, particularly focusing on the development of college men. To begin, we describe the evolution of student development theory, highlighting specific examples of scholarship on college men and masculinities grounded in each of the epistemological paradigms represented by each of the three waves of student development theory in work forwarded by Jones and Stewart (2016). Next, we briefly discuss Harper and Harris's (2010) concept of the model gender minority myth and the ways college men, certain subpopulations in particular, continue to be understudied and undertheorized in higher education literature. Finally, we conclude with an overview of theories and concepts used to understand college men while offering new directions for student affairs educators to become more gender conscious in their work with college men.

The Evolution of Student Development Theory

The founding of Harvard College in 1636 marked the start of higher education institutions in the United States, but student affairs work did not officially begin until the late 1800s (Schwartz & Stewart, 2016). Dean of women was the first student affairs position created in colleges and universities at the end of the 1800s. It was primarily a faculty position with administrative duties in overseeing the particular needs of women at their institutions and advocating for women's education (Schwartz & Stewart, 2016). In the early 1900s colleges and universities in the United States hired their first student affairs administrators, often under the title of dean of men, who were responsible for the oversight of student conduct (Schwartz & Stewart, 2016). This title was later changed to dean of students to reflect the changing student demographics. In the first four decades of the twentieth century, the foundation of what is now understood as student affairs was created with a wide array of professionalization of student services personnel and increased attention to students and their growth and development (Patton, Renn, Guido, & Quaye, 2016; Schwartz & Stewart, 2016). Since that time, there has been tremendous interest in exploring and examining how theory informs professional practice in the field of student affairs. As a result, college student development theories have historically been used by college student educators to understand aspects of the how and why students come to understand themselves, think in the ways they do, and engage in the environments they are a part of and how those environments may influence their growth (Patton et al., 2016). Jones and Stewart (2016) examined the array of various student development theories commonly used throughout the history of student affairs and framed them in three distinct waves. In the following section, we use Jones and Stewart's (2016) frame of the three waves and discuss the ways these waves of theoretical knowledge connect specifically to the attitudes, explorations, and investigations of college men and their development.

First-Wave Perspectives on Student Development

The first wave of student development theories are often-cited foundational theories and typically divided into distinct families focused on psychosocial, cognitive structure, person environment, typology, and maturity (Jones & Stewart, 2016). Often rooted in a positivist paradigm, these studies sampled largely White men on their particular developmental experiences (Jones & Abes, 2011). In particular, most of these theories reified and reinforced the experiences of a particular class of White men: those attending prestigious universities who typically come from upper-class socioeconomic backgrounds and who have influence in society (Patton et al., 2016). As Harper and Harris (2010) point out, although the development of many of these theories used samples that were primarily men, the researchers doing their scholarship typically did not use gender as a lens for their work, and if they did their view of the influence of gender was unclear.

Given the positivist approach undergirding many of these first wave theories, the scholars of the works offered in this period usually conceptualized gender as a dichotomous, independent variable. For example, Foubert, Nixon, Sisson, and Barnes (2005) used quantitative data from Winston, Miller, and Prince's (1987) Student Development Task and Lifestyle Inventory to explore gender differences in students' degree of development. In Foubert and colleagues' work, grounded by the instrument created by Winston and colleagues, gender and sex conflated as one and the same. Additionally, a binary of gender is upheld with men and women as the only options, ultimately each serving as an independent variable (Foubert et al., 2005). Yet, this perspective and view creates an erasure of individuals who do not identify as men or women and essentializes gender to a biological determinant rather than a socially constructed concept that can be dynamic and fluid in nature. This critique actually connects to the introduction of the second wave of student development theories, which we explore next.

Second-Wave Perspectives on Student Development

The second wave considers students' social identities (Jones & McEwen, 2000) and developmental trajectories that often center the experiences of underrepresented populations. Running parallel to second-wave feminism and the civil rights movements in the United States in the 1960s and 1970s, the second wave of student development theory centered the experiences of underrepresented populations, a pendulum swing in the opposite direction from the first wave that had focused nearly exclusively on men in college (Patton et al., 2016). As Jones and Stewart (2016) asserted, "Foregrounding social identities necessitated a view of identities as socially constructed because social identities are anchored in group membership that are influenced and mutually constructed by larger societal contexts" (p. 20). The research being conducted during this time was also essential in understanding the experiences of an increasingly diverse student body attending colleges and universities in the United States. In this post–World War II era, the GI Bill played a substantial role in opening college and universities' doors to historically racially minoritized students (Patton et al., 2016; Schwartz & Stewart, 2016: Thelin & Gasman, 2016).

The theories forwarded in this time period tended to have a constructivist orientation, upheld an emphasis on the social construction of identity, and promoted a holistic developmental approach: "This perspective on student development resulted in theories that shed light on the development of a diverse array of students, both related to the content (psychosocial) of their development and the meaning they made of their experiences (cognitive)" (Jones & Stewart, 2016, p. 20). For instance, Jones and Stewart (2016) pointed to Marcia Baxter Magolda's scholarship on self-authorship as an integrative, holistic approach to understanding student development.

In understanding aspects of gender during this second wave, its early period tended to focus predominantly on women (i.e., Belenky, Clinchy, Goldberger, & Tarule, 1986; Gilligan, 1982; Josselson, 1987) and how their experiences in colleges and universities informed their growth and development (Jones & Stewart, 2016). These theories foregrounded how college women made meaning of aspects of their identities and their lives. In the 1980s through the early part of the twenty-first century, an emerging group of scholars in this wave was interested in examining the lived experiences of college men, informed by pro-feminist perspectives. Masculinities scholars such as Harry Brod, James O'Neil, Michael Messner, and Michael Kimmel informed the work of higher education scholars such as Tracy Davis, Jason Laker, Shaun Harper, Frank Harris III, and Keith Edwards.

The work stemming from these scholars began to illuminate the ways the environmental influences and impact of college played a role in the socialization of college men. For instance, Davis (2002) focused on the experiences of college men and *gender role conflict*, a term coined by O'Neil (1990) and defined as "a psychological state occurring when rigid, sexist, or restrictive gender roles learned through socialization result in personal restriction, devaluation, or violation of others or self" (p. 25). Davis interviewed 10 White heterosexual college men and found the following themes among the participants: (a) the importance of self-exploration, (b) code of communication caveats, (c) fear of femininity, (d) confusion about and distancing from masculinity, and (e) a sense of challenge without support. The work stemming from Davis's study demonstrated in significant ways how many college men, particularly White and heterosexual men, struggled with gender role conflict and the ways they internalized messages of toxic masculinity that restricted their behaviors and thoughts.

Responding to criticism (e.g., Davis, 2002) that the early focus on college men and masculinities scholarship in higher education was focused on White men, scholars such as Shaun Harper, Frank Harris III, Michael Cuyjet, and T. Elon Dancy II began to focus on African American college men's experiences. Still largely rooted in constructivist stances, their work provided important insights on this particular student population. A proliferation of other scholarship on minoritized men emerged that examined sexual minority men (Duran & Pérez, 2017; Lange & Moore, 2017; Tillapaugh, 2015), Latino men (Pérez, 2014, 2017), Asian American men (Liu, 2000; Shek, 2007), and men with disabilities (Gerschick, 2011). In the past decade attention paid to college men from historically underrepresented populations increased through the framework of identity development as well as scholarship shifting from a constructivist epistemology to one grounded in critical stances, which is the third wave of student development theory.

Third-Wave Perspectives on Student Development

The third wave of student development theory departs from a developmental emphasis and foregrounds systemic oppressions and inequitable power structures (Jones & Stewart, 2016). In this wave, theories that challenge, critique, and problematize traditional student development theories are prevalent and address shortcomings of previously offered theories that did not consider or center identity in particularly meaningful ways (Patton et al., 2016). In their purview of the scholarship in this category, Jones and Stewart (2016) focused primarily on work grounded in critical or post-structural epistemes. Scholarship using a critical theoretical paradigm centers the analyses on inequitable societal structural conditions, typically on a particular identity group. The use of critical theories goes beyond the interpersonal interactions that demonstrate injustice and allow an analysis that attends to the intersections of forms of oppression. For example, critical race theory is an analytical frame used to examine how structural and institutional forms of power affect racially minoritized groups.

Harper, Wardell, and McGuire (2011) is an illustrative example of using a critical paradigm to explore college men and their development. Harper and colleagues (2011) use intersectionality as a lens to examine the narrative of Tyson, a young man attending the University of North Carolina at Chapel Hill, who identifies as biracial and gay and is negotiating particular religious and socioeconomic status issues. Intersectionality is a concept from Crenshaw (1989), grounded in a critical paradigm, to describe the ways understanding of identity is constructed and shaped by the societal interlocking power structures that create and maintain systems of power, privilege, and oppression. By framing Tyson's experiences of identity development in college using intersectionality, Harper and colleagues ultimately illuminate the complexities that Tyson faces in particular environments and the tensions that exist among his identities, such as his spiritual identity as a Christian and his sexuality. By examining the power structures that inform Tyson's understanding of himself, Harper and colleagues provide an important context for higher education professionals to understand the ways our students' multifaceted identities affect their understanding of themselves but also how they navigate their campus environments. This work, grounded in critical paradigms, shared similarities to research using post-structural perspectives.

Similar to critical paradigms, post-structural work deconstructs binaries that constrain thought and action. In particular, post-structural paradigms disrupt and problematize what is seemingly normalized as the status quo in society (Renn, 2012). Post-structuralism "seeks to encourage ambivalence and multiplicity, exceed the boundaries of what can be imagined, expose dichotomies and illusions, and advocate for resistance to subjugation" (Jones, Torres, & Arminio, 2006, p. 21). Denton's (2014) research on gay college men living with HIV/AIDS is an excellent example of post-structural work in the field. Denton deconstructed problematic discourses that link HIV/AIDS to gay men and render invisible women, trans* people, and heterosexual men living with HIV. His work interrogates the ways higher education institutions are complicit in maintaining silence about HIV/AIDS, which affected the participants in Denton's study in their negotiation of the self-concept of gay men living with HIV/AIDS.

When considering Jones and Stewart's (2016) notion of the three waves of student development, there has clearly been an evolution in those waves in thinking about and even problematizing student development theory, particularly when considering college men on campus. Professionals working in higher education can and should no longer be willing to accept monolithic conceptions of gender. As coauthors and scholars on college men and masculinity, we firmly believe that gender is a socially constructed concept that is deeply woven into the fabric of our lives and ultimately reinforces and enforces power structures in our society. As a result, we advocate and urge individuals to move away from first wave perspectives on college men and instead explore and engage in research and scholarship grounded in second and third wave perspectives, especially given the unique needs of our diverse college men living, working, and studying on our campuses today.

The Model Gender Majority Myth

College men cannot be seen and understood as a monolithic group. It is essential to interrogate why historically a societal assumption and rationale for college and university educators has been to lump together rather than disaggregate to understand the nuanced and unique needs of various college men. Harper and Harris (2010) developed the concept of the model gender majority myth, or the erroneous oversimplification of college men as a monolithic group in educational systems. Their work on the model gender minority myth was inspired by Museus and Kiang's (2009) discussion of the model minority myth commonly associated with Asian Americans, which is the stereotypes and societal assumptions imposed on all Asian Americans based on the experiences of only some Asian Americans. For instance, in educational systems, a common belief is that Asian Americans outperform their peers on standardized tests and succeed in science, technology, engineering, and mathematics coursework. Yet, this is indeed a myth centered on the experiences of some but not all Asian American students. As Museus and Kiang noted, the model minority myth's foundations are formed on five incorrect assumptions:

1. Asian Americans are all the same.
2. Asian Americans are not really racial minorities.
3. Asian Americans do not encounter major challenges because of their race.
4. Asian Americans do not require resources and support.
5. College degree completion is equivalent to success.

Using this concept as a lens, Harper and Harris (2010) argued that college men are mistakenly seen in problematic and flawed ways regarding their developmental needs and lived experiences. As a result, they proposed the model gender majority myth, which contains five flawed assumptions:

1. Every male student benefits similarly from gender privilege.
2. Gender initiatives need not include men unless they are focused on reducing violence and sexual assault against women.
3. Undergraduate men do not encounter harmful stereotypes, social and academic challenges, and differential treatment in college environments because of their gender.
4. Male students do not require gender-specific resources and support.
5. Historical dominance and structural determinism ensure success for the overwhelming majority of contemporary college men. (p. 8)

Although it cannot be denied that college men certainly do maintain power and privilege based on their gender, Harper and Harris (2010) cautioned college student educators to think critically about the anecdotal and empirical data that show that college men face dangerous and difficult challenges and obstacles in the college environment (see Kimmel, 2008, on college men struggling to negotiate manhood and masculinity). We believe that the model gender majority myth continues to exist on our campuses. Although no other studies have expanded on Harper and Harris's model, we urge researchers to focus on this concept more in future studies on college men.

Student affairs administrators and faculty members need to understand that the aggregation of college men as a monolithic group with systemic privilege because of their gender actually creates conditions of erasure of other identities of men who have oppressed and subordinated identities. As a result, college student educators need to remind themselves that the intersectional identities of college men play a significant role in shaping one's college experience. In the next section, we explore emergent research and scholarship illuminating the developmental experiences of particular groups of college men that have largely been understudied.

Emergent Student Development Research on Understudied Populations of College Men

In response to disrupting the model gender majority myth, we want to point to contemporary research that has begun to examine historically understudied and undertheorized populations of college men. Returning to Jones and Stewart's (2016) concept of the three waves, much of this emergent scholarship on college men has focused on second and third wave perspectives, emphasizing historically underrepresented identities and centering work to interrogate power and issues of inequity in higher education. In particular, we focus on the literature on men of color, transgender men, sexual minority men, and men with disabilities.

College Men of Color

As mentioned previously in this chapter, much of the early men and masculinities literature was overwhelmingly focused on White college men with scarce attention paid to men of color. Over the past two decades, attention on Black men increased (Dancy, 2012; Harper, 2004; Harris, Palmer, & Struve, 2011; McGowan, 2017; Wood & Harris, 2013) and Latino men (Cerezo, Lyda, Beristianos, Enriquez, & Connor, 2013; Pérez, 2014, 2017; Rodriguez, Lu, & Bukoski, 2016; Sáenz, Bukoski, Lu, & Rodriguez, 2013; Sáenz, Mayo, Miller, & Rodriguez, 2015). Only a small number of studies have explored Asian American men (Liu, 2000; Shek, 2007), and there has been a dearth of studies on Middle Eastern or Native American college men through the particular lens of masculinity and gender.

The literature on college men of color has been largely focused on the concept of student success in higher education. Some scholars (Harper, 2009a; Harper, Carini, Bridges, & Hayek, 2004; Harper & Quaye, 2007) centered student engagement as a key aspect of college men of color's persistence in college. Moving away from deficit model approaches to racially minoritized college men, scholars have been exploring high-achieving college men, particularly those who are Black (Harper, 2004, 2009b; Johnson & McGowan, 2017) and Latino (Pérez, 2014, 2017; Strayhorn, 2010). Across this scholarship, a central theme that emerges is the importance of these students' cultural wealth and capital, which served as rich sources of self and collective identity as well as spaces for resiliency (Pérez, 2017; Johnson & McGowan, 2017). Likewise, this scholarship has also elucidated the need for strong support networks, which can be fostered through mentoring programs (Brooms, Goodman, & Clark, 2015; LaVant, Anderson, & Tiggs, 1997; Palmer & Gasman, 2008) or through the development of interpersonal relationships with other men on campus (McGowan, 2016, 2017). For instance, McGowan's (2016, 2017) work demonstrated that Black men gain a greater sense of their racial and gender identity through the relationships established with other men (same race and cross race) throughout their college experience, leading to cultural validation. Relatedly, Sáenz and colleagues' (2015) study on Latino men in community colleges found that these men often used *caballerismo*, or positively associated characteristics of Latino masculinity grounded in chivalry, to create supportive kinship networks to succeed academically. These experiences often lead to a stronger sense of belonging for men of color on campus, which promotes higher rates of persistence in college (Strayhorn, 2008a, 2008b).

It is clear that issues of systemic and institutionalized racism still play a significant role in the development of men of color. Microaggressions from peers, faculty, and staff have continued to play a role in the academic and cocurricular experiences of men of color, leading to higher rates of attrition or disconnection from campus (Harper, 2015; Harper & Hurtado, 2007; Palmer & Gasman, 2008). Similarly, strong adherence to dominant cultural gender norms, rooted in hegemonic masculinity, can also affect college men of color's academic performance (Harris, Palmer, & Struve, 2011; Sáenz et al., 2015). As Sáenz and colleagues (2015) stated, the Latino men in their studies avoided anything feminine, adhering to strong notions of *machismo*, or hypermasculine qualities and characteristics; for some of their participants, attending college was seen as a conflict with machismo, given that finding employment and earning money was a cultural norm rather than getting a postsecondary education. In their work investigating male gender role conflict among men of color in community college, Harris, Wood, and Newman (2015) found that Asian, Mexicano, and Latino men who were more focused in college tended to view help-seeking behaviors without conflating their actions as feminine; therefore, if college student educators could help men of color think about help-seeking outreach in culturally and gender affirmative ways, there is an increased likelihood for student success.

Trans* Men

Since the early years of the twenty-first century, the number of studies focusing on transgender or trans* students in higher education have been growing (see Marine, 2011; Nicolazzo, 2017). The use of *trans* here is deliberate as this term encompasses "a wide array of identities that continues to grow and expand" (Nicolazzo, 2015, p. 13) and can include transgender, nonbinary, agender, and genderqueer individuals. In his review of the existent literature, Jourian (2018b) noted, "As the literature reviews reveal, there are only two studies currently that purposefully engaged trans* (and specifically trans men and trans*masculine) students in inquiring about constructions of manhood and masculinities, and how their campus environments informed these constructions" (p. 14), referring to work done by Catalano (2015a, 2015b) and Jourian himself (2017a).

Jourian (2017a, 2018a) discussed multiple pathways that trans*masculine individuals take in understanding and negotiating their identities, particularly when considering the intersections of race. Jourian (2017a) found that White supremacy, anti-Blackness, and racism shaped trans*masculine students of color's experiences, as well as played a role in understanding what it means to be masculine in particular cultural contexts. This was different for White trans*masculine students, where only four in the study acknowledge the privilege they have from their Whiteness and how masculinity in the United States typically centers White masculinity. In Catalano's (2015a, 2015b) and Jourian's (2017a) studies, Genderism, defined by Bilodeau (2005) as the systemic reinforcement of the gender binary through politics and practices, played a role in their daily lived experiences on campus. For the trans* men or trans*masculine students in their studies, they often negotiated messages of genderism and hegemonic masculinity to then renegotiate what it meant to be masculine in their own lives and for their own selves (Catalano, 2015b; Jourian, 2017a). One of the significant strategies used by the trans* men or trans*masculine students in these two studies was building kinship networks with other queer or trans* individuals on and off campus. This connects to recent findings for student success among trans* students by Nicolazzo, Pitcher, Renn, and Woodford (2017), who also noted the importance of virtual spaces for trans* individuals to build community and engage in resilience.

Sexual Minority Men

Concurrent with the scholarship on trans* men, expanding attention has been paid to sexual minority and queer men in the past decade. Given the critique that much of the foundational literature on college men and masculinities centered the experiences of heterosexual men, particularly those who were White, scholars have since investigated the ways that intersections of identity shaped the lived experiences of sexual minority men in college (Camacho, 2016; Chan, 2017; Duran & Pérez, 2017; Lange & Moore, 2017; Tillapaugh, 2013, 2015).

Much of the contemporary scholarship on sexual minority men discusses the sense of being othered based on their sexual identity, which Lange and Moore (2017) explained as being "outside the dominant social groups of society in terms of power and privilege" (p. 825). Sexual minority men often experience overt and covert discrimination and heterosexism on campus from peers (Camacho, 2016; Lange & Moore, 2017; Tillapaugh, 2013, 2015). In particular, their conceptualization of masculinity is seen as complex and often contradictory (Chan, 2017; Lange & Moore, 2017; Tillapaugh, 2013). As Chan (2017) stated, "Masculinity is not limited to a single mode of expression, but can involve the simultaneous existence and negotiation of multiple masculinities" (p. 87). Tillapaugh (2013) found a similar perspective but often that the gay men in his study would engage in compartmentalization of identities in various spaces and with various people, similar to code switching. This sense of navigating and negotiating multiple masculinities dependent on spaces and with particular audiences is commonly seen in the extant scholarship, particularly for sexual minority men of color (Camacho, 2016; Chan, 2017; Lange & Moore, 2017; Tillapaugh, 2013).

Later scholarship also discussed the ways in which queer men, particularly queer men of color, are negotiating their multiple social identities, especially issues of sexuality and gender, as borderlands (Camacho, 2016; Duran & Pérez, 2017; Lange & Moore, 2017). As Duran and Pérez (2017) noted from their research, queer Latino men often create extensive kinship networks made up of peers, faculty, and administrators during college that come to serve as surrogate families; these findings were similar to Camacho's (2016) work on Latino gay men, Tillapaugh's (2015) study on sexual minority men, and Lange and Moore's (2017) discussion of the importance of counterspaces for gay men. This scholarship highlights the needs for college student educators to be engaged in relationship building with sexually minoritized college men, specifically as it relates to their negotiation of multiple masculinities in various contexts on campus.

College Men With Disabilities

A dearth of information continues on college men with disabilities and the ways they negotiate the concept of masculinity. The National Center for Education Statistics (2015) reported that in the 2011–2012 academic year, 11.3% of all males enrolled in postsecondary institutions reported having some type of disability, a slight increase from 10.9% of males in 2007–2008. Ultimately, this data only relies on students who self-disclosed their disability; as Gerschick (2011) and Myers (2015) acknowledged, many students with disabilities do not understand the processes of requesting accommodations for their disabilities at college and may also be dealing with stigma about their identity of having a disability. This is particularly concerning for college men, given that we know that men, particularly those who subscribe to hegemonic masculine norms, are less likely to engage in help-seeking behaviors compared to their peers who identify as women (Juvrud & Rennels, 2017; Pederson & Vogel, 2007).

In his review of the existing literature, Gerschick (2011) acknowledged that there is a lack of empirical studies that focus on college men with disabilities attending postsecondary educational institutions. He noted the following sets of social dynamics that must be understood for these students: (a) the stigma of having a disability, (b) understanding gender as an interactional process, and (c) being aware of the use of hegemonic masculinity as the standard bearer for men and the ways that affects men with disabilities. In particular, the stigma of having a disability can also shape and affect college men's sense of self. As Taub, Blinde, and Greer (1999) found in their study of male college students with physical disabilities, participation in physical activities and sports ultimately helped the men in their study feel a greater sense of self in terms of appearance as well as a greater sense of physical competence. As a result, through their sports involvement, these men navigated issues of stigma by shifting the assumptions and perceptions of others, particularly those who do not have a disability; thus, their engagement in physical activity allows men with disabilities to demonstrate a sense of masculinity that can be liberatory (Taub et al., 1999). However, Taub and colleagues' work was only one of a small number of studies that explored men with disabilities in college. Substantial attention must be paid to this group of students in the future, who deserve to be better understood and supported in their development.

Concluding Thoughts

As individuals invested in the development of college men, we hold firmly to the belief that continued exploration and investigation in how college men grow and develop is essential. As the remainder of this book demonstrates, there can be more successful outcomes for college men if college student educators are informed by the multiple developmental theories that can be used to inform their professional practice with these students. As you continue to contemplate the ways that developmental theories, particularly the three waves of theoretical paradigms, may inform your work, we encourage you to also be thoughtful about a few particular lenses that may be useful to help you understand your students in the context of their holistic sense of self.

Additionally, much of the literature on college men and masculinities is still centered in what Jones and Stewart (2016) would classify as second wave. There is a distinct need for more critical and post-structural understandings of college men. Particularly given that the scholarship is increasingly focusing on the intersectionality of multiple social identities among college men, there is a distinct advantage in reckoning with the ways power, privilege, and oppression influence college men's lives and how their college environments, such as institution types, peer groups, and geographical domains, affect some of these dynamics. With powerful examples from scholars such as Means and Jaeger (2015), Lange and Moore (2017), and Duran and Pérez (2017), we are seeing the possibilities of what critical and post-structural lenses can offer to higher education professionals in rethinking what we know about our students. In particular, much of this emergent scholarship offers important implications for how we as college student educators must be aware of how we reinforce and reify power structures, sometimes unnecessarily, which perpetuate programs, services, and initiatives that may negatively affect students when our intent may have been just the opposite.

Finally, we urge college student educators to become critical consumers of theory and its application to practice. As noted in chapter 1, you the reader are constantly approaching your professional practice informed by an epistemological approach, whether you're conscious of this or not. The theories you resonate with and use in your work also are grounded in a particular epistemological paradigm. We urge you to think critically about those theories. In what ways do they elicit some helpful information about your potential work with college men and their development? In what ways may they limit your understanding of college men? Do these theories account for all college men or only a select few or specific groups? Asking these questions and doing critical self-reflection on why you gravitate to these theories is an important step in engaging in more gender-conscious work. As Nicolazzo writes in chapter 11, there is a distinct need for college student educators to question what they have been taught or what they think they know. Development is an evolution; we believe that student development theory can be a helpful way to shape and inform our work, but it must be done in inclusive, meaningful ways that promote learning and understanding for our students. As you read the remaining chapters, we hope you approach them with the various lenses we have described here. What questions remain for you? What work do you need to do in investigating certain theories and digging deeper into them? How would you like to begin your work in strengthening the programs and services you can offer to college men, informed by theories and epistemological paradigms? Whatever your questions, we wish you well. Your students need you.

References

Anthony, R. C. H. (2013). *Searching for the new Black man: Black masculinity and women's bodies.* Jackson, MS: University Press of Mississippi.

Belenky, M. F., Clinchy, B. M., Goldberger, N. R., & Tarule, J. M. (1986). *Women's ways of knowing: The development of self, voice, and mind.* New York, NY: Basic Books.

Bilodeau, B. (2005). Beyond the gender binary: A case study of two transgender students at a midwestern research university. *Journal of Gay & Lesbian Issues in Education, 3*(1), 29–44.

Brooms, D. R., Goodman, J., & Clark, J. (2015). "We need more of this": Engaging Black men on college campuses. *College Student Affairs Journal, 33*, 105–123.

Camacho, T. (2016). *Navigating borderlands: Gay Latino men in college* (Doctoral dissertation). Available from Proquest Dissertations and Theses database. (UMI No. 10143427)

Catalano, D. C. J. (2015a). Beyond virtual equality: Liberatory consciousness as a path to achieve trans* inclusion in higher education. *Equity & Excellence in Education, 48,* 418–435.

Catalano, D. C. J. (2015b). "Trans enough?": The pressures trans men negotiate in higher education. *Transgender Studies Quarterly, 2,* 411–430.

Cerezo, A., Lyda, J., Beristianos, M., Enriquez, A., & Connor, M. (2013). Latino men in college: Giving voice to their struggles and triumphs. *Psychology of Men & Masculinity, 14,* 352–362.

Chan, J. (2017). "Am I masculine enough?": Queer Filipino college men and masculinity. *Journal of Student Affairs Research and Practice, 54*(1), 82–94.

Crenshaw, K. (1989). Demarginalizing the intersection of race and sex: A Black feminist critique of antidiscrimination doctrine, feminist theory and antiracist politics. *University of Chicago Legal Forum, 140,* 139–167.

Dancy, T. E. II. (2012). *The brother code: Manhood and masculinities among African American males in college.* Charlotte, NC: Information Age.

Davis, T. L. (2002). Voices of gender role conflict: The social construction of college men's identity. *Journal of College Student Development, 43,* 508–521.

Denton, J. M. (2014). *Living beyond identity: Gay college men living with HIV* (Doctoral dissertation). Retrieved from http://rave.ohiolink.edu/etdc/view?acc_num=miami1406656558

Duran, A., & Pérez, D. II. (2017). Queering la familia: A phenomenological study reconceptualizing familial capital for queer Latino men. *Journal of College Student Development, 58,* 1149–1165.

Edley, N. (2017). *Men and masculinity: The basics.* New York, NY: Routledge.

Foubert, J., Nixon, M. L., Sisson, V. S., & Barnes, A. C. (2005). A longitudinal study of Chickering and Reisser's vectors: Exploring gender differences and implications for refining the theory. *Journal of College Student Development, 46,* 461–471.

Gerschick, T. J. (2011). Disability identity intersections with masculinities. In J. A. Laker & T. Davis (Eds.), *Masculinities in higher education: Theoretical and practical consideration* (pp. 130–144). New York, NY: Routledge.

Gilligan, C. (1982). *In a different voice.* Cambridge, MA: Harvard University Press.

Harper, S. R. (2004). The measure of a man: Conceptualizations of masculinity among high-achieving African American male college students. *Berkeley Journal of Sociology, 48*(1), 89–107.

Harper, S. R. (2009a). Institutional seriousness concerning Black male student engagement: Necessary conditions and collaborative partnerships. In S. R. Harper & S. J. Quaye (Eds.), *Student engagement in higher education: Theoretical perspectives and practical approaches for diverse populations* (pp. 137–156). New York, NY: Routledge.

Harper, S. R. (2009b). Niggers no more: A critical race counternarrative on Black male student achievement at predominantly White colleges and universities. *International Journal of Qualitative Studies in Education, 22,* 697–712.

Harper, S. R. (2015). Black male college achievers and resistant responses to racist stereotypes at predominantly White colleges and universities. *Harvard Educational Review, 85,* 646–674.

Harper, S. R., Carini, R. M., Bridges, B. K., & Hayek, J. C. (2004). Gender differences in student engagement among African American undergraduates at historically Black colleges and universities. *Journal of College Student Development, 45,* 271–284.

Harper, S. R., & Harris, F., III. (2010). *College men and masculinities: Theory, research, and implications for practice.* San Francisco, CA: Jossey-Bass.

Harper, S. R., & Hurtado, S. (2007). Nine themes in campus racial climates and implications for institutional transformation. *New Directions for Student Services,* 120, 7–24.

Harper, S. R., & Quaye, S. J. (2007). Student organizations as venues for Black identity expression and development among African American male student leaders. *Journal of College Student Development, 48,* 127–144.

Harper, S. R., Wardell, C. C., & McGuire, K. M. (2011). Man of multiple identities: Complex individuality and identity intersectionality among college men. In J. A. Laker & T. Davis (Eds.), *Masculinities in higher education: Theoretical and practical consideration* (pp. 82–96). New York, NY: Routledge.

Harris, F. III, Palmer, R. T., & Struve, L. E. (2011). "Cool posing" on campus: A qualitative study of masculinities and gender expression among Black men at a private research institution. *Journal of Negro Education, 80*(1), 47–62.

Harris, F. III, & Wood, J. L. (2013). Student success for men of color in community colleges: A review of published literature and research, 1998–2012. *Journal of Diversity in Higher Education, 6,* 174–185.

Harris, F. III, Wood, J. L., & Newman, C. (2015). An exploratory investigation of the effect of racial and masculine identity on focus: An examination of White, Black, Mexicano, Latino, and Asian men in community colleges. *Culture, Society, & Masculinities, 7*(1), 61–72.

Howes, L. (2017). *The mask of masculinity: How men can embrace vulnerability, create strong relationships, and live their fullest lives.* Emmaus, PA: Rodale.

Innes, R. A., & Anderson, K. (Eds.) (2015). *Indigenous men and masculinities: Legacies, identities, regeneration.* Winnipeg, Manitoba, Canada: University of Manitoba Press.

Johnson, J. M., & McGowan, B. L. (2017). Untold stories: The gendered experiences of high achieving African American male alumni of historically Black colleges and universities. *Journal of African American Males in Education, 8*(1), 23–44.

Jones, S. R., & Abes, E. S. (2011). The nature and uses of theory. In J. H. Schuh, S. R. Jones, & S. R. Harper (Eds.), *Student services: A handbook for the profession* (5th ed., pp. 149–167). San Francisco, CA: Jossey-Bass.

Jones, S. R., & McEwen, M. K. (2000). A conceptual model of multiple dimensions of identity. *Journal of College Student Development, 41,* 405–414.

Jones, S. R., & Stewart, D.-L. (2016). Evolution of student development theory. New Directions for Student Services, 154, 17–28.

Jones, S. R., Torres, V., & Arminio, J. (2006). *Negotiating the complexities of qualitative research in higher education: Fundamental elements and issues.* New York, NY: Routledge.

Josselson, R. (1987). *Finding herself.* San Francisco, CA: Jossey-Bass.

Jourian, T. J. (2017a). Trans*forming college masculinities: Carving out trans* masculine pathways through the threshold of dominance. *International Journal of Qualitative Studies in Education, 30,* 245–265.

Jourian, T. J. (2017b). Trans*ing constructs. *Tijdschrift voor Genderstudies, 20,* 415–434.

Jourian T. J. (2018a). Sexua-romanticised pathways of transmasculine college students in the USA. *Sex Education, 18,* 360–375.

Jourian, T. J. (2018b). Trans*forming higher education men and masculinities studies: A critical review. *NORMA, 13*(1), 3–22.

Juvrud, J., & Rennels, J. L. (2017). "I don't need help": Gender differences in how gender stereotypes predict help-seeking. *Sex Roles, 76*(1/2), 27–39.

Keith, T. (2017). *Masculinities in contemporary American culture: An intersectional approach to the complexities and challenges of male identity.* New York, NY: Routledge.

Kimmel, M. (2008). *Guyland: The perilous world where boys become men.* New York, NY: HarperCollins.

Kimmel, M. (2010). *Misframing men: The politics of contemporary masculinities.* New Brunswick, NJ: Rutgers University Press.

Lange, A. C., & Moore, C. M. (2017). Kaleidoscope views: Using the theoretical borderlands to understand the experiences of gay cis-men. *Journal of College Student Development, 58,* 818–832.

LaVant, B. D., Anderson, J. L., & Tiggs, J. W. (1997). Retaining African American men through mentoring initiatives. *New Directions for Student Services, 80,* 43–53.

Levant, R. F., & Wong, Y. J. (Eds.). (2017). *The psychology of men and masculinities.* Washington, DC: American Psychological Association.

Liu, W. M. (2000). *Exploring the lives of Asian American men: Racial identity, male role norms, gender role conflict, and prejudicial attitudes* (Doctoral dissertation). Available from ProQuest Dissertations and Theses database. (UMI No. 3001389)

Marine, S. B. (2011). Stonewall's legacy: Bisexual, gay, lesbian, and transgender students in higher education. ASHE Higher Education Report, *37*(4).

McGowan, B. L. (2016). Interpersonal relationships: Exploring race and relationship decisions among African American men. *Journal of Student Affairs Research & Practice, 53,* 243–255.

McGowan, B. L. (2017). Visualizing peer connections: The gendered realities of African American college men's interpersonal relationships. *Journal of College Student Development, 58,* 983–1000.

Means, D. R., & Jaeger, A. J. (2015). Spiritual borderlands: A Black gay male college student's spiritual journey. *Journal of Student Affairs Research & Practice, 52*(1), 11–23.

Museus, S. D., & Kiang, P. N. (2009). Deconstructing the model minority myth and how it contributes to the invisible minority reality in higher education research. *New Directions for Institutional Research, 142,* 5–15.

Myers, J. (2016). *The future of men: Masculinity in the twenty-first century.* San Francisco, CA: Inkshares.

Myers, K. A. (2015). Students with disabilities: From success to significance. In P. A. Sasso & J. L. DeVitis (Eds.), *Today's college students: A reader* (pp. 141–150). New York, NY: Peter Lang.

National Center for Education Statistics. (2015). *Students with disabilities.* Retrieved from https://nces.ed.gov/fastfacts/display.asp?id=60

Neal, M. A. (2015). *New Black man* (10th anniversary edition). New York: Routledge.

Nicolazzo, Z. (2015). *"Just go in looking good": The resilience, resistance, and kinship-building of trans* college students* (Doctoral dissertation). Miami University, Oxford, OH.

Nicolazzo, Z. (2017). *Trans* in college: Transgender students' strategies for navigating campus life and the institutional politics of inclusion.* Sterling, VA: Stylus.

Nicolazzo, Z., Pitcher, E. N., Renn, K. A., & Woodford, M. (2017). An exploration of trans* kinship as a strategy for student success. *International Journal of Qualitative Studies in Education, 30,* 305–319.

O'Neil, J. M. (1990). Assessing men's gender role conflict. In D. Moore & F. Leafgren (Eds.), *Problem-solving strategies and interventions for men in conflict* (pp. 23–38). Alexandria, VA: American Counseling Association.

Palmer R., & Gasman, M. (2008). "It takes a village to raise a child": The role of social capital in promoting academic success for African American men at a Black college. *Journal of College Student Development, 49,* 52–70.

Pascoe, C. J., & Bridges, T. (2016). *Exploring masculinities: Identity, inequality, continuity, and change.* Oxford, England: Oxford University Press.

Patton, L. D., Renn, K. A., Guido, F. M., & Quaye, S. J. (2016). *Student development in college: Theory, research, and practice* (3rd ed.). San Francisco, CA: Jossey-Bass.

Pederson, E. L., & Vogel, D. L. (2007). Male gender role conflict and willingness to seek counseling: Testing a mediation model on college-aged men. *Journal of Counseling Psychology, 54,* 373–384.

Pérez, D., II. (2014). Exploring the nexus between community cultural wealth and the academic and social experiences of Latino male achievers at two predominantly White research universities. *International Journal of Qualitative Studies in Education, 27,* 747–767.

Pérez, D., II. (2017). In pursuit of success: Latino male college students exercising academic determination and community cultural wealth. *Journal of College Student Development, 58,* 123–140.

Renn, K. A. (2012). Creating and re-creating race: The emergence of racial identity as a critical element in psychological, sociological, and ecological perspectives on human development. In C. L. Wijeysinghe & B. W. Jackson, III (Eds.), *New perspectives on racial identity development: A theoretical and practical anthology* (2nd ed., pp. 11–22). New York: New York University Press.

Rodriguez, S. L., Lu, C., & Bukoski, B. E. (2016). "I just feel like I have to duke it out by myself": How Latino men cope with academic and personal obstacles during college. *Journal Committed to Social Change on Race and Ethnicity, 2*(2), 64–101.

Rudolph, J. D. (2012). *Embodying Latino masculinities: Producing masculatinidad.* New York, NY: Palgrave Macmillan.

Sáenz, V. B., Bukoski, B. E., Lu, C., & Rodriguez, S. (2013). Latino males in Texas community colleges: A phenomenological study of masculinity constructs and their effect on college experiences. *Journal of African American Males in Education, 4*(2), 82–102.

Sáenz, V. B., Mayo, J. R., Miller, R. A., & Rodriguez, S. L. (2015). (Re)defining masculinity through peer interactions: Latino men in Texas community colleges. *Journal of Student Affairs Research & Practice, 52,* 164–175.

Schwartz, R., & Stewart, D.-L. (2016). The history of student affairs. In J. H. Schuh, S. R. Jones, & V. Torres (Eds.), *Student services: A handbook for the profession* (6th ed., pp. 20–38). San Francisco, CA: Jossey-Bass.

Shek, Y. L. (2007). Asian American masculinity: A review of the literature. *Journal of Men's Studies, 14,* 379–391.

Strayhorn, T. L. (2008a). Fittin' in: Do diverse interactions with peers affect sense of belonging for Black men at predominantly White institutions? *NASPA Journal, 45,* 501–527.

Strayhorn, T. L. (2008b). The role of supportive relationships in facilitating African-American males' success in college. *NASPA Journal, 45,* 26–48.

Strayhorn, T. L. (2010). When race and gender collide: Social and cultural capital's influence on the academic achievement of African American and Latino males. *Review of Higher Education, 33,* 307–332.

Taub, D. E., Blinde, E. M., & Greer, K. R. (1999). Stigma management through participation in sport and physical activity: Experiences of male college students with physical disabilities. *Human Relations, 52,* 1469–1484.

Thelin, J. R., & Gasman, M. (2016). Historical overview of American higher education. In J. H. Schuh, S. R. Jones, & V. Torres (Eds.), *Student services: A handbook for the profession* (6th ed., pp. 3–19). San Francisco, CA: Jossey-Bass.

Tillapaugh, D. (2013). Breaking down the "walls of a facade": The influence of compartmentalization on gay college males' meaning-making. *Culture, Society, & Masculinities, 5,* 127–146.

Tillapaugh, D. (2015). Critical influences on sexual minority college males' meaning-making of their multiple identities. *Journal of Student Affairs Research and Practice, 52,* 64–75.

Winston, R. B., Miller, T. K., & Prince, J. S. (1987). *Student Developmental Task and Lifestyle Inventory [SDTLI], Form W-87.* Athens, GA: Student Development Associates.

Wood, J. L., & Harris III, F. (2013). The Community College Survey of Men: An initial validation of the instrument's non-cognitive outcomes construct. *Community College Journal of Research and Practice, 37*(4), 333–338.

PART TWO

PROGRAM DESIGN

We need first a public discourse about masculinity that illuminates the price of blindly consuming masculine hegemony and raises consciousness so that boys and men can become the authors of their lives not some fictional character created by ghost writers. We need teachers, parents, counselors, bosses, coaches, and administrators to understand what is happening in boys and men's lives, the pressure they feel to live up to unattainable ideals of masculinity, and the feelings of doubt, anxiety, and shame that often accompany that quest. (M. Kimmel & T. Davis, "Mapping Guyland in College," in J.A. Laker and T. Davis (Eds.), Masculinities in Higher Education: Theoretical and Practical Considerations, *New York, NY: Routledge, pp. 3–15)*

3

BUILDING A CAMPUS
COALITION

Keith E. Edwards, Zak Foste, and Chris Taylor

Agrowing body of evidence documents the numerous challenges undergraduate college men face in navigating restrictive and rigid gendered expectations (Edwards & Jones, 2009; Foste & Jones, 2018; Harris, 2009; Kimmel, 2008). These narrow and limiting expectations have consequences not only for college men but also for cisgender women; the lesbian, gay, and bisexual community; and transgender students. Because definitions of appropriate masculine behavior are so frequently rooted in a rejection of being perceived as feminine or gay (Davis, 2002; Kimmel, 1994), how college men make sense of masculinity has implications for the entire campus community (Harris & Edwards, 2010). That is, campus cultures of patriarchy, homophobia, and transphobia cannot be divorced from the dominant culture's definition of *manhood* or what scholars refer to as *traditional hegemonic masculinity* (Connell, 1987). By failing to name the gendered experiences of college men, institutions of higher education further perpetuate the normative, privileged status of men (Davis & Laker, 2004). Thus, colleges and universities are beginning to acknowledge and respond to the consequences of hegemonic masculinity on campus.

The purpose of this chapter is to explore how educators can intentionally cultivate campus coalitions that address issues pertaining to college men and masculinities. We offer seven key considerations we believe to be important in building such coalitions. These considerations reflect theoretical and empirical scholarship as well as our own experiences engaging college men on gender and masculinity. We hope this chapter serves as a tool that faculty and staff can use to work toward campus climates that are more welcoming and affirming for people of all genders.

Because the key considerations we discuss in this chapter are based on scholarship as well as our own experiences doing this work, we want to be transparent about our own positionality and experiences. Identities and experiences shape our perspective and meaning-making in ways that offer us connection and insight and that perpetuate limitations and lack of consciousness of privilege. The three of us each identify as White cisgender heterosexual men. We have each worked on initiatives focused on college men in a variety of contexts. Keith Edwards has directly worked with and advised several student organizations focused on men and masculinities and has indirectly worked with dozens of campuses starting these initiatives as a speaker and consultant. Zak Foste has worked in a variety of contexts with college men, including sexual assault prevention and fraternities. Chris Taylor cocreated the Masculinities Committee at Miami University and served as its cochair for three years.

Key Consideration 1: Accounting for Your Own Identities and Learning

When building a campus coalition, we encourage those involved to start by looking inward, reflecting on their own social identities, perspectives, and motivations to engage in the work. We have often observed that men in particular are drawn to this work in large part because of their own experiences navigating the tensions of rigid gendered expectations. Drawing on our personal histories offers an important lens when beginning to engage the campus community on issues pertaining to college men and masculinities. However, without reflecting on how their own identities bring them to this work, educators risk crafting one-size-fits-all approaches to working with college men that are void of any critical reflexivity. We must engage in praxis with constant action and reflection (Freire, 1972); each without the other can be both ineffective and harmful. This is particularly important for those at the intersection of multiple dominant identities, such as race, sex, gender, and sexual orientation.

Accounting for our own identities can guard against the potential of essentializing all men as experiencing gender in similar ways. For instance, a committee composed almost exclusively of White, cisgender men who rely solely on their own experiences is likely to elevate the priorities of the men who look most like themselves. It is critically important to avoid such oversimplification. An individual's identities and experiences can shape and influence the purpose for someone engaging in men and masculinities work. Cisgender men may approach this work very differently from women and transgender individuals, who might be interested less in explicitly supporting college men and more in addressing patriarchy, misogyny, transphobia, and sexual violence. Additionally, scholarship has long documented how other social identities such as race (Harper, 2009), sexual orientation (Tillapaugh, 2015), and gender identity (Catalano, 2015) influence how college men interact with and experience gender. For instance, racism intersects with gender in a way that mitigates many of the privileges typically associated with masculinity for men of color. For example, Black men on campus frequently encounter racialized and gendered expectations that frame them as dangerous, deviant, unintelligent, and outsiders of the campus community (Harper, 2009). Some institutions have launched initiatives specifically directed at men of color with the goals of improving persistence and retention and helping these men navigate racialized experiences. Similarly, Catalano's (2015) work has examined how transgender men struggle with being perceived as trans enough. Catalano critiqued higher education's commitment to trans men, noting that "the real and central concern for the trans men in this research is the lack of space, time, and effort put forth by institutions to actually understand their needs" (p. 426). In beginning to build a campus coalition, educators need to be mindful of the impact of intersecting forms of oppression and how multiple social identities affect the different ways college men experience and interact with gender norms and conceptualize their gender identity.

To advocate for college men, and people of all genders on campus who are affected by toxic forms of masculinity, immersing oneself in preexisting literature is a useful first step. We encourage educators to spend a considerable amount of time familiarizing themselves with conceptual and empirical work on issues pertaining to college men and gender. Although it is tempting to rush toward actionable steps, sustained engagement with prior literature can add important nuance and complexity to formulating a coalition's goals and purpose. Further, this can provide a conceptual tool kit of sorts that will assist in providing the rationale and making the case to key stakeholders on campus and beyond.

When Chris Taylor began a committee on college men and masculinities at his own institution, he suggested that the committee spend considerable time with preexisting literature on the subject. For several months, the committee focused on the group's collective learning and emerging understanding of college men, gender, and masculinities. The committee members also held a retreat to dig into the scholarship and their own individual and collective meaning-making.

In addition to immersing oneself in conceptual and empirical work on college men, we also encourage individuals to construct a diverse coalition of stakeholders. In our own experiences, we have been fortunate enough to have, and incredibly grateful for, individuals who have pointed out the areas we are unaware of because of our own privileged locations in crafting educational interventions for college men. We encourage those who are beginning this work to construct a coalition of people who are truly interested in and representative of the diversity of experiences under the umbrella terms of *men* and *masculinity* on campus.

Key Consideration 2: Goals and Framing

Grounding our learning and accounting for our own identities and experience prepares us to begin framing and articulating goals for a campus initiative. Most of these campus initiatives have an overall goal of trying to address patriarchy and sexism as well as reduce gender norm expectations. In our experience, discussions regarding framing and goal setting should occur as close to the creation of a coalition as possible. Mizrahi and Rosenthal (2001) noted that organizations that possess a shared sense of ideology often have increased longevity in terms of a willingness to devote time and energy to the collective work. For groups that have already been engaging in this work, it is certainly possible to have these discussions at a later time and revisit them as the group grows or changes focus. How this is articulated may vary from learning goals and outcomes for one initiative to mission and values for another. Setting aside time and space to do this work around a core mission and purpose through retreats may be beneficial.

The purpose and goals of individual coalitions will vary based on the needs of a campus or groups on a campus. Purposes could potentially include radical deconstruction of gender, discussions and action surrounding retention of men, alcohol use and the overrepresentation of men in conduct systems, creating a first-time space for reflection among men, programming initiatives, sexual violence prevention, and initiatives focused on men of color as well as many others.

Several considerations are necessary to locate the goals of the work. Foremost, the broad campus context should be considered, including factors such as history, demographics, institutional type, and geographic location. An initiative might also consider any past or current initiatives that are focused on men. A campus climate survey may also be an effective and low-cost option for gaining insight into men's experiences on campus. In addition to general demographics, areas to consider in such an effort might include the use of general campus services (learning centers; academic advising; lesbian, gay, bisexual, transgender office; residence life staff; women's center;

career services; health services; etc.), class attendance, level of faculty contact, awareness of initiatives for men on campus, and initiatives men would like to see on campus.

Regardless of the means that are used to gain information, data can be used to assist in connecting to other important stakeholders on campus. It is likely that as a group defines the purpose and goals of a coalition, compelling interests across different functional areas will become apparent, including student conduct, men's health, service-learning, sexual violence prevention, retention and persistence, and fraternity and sorority life. Units that advocate for traditionally marginalized populations that are often harmed by dominant conceptualizations of masculinity, such as women's centers and lesbian, gay, bisexual, and transgender centers, are particularly important stakeholders to connect with as a coalition.

Finally, when considering framing a coalition and its work, it is vital to consider the power of language. In other words, what do you call your group? Issues of inclusion and power, as well as audience and marketing, form a complicated crossroads that must be addressed. Terms including *men, male, male identified*, and *masculinity* all have potential implications for who will feel included or excluded in a group. Although this chapter discusses coalitions, a group may also find language that better suits its purpose and goals such as a men's programming group, men's discussion groups, masculinity committees, or others. Marketing is also important, and an appealing name, particularly if a goal is to involve students, could be one key to success. It is important to safeguard against language that reifies problematic gender norms.

Key Consideration 3: Different Models

A clear purpose and vision should guide the initiative model that best helps you reach your goals and fits your campus environment. This may come organically as the coalition forms or as a result of the work on mission and vision. Different campus contexts, history, and group goals will result in a particular model or hybrid model that makes the most sense. This is not a-one-size-fits-all (or even most) approach.

Each model has benefits and challenges. If there is a desire to involve students, which is likely, a group should carefully consider what models may encourage students to become involved and any that may detract from a student's experience. If climate study data is available, it may be helpful giving direction to the types of experiences or services students are seeking. Other challenges may involve the credibility of this work in your setting, whether resources exist, and if efforts may receive resistance. The following represent possible models that may be used alone or in combination.

Resource Library

This may be the least difficult model to achieve because many resources are available for free from an institutional library or online. Articles, books, films, and other media can be collected in a common location (physical or virtual) and help a variety of campus groups or individuals who want to learn more or engage in programming on their own.

Student Organizations

A student organization could come in the form of masculinity-focused student groups that promote healthy relationships, discussion groups, social justice theater groups, sexual violence prevention groups, and many others. Because many college-age men may still be forming their personal concepts of masculinity, it is important for groups to have an adviser who has the awareness of and ability to foster men's identity development.

Peer Educators

Although this is a student-focused model, creating a group of peer educators who concentrate on healthy masculinity should also involve faculty or staff to provide the necessary training and advising (see chapter 8 for more discussion on this). This staff presence makes this model more sustainable, but it also requires more dedication from student and faculty and staff participants.

Committees or Programming Groups

This model allows the possibility of a cross-section of interested parties to come together and centralize educational and programmatic efforts on a campus. It can potentially work as a standing committee, possibly in a student affairs division, or on an ad hoc basis. Sustaining membership and leadership is often a challenge with committees.

Retreat

Retreats can be part of many of these strategies and could be useful while a group is creating its vision or for more in-depth experiential learning as a coalition (see chapter 6 for more on retreats). Some institutions have created retreats for college-age men to serve as an opportunities to discuss and learn in a setting that is somewhat removed from day-to-day campus life.

Regional Conferences or Coalitions

Some coalitions host regional conferences that focus on masculinity. We have found that often several people in a given area are anxious to engage in this work but feel overwhelmed or lack resources. The opportunity to share ideas, gain knowledge, and have a core group or electronic mailing list for follow-up is desirable. In some cases, this can lead to a regional coalition.

Offices or Centers

These units require a great deal of time, resources, and institutional support and often come after other masculinity work has been done on campus. It is obviously necessary to provide proof of a need for this type of structure, which may be linked to academic programs or departments that provide additional layers of complexity. Sustainable funding may be necessary, such as an endowed fund with institutional advancement. However, these entities can also act as a campus or even regional hub for programming, education, and activism regarding healthy masculinity.

Depending on the goals and the campus context, one of these units may be a better fit, or perhaps a hybrid model combining different aspects may be best for your campus community. It is important to note that one size will not fit all settings, and consideration of a variety of factors as well as some trial and error is necessary.

Key Consideration 4: Logistics

Once clear goals are outlined and a model that matches those goals identified, there are important logistics to consider. Just as there is no model that is ideal for every goal or campus community, there is no one-size-fits-all approach to these logistical considerations either. Based on our experiences we turn now to some of the logistical aspects as well as some possibilities to consider including time lines, members, funding, meeting logistics and structure, and possible programs and events to organize.

Time Line

In our experience college men in particular are often reluctant to start an initiative but are willing to join one that has already been established. For this reason, it may be worth considering pulling together a small group of very committed folks to organize and lay the foundation before a formal launch. For student organizations, this could consist of recruiting three or four students, identifying an adviser, submitting paperwork to become a student organization, applying for a budget in the spring semester, and then doing a full launch at the beginning of the fall semester as an established organization.

Members

Representation from and the reach to different communities on campus is key to the type of cultural change on hegemonic masculinity that these initiatives are often seeking. It is important to seek a variety of perspectives from different social identity groups such as race, age, gender, sexual orientation, social class status, religion, abilities, and more. It is also important to bring in and connect with a variety of campus constituents. For a faculty and staff steering committee this could mean a blend of staff from different academic departments, divisions of the institution, staffing, and promotion and tenure levels. For a student organization, this means contacting student athletes, fraternity and sorority members, formal and informal student leaders, resident assistants, those involved with music and theater, the Reserve Officers' Training Corps, and more. If the initiative comes to be seen as solely focused on student athletes, resident assistants, or other subgroups, it will lose credibility in other communities. It is important to be mindful that individuals may be interested in these initiatives for a variety of reasons including identity struggles, being survivors of sexual violence, seeking connection and community, promoting their own agenda, or a desire for learning and growth.

Funding

Many of the models require modest funding to achieve their goals. A student organization may be able to operate with as little as $200 per semester, making larger requests for major events or speakers. A campus committee may need no new funding and be able to support larger initiatives by collaborating with the existing funds of the offices and departments represented. In fact, we have often observed collaborative funding helps not only generate financial support for an initiative but also create ownership and acceptance from broader campus constituents. A model with physical space and staffing would need to identify budget line sources of funding or seek sustainable support through alumni giving or even endowed funding.

Meeting Logistics and Structure

Setting consistent meeting times and locations can be key to the success of these initiatives. Meeting on a regular schedule in a consistent location can help those involved build it into their routine. It is key to also model a different way of leading these meetings and initiatives so that the leadership approach does not reinforce and may even provide a counternarrative to the hierarchical traditional leadership often associated with men.

Meeting structures should be carefully considered and tied to the goals and the model. For a campus committee, sharing articles, blog posts, videos, or assessment data before the meeting can help the group use time efficiently and focus on discussion toward action. For a peer education model, devoting significant time to the learning and development of members of the group aligns well with the purpose. For a student organization, we have found it important to split meeting time between discussion and action. As students will attend for different reasons, it is important to incorporate discussion and action into each meeting. Those more focused on action to plan an event or host a speaker can learn and grow by participating in the discussions. Similarly, those eager to reflect on and discuss their experiences as men may be interested in discussing current events related to masculinity, provocative topics such as pornography or men's violence in video games, or their experiences of men on campus. These discussions can benefit the participants and others by turning that learning and reflection into action to benefit other members of the campus communities.

Programming

In regard to planning programs and events, coalitions have many possibilities from the simple to complex. Designing posters, T-shirts, and logos to represent the group or initiative can be helpful. One group required participants to attend four meetings before they were eligible to purchase a T-shirt, which generated commitment and also elevated the social status of the T-shirts significantly. Another campus group held a concert featuring local bands that played for free; proceeds from all ticket sales were used to purchase clothing to donate to local sexual assault nurse examiners so that survivors didn't have to wear the clothes they were assaulted in going home from the exam. Super Bowl viewing parties, in which poor messages about masculinity are transmitted to viewers, can also be fun, build community, and raise awareness.

Supporting events on campus organized by women-led or feminist organizations can be helpful and rewarding, but it is important to consult with these organizations so that men's voices and masculinity are not unintentionally recentered. It is also important to understand and respect the fact that women's organizations may not want any help from individual men or men's groups. For example, a student group focused on engaging men might offer to usher or take tickets for performances of *The Vagina Monologues*.

Another group might offer to contribute to building a structure for the Clothesline Project, a program where interpersonal violence survivors display their experiences on a T-shirt in a public area on campus, or monitoring the exhibit during off hours. These contributions can be a way to demonstrate a commitment to supporting women and women's leadership.

Key Consideration 5: The Role of Developmental Readiness

Rarely have college men been asked to critically reflect on dominant gendered expectations related to men and masculinity (Edwards & Jones, 2009; Harris, 2009). For many, a weekend retreat, classroom discussion, or guest speaker may be the first-time college men have been invited to consider how gender structures and informs the ways they move through the world. Because of this lack of critical reflection, coupled with the powerful conditioning of masculinity, we advocate for developmentally appropriate interventions that account for where college men are in their own development.

Kegan (1994) offered a developmental bridge as an important metaphor for learning and meaning-making, which considers where students are and where we hope for them to be in developmental terms. He explained that this type of support constitutes *"a holding environment that provides both welcoming acknowledgement to exactly who the person is right now as he or she is, and fosters the person's psychological evolution"* [emphasis in original] (p. 43). Applied to work with college men, particularly those at the nexus of multiple dominant identities who have rarely encountered the dissonance necessary for such critical reflection, educators must acknowledge developmental considerations when crafting educational interventions. What does it mean for students to receive information that contradicts current paradigms learned from and reinforced by credible, trusted sources of authority (e.g., parents, coaches, friends, the media)?

Educators should consider a number of questions in crafting developmentally appropriate interventions, including the following:

1. What do we know about the prior knowledge of those we are trying to reach?
2. Are the interventions consistent with what we know about developmental theory?
3. Do the interventions acknowledge the different ways college men performed and perceived gender and masculinity?

4. Do the interventions disrupt traditional understandings of masculinity as the sole property of male bodies and femininity as the sole property of female bodies?

Each of these, we believe, offers helpful guidance as campus coalitions begin taking steps to engage college men in the powerful role of gender broadly and masculinity in particular in shaping attitudes, behaviors, and understandings of the self. Most important, accounting for development can avoid a too-much, too-soon approach that might overwhelm students who have rarely, if ever, reflected on dominant meanings of masculinity. Although at times overly simple and reductionist, basic discussions on gender roles may offer an important entry point for college men during new student orientation or during the first-year experience. This can provide the foundation later during a student leader or peer educator training to illuminate the socially constructed nature of gender and prompt a larger discussion on how such binary understandings limit men's ability to access a wide range of feelings.

Unlearning the powerful conditioning of masculinity cannot occur over a weekend retreat or a semester's worth of coursework. It is a lifelong process of continual reflection and self-critique. We encourage coalitions to consider their work with college men as the likely starting point for this process. Acknowledging the complexity and messiness of development necessitates a coalition to secure campus support for this type of work across the institution. Offering students opportunities to reflect on matters of masculinity across multiple contexts can ensure that engagement is sustained, with the possibility of cultivating increasingly complex ways of thinking about the gendered self.

Key Consideration 6: Sustainability

Once any initiative is established, maintaining momentum, motivation, and sustainability is challenging. In higher education students are by design transient, and staff, particularly entry to midlevel, often are as well. Faculty may be more lasting, but they have multiple competing interests, especially those in tenure-track positions. Like much social activism, this work is often born of passion and personal interest in a single individual or a small group. If that individual or group leaves or disengages from the work, a coalition can fizzle. Successful coalitions anticipate turnover and plan how they will maintain sustainability.

Although an individual's passion may serve as the initial motivation, a successful coalition needs to be focused on more than the individual leader or adviser. Shared leadership among cochairs or coadvisers can be helpful in fostering sustainability. This may also provide an opportunity to interrogate traditional, patriarchal leadership models as the group establishes itself. Shared leadership across individuals, organizational structures, and positionality can help prevent loss of momentum as the work becomes interwoven into the fabric of the institution. Gaining this acceptance can provide a support structure that includes staff, advisers, physical space, funding, and other resources. Collaboration among student organizations and multiple offices can provide shared ownership, collaborative advising, and a diverse funding stream from multiple sources.

Ongoing attention is needed as the meaning of a coalition may evolve over time and members come and go. In addition to providing data to justify the use of resources, assessment of coalition efforts as well as member satisfaction can aid in providing direction for sustainability.

Key Consideration 7: Systemic Accountability

Kivel (1992, 2002, 2013) is one of the original critical scholars of men and masculinities. He has written about issues of masculinity, Whiteness, religious privilege and oppression, and other social justice subjects. Kivel once asked Keith E. Edwards, "How are you setting up systems of accountability so that you are being held accountable to those you aspire to be an ally with, without placing the burden of your accountability on those who are already being oppressed?" (P. Kivel, personal communication, October 11, 2005). This is a powerful question without easy answers, and even if we don't have an immediate answer, our social justice efforts are much improved if we keep this question in mind.

Systemic accountability is about moving beyond openness to feedback. It is about setting up systems that provide input about how you are doing whether or not you are seeking it, open to it, or want it. This kind of accountability is especially important for those of us operating from a place of social privilege for two reasons. First, our social privilege can leave us unaware of many of the ways that privilege and oppression function, even if we are educated, open, and committed to our own unlearning. Second, when those of us with privilege challenge social oppression we often receive far more credit than those who experience that oppression. Many of us doing anti-oppression men's work are well aware that we get far too much credit for doing far too little. These are just two of the reasons systemic accountability is so critical. We must hold a critical orientation, pay attention to power dynamics, continue to tend to our own unlearning, and create systems of accountability.

Doing work on men and masculinities and being a part of launching initiatives on campuses related to this means establishing systems to be held accountable, particularly to the leadership of women and transgender people. This can feel risky, vulnerable, and raise our concerns that our sexism, genderism, and other internalized dominance may be revealed, named, and made public. It is important to remember that we do this work not to advance ourselves and be held up as experts but to make progress in addressing systemic sexism, liberating us all from oppressive and limiting gender norms, and not doing additional harm in the process. We do not want to reify the very systems of oppression (e.g., sexism and genderism) that we seek to challenge and deconstruct on campus. We also do not want to fall into the trap of reifying other systems of oppression when our attention and focus is on sexism and genderism, which is all too easy to do. The criticism we receive may also not be about us specifically or about this particular initiative. It might be about the systemic structures and history (often personally lived) that may very reasonably instill fear, trepidation, and mistrust among women and transgender folks toward this type of work being done by men. Skepticism and cautiousness are warranted. Collectively men have a history of not getting this type of work right, an unfortunate reality that far too often has inflicted harm on the very populations we seek to work with.

Conclusion

Because each campus context is different, there is no a universal paradigm, approach, or strategy that will work on every campus. The purpose of this chapter is to offer some key considerations we have found useful in being more intentional, aware, and effective in cultivating sustainable campus coalitions for men and masculinities work. When effective, these coalitions can support men and people of all genders through their individual development and begin addressing systemic sexism, genderism, and intersecting forms of oppression on campus.

To be effective in interrogating masculinities broadly, we must develop a willingness to be vulnerable as a key starting point for coalition building on masculinities. Without the willingness to acknowledge our socialization, our internalized dominance, and how it shows up, we cannot move toward individual and collective liberation including our own. Vulnerability can serve as the foundation for a stronger sense of humility and uncertainty, which may be uncomfortable but will help us be more effective in reaching the goals of these initiatives. As Yancy (2015) said, "Humility is about strength. It provides us with the ability to recognize that our knowledge is always limited, which is not a deficit but a crucial source of information" (p. 107). Vulnerability and humility allow growth and compassion and opens us to what we do not know and cannot know because of our experiences in systems of oppression. Once we are open, we can see the critique and feedback not as a threat to be defensive about but as a gift toward our own liberation (Edwards, 2006). We offer these considerations in the hope that they can help you foster more intentional, critically reflective, and successful initiatives and campus coalitions.

References

Catalano, D. C. J. (2015). "Trans enough?" The pressures trans men negotiate in higher education. *Transgender Studies Quarterly, 2*, 411–430.

Connell, R. W. (1987). *Gender and power.* Palo Alto, CA: Stanford University Press.

Davis, T. L. (2002). Voices of gender role conflict: The social construction of college men's identity. *Journal of College Student Development, 43*, 508–521.

Davis, T. L., & Laker, J. (2004). Connecting men to academic and student affairs programs and services. *New Directions in Student Services, 107*, 47–57.

Edwards, K. E. (2006). Aspiring social justice ally identity development. *NASPA Journal, 43*(4), 39–60.

Edwards, K. E., & Jones, S. R. (2009). "Putting my man face on": A grounded theory of college men's gender identity development. *Journal of College Student Development, 50*, 210–228.

Foste, Z. H., & Jones, S. R. (2018). Isn't that for sorority girls? Narratives of college men in service-learning. *Journal of Student Affairs Research and Practice, 55*, 65–77.

Freire, P. (1972). *Pedagogy of the oppressed* (M. B. Ramos, Trans.). New York, NY: Herder and Herder.

Harper, S. R. (2009). Niggers no more: A critical race counternarrative on Black male student achievement at predominantly White colleges and universities. *International Journal of Qualitative Studies in Education, 22*, 697–712.

Harris, F., III. (2009). Deconstructing masculinity: A qualitative study of college men's masculine conceptualizations and gender performance. *NASPA Journal, 45*, 453–474.

Harris, F., III, & Edwards, K. E. (2010). College men's experiences as men: Findings from two grounded theory studies. *Journal of Student Affairs Research and Practice, 47*, 43–62.

Kegan, R. (1994). *In over our heads: The mental demands of modern life.* Cambridge, MA: Harvard University Press.

Kimmel, M. S. (1994). Masculinity as homophobia: Fear, shame, and silence in the construction of gender identity. In H. Brod & M. Kaufman (Eds.), *Theorizing masculinities* (pp. 119–141). Newbury Park, CA: Sage.

Kimmel, M. S. (2008). *Guyland: The perilous world where boys become men.* New York, NY: HarperCollins. Kivel, P. (1992). *Men's work: How to stop the violence that tears our lives apart.* Center City, MN: Hazelden.

Kivel, P. (2002). *Uprooting racism: How White people can work for racial justice* (Rev. ed.). Gabriola Island, British Columbia, Canada: New Society.

Kivel, P. (2013). *Living in the shadow of the cross: Understanding and resisting the power and privilege of Christian hegemony.* Gabriola Island, British Columbia, Canada: New Society.

Mizrahi, T., & Rosenthal, B. B. (2001). Complexities of coalition building: Leaders' successes, strategies, struggles, and solutions. *Social Work, 46,* 63–78.

Tillapaugh, D. (2015). Critical influences on sexual minority college males' meaning-making of the multiple identities. *Journal of Student Affairs Research and Practice, 52,* 64–75.

Yancy, G. (Ed.). (2015). *White self-criticality beyond anti-racism: How does it feel to be a White problem?* Lanham, MD: Lexington Books.

4

TOWARD AN INTERSECTIONAL MODEL OF COLLEGE MEN AND MASCULINITIES PROGRAMMING

Kyle C. Ashlee and Rachel Wagner

Headlines about toxic masculinity pepper news feeds as journalists and pundits seek to explain the sexually abusive and violent behavior of men across a variety of contexts and professions. In popular usage, *toxic masculinity* acts as a placeholder for the problematic attitudes and behaviors associated with hegemonic forms of masculinity that cisgender men are socialized into. These behaviors include obsession with power and control, emotional stoicism, heterosexual promiscuity, and fear of femininity (Brannon, 1976; Connell, 2005; Kimmel, 2008). Calls for replacing toxic masculinity abound in many social environments including college campuses. Monaghan (2017) notes that a growing number of campuses are relying on initiatives informed by men and masculinities scholarship to address questions such as, How might we teach young men that the cultural programming and conditioning they have received is (a) not the only route to manhood and (b) a price too high to pay?

Researchers have argued for more comprehensive men's programming in higher education to transform hegemonic masculinity on college campuses (Edwards & Jones, 2009; Harris & Struve, 2009) and for initiatives specifically addressing the needs of marginalized men, including men of color (Harper & Harris, 2010), queer men (Berila, 2011), and men with disabilities (Gerschick, 2011). Cisgender college men are responsible for alarming rates of high-risk behavior, including binge drinking, sexual assault, and violence, which require significant institutional resources (Capraro, 2000; Harris & Edwards, 2010). Davis and Laker (2004) noted that the many educational needs related to college men are often difficult to achieve because of limited staffing and a lack of understanding regarding men's identity development. Thus, many college educators charged with creating men's programming find themselves conflicted about what types of initiatives to create, what population of students to target, and what learning outcomes to pursue.

In this chapter we review various formats, intended audiences, and learning outcomes of college men and masculinities programs and analyze the inherent challenges and benefits associated with these approaches to men's programming in higher education. Although broad initiatives aimed at college men have some positive outcomes, without intentional critical frameworks these programs can undermine emancipatory efforts by recentering patriarchy, White supremacy, heteronormativity, and other forms of dominance. As a result, we argue that an intersectional approach to men's programming that situates multiple identities in systems of power and oppression is more suitable to facilitating college men's identity development (Jones & Abes, 2013). An intersectional model of college men's programming uses intersectionality theory (Crenshaw, 1991) to center the experiences of individuals in marginalized groups, complicate unexamined notions of social identity, unveil systems of power, and ultimately promote social justice (Dill & Zambrana, 2009). In addition to this intersectional model for college men and masculinities programming, we offer programmatic learning outcomes, examples, and theoretical and practical considerations. This chapter aims to address some of the most persistent questions faced by college men and masculinities educators while providing a social justice framework for men's programming in higher education.

Men's Programming on Campus

There is a dearth of literature on college men and masculinities programming that addresses men's gender identity, expression, socialization, and performance. The majority of research on programming that targets men as an audience focuses on sexual assault prevention, including violence prevention, bystander intervention, and risk reduction efforts (Berkowitz, 2011; Foubert, Garner, & Thaxter, 2006). In the absence of empirical publications evaluating the effectiveness of various programs that target college men, we were able to find several programs through national organizations, news articles, and Web searches. Specifically, we found 25 different programs, but this

TABLE 4.1
Types of College Men Programming on Campus

Type	Category	Purpose	Example
1	Gender socialization	Raising consciousness and sensitizing men to how gender broadly and masculinity specifically organize social life and relationships	Gender Box activities that increase participants' understanding of the messages and enforcements that circumscribe what is authoritatively masculine
2	Success programs	Increase support with the goal of improving persistence and graduation rates for men of color	Mentoring programs that aim to develop social and cultural capital to be successful in college and work placement
3	Violence prevention	Involve men in addressing and eliminating rape culture	Peer education and bystander intervention training

is not a comprehensive list. Examples fall into three distinctive categories or types of programs (see Table 4.1).

Type 1 programs seek to disrupt and deconstruct hegemonic masculinity through programmatic offerings that encourage men to interrogate their gender socialization. These programs are built on activities that compel students to identify and explore the messages they received about what it means to be a man and attempt to respond to calls to activate men's consciousness about gender (Davis, 2002). Type 2 programs provide targeted support in the vein of mentoring, tutoring, peer networking, and leadership development curricula for men with marginalized identities to increase persistence and success rates. These important initiatives seek to redress the alarming rates of attrition of African American and Latinx men, although they rarely target the structural issues that create untenable circumstances, such as underresourced school districts that fall short of delivering college preparatory curricula, intergenerational poverty that cannot offset the rising costs of college, and pervasive racism that buttresses a hostile campus climate. Type 3 includes national and campus-based organizations that center men's role in sexual and domestic violence prevention. Through peer education strategies and social norms initiatives, prevention programs offer a space for men to disturb and actively work against rape-supportive attitudes and behaviors.

These programs support developmental, retention, and violence prevention outcomes based in scholarship on men and masculinities. However, with the exception of Type 2 programs, they conceptually organize men and masculinities as a fairly monolithic group, largely undifferentiated by social location. As a result, we offer a revised approach to masculinities programming that specifically foregrounds multiple intersections of identity using the intersectional model of multiple dimensions of identity (I-MMDI; Jones & Abes, 2013).

Theoretical Framework: The I-MMDI

The I-MMDI is a theoretical framework for understanding college student identity development (Jones & Abes, 2013). It advances previous iterations of the model, namely the model of multiple dimensions of identity (MMDI; Jones & McEwen, 2000) and the reconceptualized MMDI (R-MMDI; Abes, Jones, & McEwen, 2007). Through the captivating image of a swirling atom, the original MMDI demonstrated how the various facets of a college student's socially constructed identities, including race, class, gender, and others, can be understood only in relation to each other (Jones & McEwen, 2000). Building on the original model, the R-MMDI incorporates students' meaning-making capacity through a filter to fully capture the relationship between the context of their experiences and the salience of identity (Abes, Jones, & McEwen, 2007). The MMDI and the R-MMDI consider college student identity development as a socially constructed individual phenomenon rather than being situated in societal systems of power and oppression.

The I-MMDI applies intersectionality theory (Crenshaw, 1991) to the MMDI, providing important insights into how college students construct their identities. Although many scholars and activists have examined the intersection of various social identities, Crenshaw was the first to introduce the term *intersectionality* and thus intersectionality theory (Mitchell, Simmons, & Greyerbiehl, 2014). To capture the unique lived experiences of women of color, as opposed to typical gender-only or race-only analyses, Crenshaw noted that "the intersection of racism and sexism factors into Black women's lives in ways that cannot be captured wholly by looking at the race or gender dimensions of those experiences separately" (p. 1244). Crenshaw's analysis considered a systemic interpretation of social identity, rather than a sole focus on individual experiences. In higher education research, intersectionality theory has been applied to examine "relations of domination and subordination, privilege and agency, in the structural arrangements through which various services, resources, and other social rewards are delivered" (Dill & Zambrana, 2009, p. 5). Dill and Zambrana (2009) discussed four theoretical interventions educators can use to situate intersectionality theory in their practice, including centering the experiences of people of color and other marginalized identity groups, complicating social identity, unveiling power, and promoting social justice.

The I-MMDI allows educators to reimagine the MMDI through these four theoretical interventions of intersectionality theory. The I-MMDI stresses the importance of context, or the omnipresent macro-level matrix of domination in which all social identities are inherently embedded. Context is significant for understanding how an individual determines the salience of social identities in a sociohistorical life experience. For instance, individuals at predominantly White universities (PWI) often fail to acknowledge their institution's history of land theft and continued depiction of Native life through demeaning and racist intercollegiate sports logos and mascots (Davis, 1993). A Native student who attends such a university could very well be required to take a U.S. history course. Given individuals' lack of acknowledgment of their institution's complicity in colonization, the U.S. history course may cover battles between indigenous and colonizing nations using accounts and texts written by colonizers while silencing the voices of Native people. In this context, fulfilling such general education requirements is the latest occurrence of an intergenerational assault on Native students' humanity as well as an example of how context can determine identity salience for college students.

The I-MMDI extends intersectionality theory to understand how individual students make meaning of their multiple intersecting identities. The I-MMDI helps to explain the ways patriarchy and male dominance in the classroom serve to uphold an embedded culture of colonial racism experienced by the Native student at a PWI and also how White supremacy and settler colonialism work to maintain patriarchy. The meaning-making filter introduced in the R-MMDI implicitly connects the individual interpretation of identity salience to the larger context of systemic power and oppression represented in the I-MMDI. The I-MMDI points to the existence of multiple identities in structural systems of power as well as the intersecting nature of those identities and systems to mutually reinforce one another. As Jones and Abes (2013) noted, "The nature of the developmental process is itself qualitatively different depending on one's intersecting identities" (p. 161). Specifically, the I-MMDI captures how students' meaning-making capacity depends on how hey are situated in systems of power and oppression.

The Intersectional Model for College Men and Masculinities Programming

Inspired by the I-MMDI, we imagine a fourth intersectional type of men's programming. To guide college men's programming design and delivery efforts, we offer the intersectional model for college men and masculinities programming (see Figure 4.1).

Figure 4.1. Intersectional model for college men and masculinities programming.

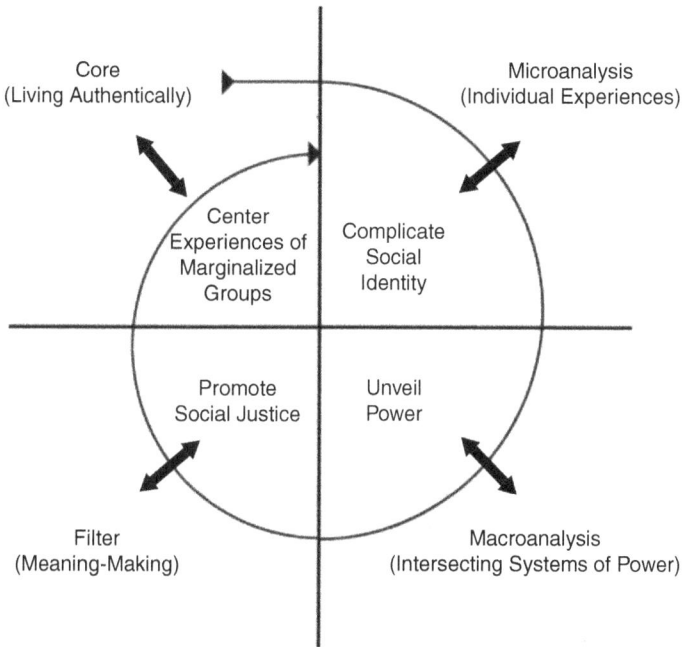

The proposed programming model informs educational programs that situate college men's multiple intersecting identities in systems of power and oppression. By overlapping tenets of the I-MMDI (Jones & Abes, 2013) and intersectionality theory (Crenshaw, 1991), this model provides a conceptual blueprint for college educators to develop men's programming that facilitates students' meaning-making capacity by centering the experiences of marginalized groups, complicating social identity, unveiling power, and promoting social justice.

Applying the I-MMDI and Intersectionality Theory

Although intersectionality theory was originally created to analyze the unique violence experienced by women of color (Crenshaw, 1991), we find it a robust theoretical tool to examine how systems of power intersect to simultaneously privilege and oppress college men in different but important ways. Specifically, college men's programming must explore the complex intersection of masculinities and other dominant and marginalized social identities (Harper, Wardell, & McGuire, 2011; Salinas & Beatty, 2013). Many scholars highlight the specific challenges experienced by college men who hold multiple marginalized identities, including men of color (Harper, 2004; Harris, 2009), queer men (Berila, 2011; Tillapaugh, 2016), men with disabilities (Gerschick, 2011) and trans* men and trans*masculine individuals (Catalano, 2014; Jourian, 2016). Applying the I-MMDI and intersectionality theory to college men's programming allows students to make meaning of their multiple intersecting social identities while also reflecting on their personal experiences with privilege and marginalization.

To develop and implement intersectional programming for college men, educators must expand their notions of gender to include individual lived experiences and the institutionalized oppressions that have affected students. Robbins and McGowan (2016) offered three insights regarding intersectional perspectives on gender integral to the creation of intersectional men's programming. First, educators creating men and masculinities programming must recognize that gender is inextricably connected to students' other social identities. Second, educators must understand that students' gender identities are shaped by social structural inequities. Finally, educators must acknowledge that students' gender identities are socially constructed through interactive processes (Robbins & McGowan, 2016). Employing intersectional perspectives of gender in college men and masculinities programming promotes the meaning-making of students' lived experiences while also promoting efforts to dismantle systemic oppression.

The following sections discuss the key theoretical components of the intersectional model of college men and masculinities programming. Each section contains an explanation, learning outcomes, and examples of programs or activities that could be used to fulfill the corresponding tenet of the model. No single program will accomplish all goals of the model. Ideally, this model will inform an ongoing educational curriculum or multiple programs over a sustained period of time. Furthermore, we do not believe the model is exhaustive or prescriptive. We encourage educators who contemplate intersectional men's programming to view our offering as a starting place to imagine and proliferate emancipatory programming that responds to the wisdom and complexity of intersectionality theory.

Centering the Experiences of Marginalized Groups

Using the intersectional model for college men and masculinities programming, educators should develop programs that center the experiences of marginalized groups. We envision two possible approaches, the first of which is targeting populations of college men with marginalized social identities. *Marginalized* describes, although imperfectly, men with oppressed identities that intersect with their masculine gender identity, including queer men, men of color, and men with disabilities. Abundant scholarship demonstrates the individual and systemic barriers to success for college students with oppressed identities (Jones & Abes, 2013; Patton, Renn, Guido, & Quaye, 2016). By framing programmatic efforts in the experiences of marginalized groups and situating masculinity in and among students' multiple intersecting identities, educators will appeal to men's core sense of belonging and offer rare opportunities for men to convene over a shared identity experience. This model allows men to be seen as whole beings and encourages them to live authentically.

- Learning outcome: Students will be recognized as individuals with multiple intersecting identities situated in systems of power and oppression.
- Examples: Men of Color Dialogue Group, Queer Men's Panel, and Working-Class Men's Poetry Writing Workshop are a few examples of programs that offer men an opportunity to know and interrogate how they have come to understand masculinity and opens up dialogue for imagining more inclusive and nonhegemonic forms.

The second approach involves creating opportunities for men to look to the experiences of marginalized groups as a vital and valid source of knowledge production. This approach recognizes the "distinctive knowledge generated by the experiences of previously excluded communities and multiple oppressed groups" (Dill & Zambrana, 2009, p. 6). By foregrounding the perspectives of individuals and groups who have been denied access to or erased from the libraries, laboratories, and classrooms of the Western academic enterprise, educators can ensure that the stories, histories, and art that inform students' sociopolitical understanding of the world includes more than dominant hegemonic narratives.

- Learning outcome: Students will be able to critically interrogate dominant narratives and meaningfully explore counternarratives from marginalized groups.
- Activities: Reading memoirs, histories, and narratives of radical social movements by participants; participating in spoken word and poetry readings; and attending performance and visual art installations are a few examples of programs or activities that offer men an opportunity to critically interrogate dominant narratives and consider the importance of marginalized experiences and ways of knowing.

Complicate Social Identity

An initial aspect of college men's programming should also focus on analyzing men's individual experiences as gendered beings with multiple intersecting identities. This process allows men to complicate their understandings of social identity by articulating the ways the sites of their intersecting identities influence and reinforce each other. Additionally, educators should help students anticipate and value the diversity in group experiences and acknowledge that a variety of social locations inform individual circumstances and experiences. For example, disabled men are not a monolithic group. The experience of a deaf man who rejects the notion of hearing loss and instead prioritizes deaf gain (Bauman & Murray, 2009) is not the same as a chronically ill man who looks for a biomedical cure to address persistent, debilitating pain.

- Learning outcome: Students will analyze their individual lived experiences, recognizing the sites of their multiple intersecting identities and the diversity in identity groups.
- Examples: Identity Map Sharing, I Am From Poems, and Take a Stand are examples of programs or activities that offer men an opportunity to meaningfully examine their lived experiences, which can be better understood by considering multiple intersections of identity.

Unveil Power

Another integral aspect of intersectional college men and masculinities programming requires providing the opportunity for men to analyze intersecting systems of power. Unveiling power in college men's programming involves illustrating the sociohistorical events that have constructed patriarchy and privilege men while oppressing women and trans* individuals, although we note that some scholars have begun to argue that trans*masculine individuals are also able to wield privilege via their gender (Catalano & Jourian, 2018). This systemic analysis also encourages college men to identify how other forms of structural oppression, like White supremacy and heteronormativity, have been established to uphold and reinforce patriarchy. This process of unveiling power can focus on sociohistorical examples of structural inequity, such as women's suffrage or Jim Crow, to unveil the power of intersecting systems to oppress individuals with marginalized identities.

- Learning outcome: Students will analyze multiple intersecting systems of power and oppression through sociohistorical examples of structural inequity.
- Examples: The Web of Oppression or the Cycle of Socialization (Harro, 2013) are programs or learning activities that can help students discover how they are situated in and potentially complicit with systems of advantage and disadvantage.

Current experiences also provide fertile ground for the exploration of how domains of power organize inequality at the structural, disciplinary, ideological, and relational levels (Dill & Zambrana, 2009). Facilitators of men's programming can help students examine how laws and policies (structural), organizational patterns and bureaucracies (disciplinary), cultural narratives and common knowledges (ideological), and everyday interpersonal acts (relational) contribute to asymmetrical power relations that disadvantage some while advantaging others.

- Learning outcome: Students will analyze multiple intersecting systems of power and oppression through an activity that documents contemporary social problems.
- Example: A collaborative action research collective seeking to document and transform elements of rape culture in student clubs and organizations is an example of a learning activity that allows students to understand and analyze various domains of power and inequity.

Promote Social Justice
Finally, college men's programming should provide students with opportunities to make meaning of their individual experiences in systems of power. This filtering process of connecting individual identity salience with systemic power and oppression illuminates students' understandings of themselves and their contexts, ultimately leading to insights about how and where they can take action to promote social justice. Given that most college men hold significant power and privilege in the existing system of higher education, they have the potential to influence and change those systems, particularly in their spheres of influence. Regardless of college men's multiple intersecting identities, their gender identity as men places them in a position to wield power. Thus, it is vitally important for masculinities programming to focus on developing college men's capacity to take action for social justice. This action should begin by centering the experiences of marginalized groups, leading to an analysis of individual lived experiences as well as intersecting systems of power, finally resulting in further action for social justice.

- Learning outcome: Students will make meaning of their multiple intersecting identities by situating themselves within systems of power and oppression.
- Examples: Four Corners Story Sharing (e.g., when student experienced oppression, perpetuated oppression, witnessed oppression, disrupted oppression), Spheres of Influence, and Action Planning

Worksheet can facilitate students' meaning-making of their multiple intersecting identities in systems of power.

Theoretical and Practical Considerations

All aspects of the model are multidirectional. For example, creating space for men to live authentically will allow them to acknowledge and embrace their marginalized identities. Complicating social identity beyond isolated or additive notions of identity will allow men to explore undiscovered aspects of their own lived experience. Unveiling power through sociohistorical examples of structural inequity will allow college men to understand how all forms of oppression are intersecting at a macro level. Finally, taking action to promote social justice will allow students to link theory and practice, enabling a process of meaning-making of their individual experiences in systems of power.

Creating educational programming for college men is inherently risky because it can easily reinforce patriarchy and other forms of oppression. College men's programming can interfere with social justice in many ways, including using money and other resources that would otherwise be used to support the needs of marginalized student populations. Additionally, college men involved in these programs may strategically use their status as members of a healthy masculinity group to earn the trust of women and perpetrate sexual assault. Educators who are responsible for creating masculinities programming must be vigilant to ensure that the intent and impact of their efforts are aligned with social justice on campus.

A promising method for maintaining accountability with men's programming is to actively invite and prioritize the perspectives of people who experience gender marginalization (women and trans* individuals) on campus. To be clear, women and trans* people should not be required to give their time or labor to support college men and masculinities programming. Rather, masculinities programming can contribute to a liberated campus community by following the leadership of women and trans* educators. If programming is in line with social justice, and women and trans* individuals are willing to collaborate, feedback should be sought during all phases of the programming process, including planning, marketing, funding, recruitment, implementation, and assessment.

Given the experiences of marginalization that these populations experience as a result of living in a gender-oppressive culture, many students, staff, and faculty who identify as women and trans* may not be interested in contributing more time and emotional labor to helping a college men's program. This does not preclude educators from seeking to retain paid feminine-identified people of a diversity of genders who offer professional consultation services on social justice and gender-related topics. Moreover, educators must consider that trans*masculine students may choose to interact with men's programming in a variety of ways. Trans*masculine individuals could feasibly choose to participate in programming, offer feedback from an accountability perspective, have no interest in engaging in or commenting on men's programming, or some combination thereof. We urge educators to acknowledge the ways trans*masculine students may benefit from programming that helps them discern their own investment in toxic or hegemonic forms of masculinity, as well as offer valuable critiques of intersectional programs.

We maintain that educators responsible for coordinating college men's programming should expect and welcome the invitation to grapple with complexities associated with creating even more educational efforts for a population of students that already benefits from patriarchy. Additionally, we encourage those who have not considered including or consulting with women and trans* individuals on their campus to determine if their efforts are truly supporting liberation. If at any point collaborators and participants indicate that the program is no longer promoting and supporting social justice efforts on campus, the coordinating educator, involved students, and university administrators must earnestly reflect on whether the program should continue.

Conclusion

Extensive research and scholarship related to high-risk and violent behavior of cisgender men has led to a resounding call for college and university educators to address toxic masculinity on campuses across the United States. In response, many student affairs and higher education professionals have developed men and masculinities educational programming, but these efforts often fall short because of a lack of resources, a lack of concrete direction, and a limited number of practical examples that have proven effective in addressing toxic masculinity. Moreover, these programs are often broadly aimed at men as a monolithic group, ignoring the needs and perspectives of college men with marginalized identities, women, and trans*-identified individuals. In an effort to address some of these challenges, this chapter discusses the existing models of college men's programming as well as the benefits and limitations of these programs. In addressing the current gap in college men's programming to prioritize the experiences of marginalized student populations and dismantle the systems that lead to barriers for these students in higher education, we also offer an intersectional model of college men and masculinities programming.

The model employs the I-MMDI (Jones & Abes, 2013) and intersectionality theory (Crenshaw, 1991; Dill & Zambrana, 2009) to (a) center the experiences of individuals in marginalized groups and appeal to their core sense of belonging, (b) complicate unexamined notions of social identity and individual experience, (c) unveil systems of power and intersecting systems, and ultimately (d) promote social justice and meaning-making. These theoretical interventions, when considered alongside the I-MMDI, provide imaginative and innovative potentialities for educators and re-create college men's programming. Previous efforts to educate and develop college men have revealed a need for more complex frameworks of masculinities programming. Just as the field of higher education no longer views college students as having isolated and discrete identity categories, the educational programming for college students must also consider students' multiple intersecting identities and the interlocking systems of power that shape students' lived experiences (Collins, 2004). We invite educators to join us in applying emerging student development theories to practice (Jones & Abes, 2013), advancing current understandings of college men and masculinities programming to match the complex and nuanced lived experiences of today's college students. In doing so, we may reduce the negative impact of toxic masculinity on college campuses while simultaneously making strides toward dismantling the systems of oppression that negatively affect everyone in higher education and beyond.

References

Abes, E. S., Jones, S. R., & McEwen, M. K. (2007). Reconceptualizing the model of multiple dimensions of identity: The role of meaning-making capacity in the construction of multiple identities. *Journal of College Student Development, 48,* 1–22.

Bauman, H. D., & Murray, J. (2009). Reframing: From hearing loss to deaf gain. *Deaf Studies Digital Journal, 1*(1), 1–10.

Berila, B. (2011). Queer masculinities in higher education. In J. Laker & T. Davis (Eds.), *Masculinities in higher education: Theoretical and practical considerations* (pp. 97–110). New York, NY: Routledge.

Berkowitz, A. (2011). Using how college men feel about being men and "doing the right thing" to promote men's development. In J. Laker & T. Davis (Eds.), *Masculinities in higher education: Theoretical and practical considerations* (pp. 161–176). New York, NY: Routledge.

Brannon, R. (1976). The male sex role: Our culture's blueprint for manhood and what it's done for us lately. In D. David & R. Brannon (Eds.), *The forty-nine percent majority: The male sex role* (pp. 1–48). Reading, MA: Addison-Wesley.

Catalano, D. C. J. (2014). *Welcome to guyland: Experiences of trans* men in college* (Doctoral dissertation). Retrieved from https://scholarworks.umass.edu/cgi/viewcontent.cgi?article=1014&context=dissertations_2.

Catalano, D. C. J., & Jourian. T. J. (2018). LGBTQ centers: A queer gender-aware approach to gender. *New Directions for Student Services, 164*, 41–50.

Capraro, R. L. (2000). Why college men drink: Alcohol, adventure, and the paradox of masculinity. *Journal of American College Health, 48*, 307–315.

Collins, P. H. (2004). Toward a new vision: Race, class, and gender as categories of analysis and connection. In L. Heldke & P. O'Connor (Eds.), *Oppression, privilege, and resistance* (pp. 529–543). Boston, MA: McGraw-Hill.

Connell, R. W. (2005). Change among the gatekeepers: Men, masculinities, and gender equality in the global arena. *Signs*, 30, 1801–1825.

Crenshaw, K. (1991). Mapping the margins: Intersectionality, identity politics, and violence against women of color. *Stanford Law Review, 43*, 1241–1299.

Davis, L. R. (1993). Protest against the use of Native American mascots: A challenge to traditional American identity. *Journal of Sport and Social Issues, 17*(1), 9–22.

Davis, T. L. (2002). Voices of gender role conflict: The social construction of collegemen's identity. Journal of College Student Development, 43, 508–521.

Davis, T. L., & Laker, J. (2004). Connecting men to academic and student affairs programs and services. *New Directions for Student Services*, 107, 47–57.

Dill, B. T., & Zambrana, R. E. (2009). Critical thinking about inequality: An emerging lens. In B. T. Dill & R. E. Zambrana (Eds.), *Emerging intersections: Race, class, and gender in theory, policy, and practice* (pp. 1–21). New Brunswick, NJ: Rutgers University Press.

Edwards, K. E., & Jones, S. R. (2009). "Putting my man face on": A grounded theory of college men's gender identity development. *Journal of College Student Development, 50*, 210–228.

Foubert, J. D., Garner, D. N., & Thaxter, P. J. (2006). An exploration of fraternity culture: Implications for programs to address alcohol-related sexual assault. *College Student Journal, 40*, 361–373.

Gerschick, T. J. (2011). Disability identity intersections with masculinities. In J. Laker & T. Davis (Eds.), *Masculinities in higher education: Theoretical and practical considerations* (pp. 97–110). New York, NY: Routledge.

Harper, S. R. (2004). The measure of a man: Conceptualizations of masculinity among high-achieving African American male college students. *Berkeley Journal of Sociology, 48*, 89–107.

Harper, S. R., & Harris, F., III. (2010). *College men and masculinities: Theory, research, and implications for practice.* San Francisco, CA: Jossey-Bass.

Harper, S. R., Wardell, C. C., & McGuire, K. M. (2011). Man of multiple identities: Complex individuality and identity intersectionality among college men. In J. A. Laker & T. Davis (Eds.), *Masculinities in higher education: Theoretical and practical considerations* (pp. 81–96). New York, NY: Routledge.

Harris, F., III. (2009). Deconstructing masculinity: A qualitative study of college men's masculine conceptualizations and gender performance. *Journal of Student Affairs Research and Practice, 45*, 453–475.

Harris, F., III, & Edwards, K. E. (2010). College men's experiences as men: Findings and implications from two grounded theory studies. *Journal of Student Affairs Research and Practice, 47,* 43-62.

Harris, F., III, & Struve, L. E. (2009). Gents, jerks, and jocks: What male students learn about masculinity in college. *About Campus, 14*(3), 2–9.

Harro, B. (2013). The cycle of socialization. In M. Adams, W. Blumenfeld, C. Castaneda, H. W. Hackman, M. L. Peters, & X. Zuniga (Eds.), *Readings for diversity and social justice* (3rd ed., pp. 14–21). New York, NY: Routledge.

Jones, S. R., & Abes, E. S. (2013). *Identity development of college students: Advancing frameworks for multiple dimensions of identity.* San Francisco, CA: Jossey-Bass.

Jones, S. R., & McEwen, M. K. (2000). A conceptual model of multiple dimensions of identity. *Journal of College Student Development, 41,* 405–415.

Jourian, T. J. (2016). *"My masculinity is a little love poem to myself": Trans*masculine college students conceptualizations of masculinities* (Doctoral dissertation). Available from ProQuest Dissertations and Theses database. (UMI No. 10188206)

Kimmel, M. S. (2008). *Guyland: The perilous world where boys become men.* New York, NY: HarperCollins.

Laker, J. A., & Davis, T. (2011). *Masculinities in higher education: Theoretical and practical considerations.* New York, NY: Routledge.

Monaghan, P. (2017, December 10). The fight against "toxic masculinity." *Chronicle of Higher Education.* Retrieved from https://www.chronicle.com/article/The-Fight-Against-Toxic/242017

Mitchell, D., Jr., Simmons, C. Y., & Greyerbiehl, L. A. (Eds.). (2014). *Intersectionality & higher education: Theory, research, and praxis.* New York, NY: Peter Lang.

Nicolazzo, Z. (2016). "I'm man enough; are you?": The queer (im)possibilities of Walk a Mile in Her Shoes. *Journal of Critical Scholarship on Higher Education and Student Affairs, 2*(1), 5–10.

Patton, L. D., Renn, K. A., Guido, F. M., & Quaye, S. J. (2016). *Student development in college: Theory, research, and practice.* San Francisco, CA: Jossey-Bass.

Robbins, C. R., & McGowan, B. L. (2016). Intersectional perspectives on gender and gender identity development. *New Directions for Student Services, 154,* 71–83.

Salinas, C., & Beatty, C. C. (2013). Constructing our own definition of masculinity: An intersectionality approach. In Z. Foste (Ed.), *Looking forward: A dialogue on college men and masculinities* (pp. 24–29). Washington, DC: College Student Educators International Standing Committee on Men and Masculinities.

Tillapaugh, D. (2016). Understanding sexual minority male students' meaning-making about their multiple identities: An exploratory comparative study. *Canadian Journal of Higher Education, 46,* 91–108.

ASSESSMENT AND EVALUATION

Lucas Schalewski, Brian Lackman, and Jamie Utt

The past decade has seen a blossoming of collegiate men and masculinities practices designed to engage masculine-identifying students. Programs and services aim to support and develop the whole student from persistence to completion, violence prevention, and critical power and privilege examination. Simultaneously, student services and universities more broadly have come to expect robust forms of assessment to demonstrate the effectiveness of programs and services. It is not uncommon for division or department leadership to expect evidence documenting the impact of programs to justify continued support. This chapter offers an outcome-based assessment framework that can be applied to such programs and services that focus on men and masculinities.

There are several different types of assessments (needs, satisfaction, campus climate, formative, learning and development). Formative assessment often is accomplished by applying classroom assessment techniques (Angelo & Cross, 1993) in student learning. This chapter frames assessment of programs and services as *outcomes-based assessment*, which is defined by Bresciani, Gardner, and Hickmott (2009) as a "systematic and intentional process" (p. 15) where outcomes are planned and determined if they are achieved based on results from implemented methods. Results are then used to inform decision-making that improves policies, programs, services, and other practices to support defined goals. Assessment cycles are often used as a way to conceptualize outcomes-based assessment that can be applied to practice (Bresciani et al., 2009; Maki, 2004). The following explains our systematic and intentional approach to outcome-based assessment as an assessment cycle (see Figure 5.1) on a recurring model with six sequential phases.

Figure 5.1. The assessment cycle.

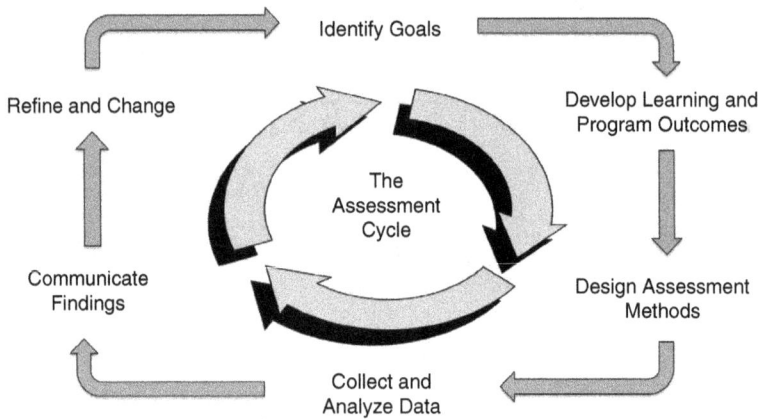

The assessment cycle is flexible enough to be implemented at any phase in your programming and evaluation process but is best used from the beginning as the most effective assessment efforts are woven into the fabric of a program from the start. To demonstrate how this cycle can be used in assessing men and masculinities programs, we describe each step using the following example of a program called Taking Off the Masc (see Box 5.1).

Phase 1: Identify Goals

To maximize your program and service impact, one of the most critical foundations for work in masculinities is to approach the development and implementation of programs with clear goals in mind. A goal describes what a program is expected to accomplish and guides the development of curriculum and educational activities. Although this may seem obvious, it is important to take time to carefully think through and document a program's goal. An example of this is in Box 5.2.

College men and masculinities goals should also ensure alignment with department, division, and institutional goals. This alignment supports the need to demonstrate contribution toward priorities of institutions that are often determined in strategic planning, mission statements, and institutionally established learning outcomes. Once goals are clearly stated, learning and program outcomes are used to measure them and determine if they were accomplished.

BOX 5.1
Taking Off the Masc

Program Overview: Taking Off the Masc

Taking Off the Masc is a program offered through the Gender Resource Center and the New Student Experience Office. A total of 25 first-year masculine-identifying college students are provided with opportunities to better understand masculinities in society and a college environment while being exposed to healthier alternatives to toxic expressions of masculinity that better support their personal and academic lives. The goal of Taking Off the Masc is to advance college men's healthy masculinities development and student success.

Fall semester program activities include capturing masculinities in college through photography, movie screenings and discussions, biweekly gatherings to reflect and discuss selected masculinity topics (i.e., precollege socialization, gender and college student experiences, masculinity in the media), and an ongoing digital journal with reflective prompts. The program ends with a final capstone project encapsulating students' own self-defined masculine identities as they relate to their academic and personal lives.

BOX 5.2
Program Goal

Taking Off the Masc

Advance college men's healthy masculinities development and student success.

Phase 2: Develop Learning and Program Outcomes

Learning outcomes define what students will know or do, whereas program outcomes cover additional expectations as a result of program participation. Examples of program outcomes that college men and masculinities programs may seek to achieve include participation rates, grade point average (GPA), satisfaction, student development, and sense of belonging. It is beneficial to include success criteria in outcomes that balance challenge with reasonable achievement of what is expected from students or a program. Success criteria represent the measurable degree to which outcomes are determined to be achieved or not. If a program is expected to increase participants' GPA, the success criteria of a program outcome specify what GPA cutoff will be used to determine if the outcome is met.

Writing learning outcomes at first glance may sound easy but requires a careful approach with continued revisions to establish outcomes that will clearly describe measurable intended student learning. One framework to assist in capturing the learning that programs seek to have students demonstrate is Bloom's taxonomy (Bloom & Krathwohl, 1956). The revised taxonomy categorizes learning in six different dimensions: create, evaluate, analyze, apply, understand, and remember (Anderson & Krathwohl, 2001). Dimensions increase in cognitive processes from lower order thinking skills to higher order thinking skills. Each of the six dimensions is accompanied with verbs that allow student learning to be demonstrated and measured with methodology (see Appendix 5.A).

Bloom's taxonomy verbs are helpful when writing learning outcomes using the ABCD approach:

> The Audience of learners . . . specifies the Behavior or capability to be demonstrated and the Conditions under which the behavior or capability will be observed . . . [and] the Degree to which the new skill must be mastered. (Heinich, Molenda, & Russell, 1989, p. 36)

You can identify your ABCD with the following questions about your program and intended learning:

- Audience: Who are the intended student learners of the program?
- Behavior: Using Bloom's (Bloom & Krathwohl, 1956) taxonomy verbs, what will students be able to think, know, or do?
- Condition: What is the program, service, or educational activities students will experience?
- Degree: What is the degree, or success criteria, students are expected to use to demonstrate their learning?

Having well-thought-out learning and program outcomes informs the next steps of identifying and implementing a methodology (see Box 5.3).

Bresciani and colleagues (2009) recommended commonly used classroom assessment mapping (Maki, 2004) in cocurricular settings. These assessment mapping techniques can easily be applied to college men and masculinities program and service assessments. Assessment mapping of learning outcomes for one's program and service is a helpful strategy to ensure correct alignment between educational activities and the intended outcomes. This process helps identify gaps where outcomes may need to be reinforced with educational activities. It also prevents the unplanned consequence of discovering unfavorable results that may not necessarily be because of a lack of learning but

BOX 5.3
Student Learning Outcomes and Program Outcome

Student Learning Outcomes

On completion of Taking Off the Masc, students at a proficient level will be able to

- explore how precollege experiences lead to the development of masculinity identities and subsequent behaviors;
- describe how gender identity relates to power, privilege, and oppression in society and on campus; and
- integrate self-defined masculinities supportive of healthy behaviors into their personal and academic lives.

Program Outcome

Taking Off the Masc student participants will achieve a 90% persistence rate to their sophomore year.

instead a misalignment between outcomes and the activities students experience. The assessment map (see Table 5.1) includes outcomes on the left-hand side with educational experiences and activities on the top row.

Phase 3: Design Assessment Methods

Assessment methods should be selected based on their ability to collect data that best measure intended outcomes. Applying the most appropriate method to measure intended outcomes supports continued progress in the assessment cycle. Qualitative, quantitative, or mixed-methods approaches can be used to capture intended outcomes. We pay particular attention to rubrics as a promising tool to measure more complex outcomes that college men and masculinities programs and services intend to measure among student participants (i.e., leadership, intercultural competencies, healthy masculinities identity). Designing assessment methods should also take into consideration how direct and indirect measures are incorporated to elicit evidence that demonstrates learning outcomes are achieved.

Qualitative methods are often well suited to measure the complex and convoluted ways student learning occurs. Schuh, Biddix, Dean, and Kinzie (2016) described qualitative techniques as data gathered as visuals or words

TABLE 5.1
Assessment Map

Student Learning Outcomes	Educational Activities				
	Digital Journal	Topical Group Discussion	Capture Masculinity Using Photography	Movie Screening and Discussion	Capstone Project
1. Explore how precollege experiences lead to the development of masculinity identities and subsequent behavior.	X	X		X	X
2. Describe how gender identity relates to power, privilege, and oppression in society and on campus.	X	X	X	X	X
3. Integrate self-defined masculinities supportive of healthy behaviors into their personal and academic lives.	X	X			X

and later analyzed to produce categories and themes. One main advantage to using qualitative methods is that they collect data in subjective ways that recognize college men's own unique experiences, interpretations, and feelings based on their engagement in a program or service. These approaches typically are best suited for smaller groups of participants. Common examples of qualitative methods include journals, focus groups, open-ended survey questions, observations, portfolios, or case studies.

Quantitative methods, discussed in additional detail by Schuh and colleagues (2016), collect numerical data that are analyzed using statistics and often presented in tables, graphs, or charts. One main advantage to using quantitative methods is the ability to apply generalized findings to a larger population, such as an institution's student population of college men. Quantitative methods are often used in student affairs assessment because of the typically lower amount of time necessary to conduct them and expressed preferences from supervisors and university leadership. These methods are helpful in measuring student learning in the lower order thinking skills (i.e., define, list, identify). Common examples of quantitative methods includes developing surveys, pre- and posttests, institutional data (e.g., GPA, persistence), and existing instruments.

Mixed-methods approaches are often found to be successful ways to measure outcomes given the complementary benefits of qualitative and quantitative methods (Schuh, 2009). For example, patterns in student narratives can add nuance or perspective to quantitative results, generalizing findings to a student population. This tactic, compared to presenting results from one method, seeks to provide a more well-rounded and powerful representation of assessment results through triangulation of data.

Rubrics are surprisingly underused, given their advantages to assess student learning or development outcomes and should be highly considered as a method in college masculinities program and service-learning outcome assessments. Rubrics are able to assess student learning through clearly defined categories with a set scoring strategy (Suskie, 2009). Students demonstrate their learning through an artifact (e.g., essay, project, presentation) that is then scored using assigned categories in a consistent manner. One of the main reasons rubrics are well suited for college masculinities programs and services is their ability to capture higher order thinking skills (i.e., synthesize, formulate, design) and more complex outcomes, similar to many qualitative methods. Rubrics have additional benefits when shared with students. This transparency supports student understanding of intended learning or development outcomes from the programs and the criteria that will be used in their assessment. After recognizing the outcomes and rubric, results shared and discussed with students will further facilitate their reflection and learning. As a direct measure, rubrics provide credible evidence of learning and development outcomes.

Direct measures collect data that demonstrate student learning in an observable manner, whereas indirect measures require students to reflect on the learning that may have occurred (Schuh et al., 2016; Suskie, 2009). An example of a direct measure is asking students to produce an artifact (e.g., essay, website, video blog) that explains how gender is related to privilege, which is then evaluated using a rubric (see Box 5.4). A survey that asks students to report their level of agreement using a Likert-type scale (1 = *strongly disagree* to 5 = *strongly agree*) with the statement "I understand the relationship between gender and privilege" is an indirect measure. Outcomes-based assessments measuring learning should prioritize direct measures, whereas indirect measures are better suited for measuring students' perceptions, feelings, or opinions.

BOX 5.4
Assessment Methods

Student Learning Outcomes

In support of the program's goal to advance healthy masculinities development, a capstone project requires students to produce an artistic representation of their choice that represents their masculinity while responding to the following questions:

- How has your masculinity identity developed over time?
- What factors contributed to your development?
- In what ways does your masculine identity connect with power, privilege, and oppression within society and on campus?
- How does your masculinity identity relate to your personal and academic life?

Students are asked to present their project. A rubric (see Appendix 5.B) is used to evaluate the capstone project and supplemental question responses to determine if the learning outcomes were met.

Program Outcome

Use institutional data in the following fall semester to determine how many student participants return to campus in their sophomore year.

Phase 4: Collect and Analyze Data

Before collecting data, it is important to determine if existing information is already available for use. Assessments seeking to measure student engagement, campus climate, or use of services should begin by using data sets often available from commonly administered institutional or department surveys. Once you receive the data, you are able to disaggregate them by gender, if the demographic is available, to better understand how college men uniquely experience behaviors, perceptions, and outcomes. Readily available institutional data can pair well with programs and services when intended outcomes measure academic success (e.g., GPA, academic probation) and student persistence (e.g., retention, graduation rates). Preexisting institutional data can also offer the longitudinal benchmarking of experiences and outcomes (increased men's student engagement) you seek to develop or change through men and masculinities programs. Examining outcomes through these data sets may provide valuable data sources already available to you.

If data do not already exist, the collection and analysis processes must align with the methods employed. The assessment plan will include an outline of a time line and identify staff responsible for carrying out specific data collection and analysis tasks. Too often assessment stops with data collection because of a lack of planning in time or resources to conduct analysis that transforms the data into meaningful, action-oriented information. Taking the time to document a clear plan in the data collection and analysis phase is important to ensure the assessment cycle progresses. The plan will also identify the skill sets, tools, and time that are required to successfully conduct data collection and analysis.

Compared to classroom assessment, men and masculinities assessment methods are best served by using more strategic approaches as students may be involved in programs and services on a volunteer basis. Final papers and exams are not commonly expected in cocurricular settings and may have negative connotations among students. Therefore, technologically modern and interactive assessment techniques are more welcome ways to collect data among college men about their program and service participation. More innovative and student-centered methods and data collection approaches of student learning and development for men and masculinities programs include digital storytelling, video blogging, photography, poetry, and other forms of performance art. These methods allow differing ways of demonstrating learning and can be more easily embedded in the experience and not necessarily feel like an assessment (e.g., see Box 5.5).

BOX 5.5
Data Collection and Analysis Plan

Student Learning Outcomes

The program coordinator will collect and analyze the data using a developed rubric assessing the capstone project. The rubric will be analyzed to determine individual and average learning outcomes achievement among all participants after completion of the program.

Program Outcome

The program coordinator will contact the Office of Institutional Research in the following year and request data determining if student participants were retained. Results will be analyzed by calculating the average of students enrolled in the sophomore year to determine the retention rate.

Taking a strategic approach to method and data collection by keeping in mind the student population and program contexts will benefit the assessment. Students may feel more engaged with a method when it is embedded in the experience and more willing to participate compared to traditional assessment methods often found in the classroom.

Phase 5: Communicate Findings

One must effectively communicate results to enable action and use by stakeholders. Take the time to document a communication plan of your results. The following four-step framework by Livingston (2016) will support effective communication of your assessment findings.

First, identify your story. A data-informed story sets a narrative for the assessment findings. A story may be framed by deciding on the title for your assessment findings that you desire audiences to know. Additional data-driven findings will be included in your communication product that supports this overall narrative. Ask yourself, what do the stakeholders (i.e., students, supervisors, chief student affairs officer, community members) want and need to know based on the assessment results? One useful approach is to align the story with timely issues and larger goals that stakeholders are currently or will be invested in.

Second, spend time interpreting the data. Data presented as bite-size actionable insights support the use of assessment results. The audiences should be able to quickly and easily interpret your data. Do not assume audience members have the required level of data literacy to understand what is being reported. Take the extra effort to make meaning of the data by reporting clear interpretations audiences will accurately understand and act on.

Third, know your audience. It is important to identify not only who your audience is but also how they prefer information communicated from assessment results. Tailoring the communication of results to audiences in ways that ensures relevance and reception in a preferred format advances the goal of using the findings (Schuh et al., 2016). University staff members and students may gain more insights from receiving an infographic, supervisors may prefer a full report, and chief student affairs officers are often best served with a one-page executive summary of key findings and recommendations. Take the time to understand your own context as it relates to your program and service stakeholders and preferred communication products. A tool to consider using or adapting from the University of Arizona presents different forms of communication as a matrix of various audiences (see goo.gl/xLqGwE).

Fourth, keep it focused. With the increase of assessment in student affairs and higher education, the availability and communication of information stakeholders receive on a daily basis has also increased. It is important to focus the story you identified and maintain a simple communication of the message to audiences. Incorporating data visualization components that amplify your results and interpretations is highly recommended. For occasions when you have abundant data, your communication strategy may include various audiences that receive targeted communication products dispersed throughout the year instead of all at once.

Effective communication of actionable insights and the ability to demonstrate the impact of programs and services are critical to assessment and evaluation of college men's programs and services. Successful communication of results is meant to inform changes in the program or service that improves defined goals and establishes continued or even increased investments in college men and masculinities efforts (see Box 5.6). College masculinities programs and services produce critical learning, development, and student success outcomes that directly relate to larger student affairs divisional and institutional goals. However if these evidence-based stories are not shared in an effective manner, results remain unknown among students and university leaders who are often stakeholders in their success and growth.

Phase 6: Refine and Change

Although the communication of findings to stakeholders helps to ensure the long-term success of our men and masculinities initiatives, some of the

BOX 5.6
Communication Plan

Stakeholder: Students and Campus Community

Student learning results will be reported with examples of the capstone projects as permitted by participants. The department website will host this content and distribute it through social media outlets to reach campus community members. The results will be used next year as a marketing tool to recruit participants in next year's program.

Stakeholder: Department Head and Senior Leadership

Results will be concisely described in a one-page summary that captures the high-impact learning and development related to institutional learning outcomes. Retention results will be particularly highlighted in a way that advocates for programs to continue their role in promoting healthy student behaviors in the campus community, which supports persistence to sophomore year.

Stakeholder: Program Coordinator and Campus Partners

At the end of the Taking Off the Masc, the program coordinator and campus partners in the Gender Resource Center and the New Student Experience Office will meet to discuss the assessment results. Based on the findings, an internal document will be prepared to document the program's assessment results and implications for next year to improve Taking Off the Masc's goal and outcomes.

most important work in assessment is how we respond internally to findings. Assessment results should lead to program and service improvements that advance student learning outcomes and defined goals. One strategy to support use of the results is deciding what a program will start, stop, and continue to do based on the assessment results. Refinement should also happen in the assessment plan itself as shown in Box 5.7.

Take time to develop the knowledge and skills to create and implement assessment plans that can inform the work for coming years with the resources available through your university and professional organizations, which increasingly recognize the importance of programs that address college men specifically. This can help to ensure an ongoing and sustainable

BOX 5.7
Refining and Changing the Taking Off the Masc Program

Student Learning Outcomes

Student-level outcomes reveal that most participants showed stronger understanding of their personal masculine identity and its connection to other identities and communities but struggled to link that understanding to systems of oppression or to challenges with behavior of men on campus as intended in the second learning outcome. To enhance the connections between how gender relates to communities and society and improve results for Student Learning Outcome #2, we are starting to incorporate a service project that will actively involve participants through discussions and reflection. More activities will be planned to address power and privilege from an intersectional perspective and will be tailored to offer different approaches for men of color, White men, and queer men.

Program Outcomes

The retention rate for participating students was 84% ($n = 21$). Spring semester activities will be enhanced and offer a mentorship program with staff and faculty, who will be given meal cards to connect with students to build relationships with the campus community and increase connections to campus resources.

---

assessment and evaluation practice. It also means, though, that budgeting for growing programs must include resources for assessment. Far too often student affairs programming collects data that are never effectively analyzed, communicated, or used. Thus, it is important to build capacity for staff who are conducting assessments, ideally assessment staff who also have a strong theoretical grounding in your reasoning for building programming around men and masculinities. Further, the refinement of curriculum and program delivery should also include revision of program assessment goals, outcomes, and methods.

Theoretical Considerations in Assessing Men and Masculinities Programs

Too often in assessment the program's guiding theoretical framework is forgotten and seen only as guiding the development of the curriculum.

Every aspect of men and masculinities programming, including its assessment and evaluation, needs to be guided by a critical theoretical framework, ideally rooted in intersectional feminist perspectives on gender and oppression. Assessing men and masculinities work without critical intersectional lenses on gender, race, sexuality, and other identities can lend itself to findings that simply reinforce problematic patterns. For instance, if assessment of a program that focuses on men of color ends up reflecting only deficit narratives, the program will inevitably result in further stratifying our campuses and categorizing men of color as a problem population. Similarly, if we were to assess attitudes toward traditional notions of masculinity without a critical feminist lens, we might see minor shifts through a myopic lens of narrowly defined good outside the wider context of hegemonic masculinity.

Assessment should take account of equity and the student populations served throughout the assessment cycle. Montenegro and Jankowski (2017) provide a helpful illustration of this through culturally responsive assessment practices. They said that being culturally mindful with assessment ensures that the overall process recognizes differences of student populations and uses methods that are best suited for the different student communities being served. Assessment methods used to measure intended learning outcomes should take into account the different ways students demonstrate their knowledge because ways of knowing are informed by culture and identity. They also recommend including students throughout the assessment process from developing outcomes to determining the assessment method to sharing and using the results (see Box 5.8).

BOX 5.8
Theoretical Considerations in Taking Off the Masc Assessment

Taking Off the Masc's assessment includes critical evaluation of masculine socialization rooted in feminist critiques of masculinity (e.g., hooks, 2004) to understand how the retention challenges might be affected by student conformity to traditional masculinity norms. The capstone project supports culturally responsive assessment by welcoming and validating multiple ways for students to demonstrate their learning. Results are disaggregated to identify how different student populations achieved learning outcomes and were retained to sophomore year. Findings are used to make improvements, keeping in mind the various student communities that participate in Taking Off the Masc.

Common Barriers to Effective Assessment

Despite our best efforts, there can be significant barriers to assessing programs, interventions, and services on campus, and educators may struggle with this work. Assessment challenges may arise from a lack of capacity in regard to one's role, time, and staffing. Other professionals may not have received assessment training prior to their role and may not be fully equipped to effectively implement and interpret data. Some may be challenged by a lack of institutional support, whether in human resources, financial constraints, or other issues. However, there are several ways to overcome these issues.

Human capacity is an undeniably important resource on any campus, no matter the institutional size or type. An important means of enhancing human resources is effectively tapping into what is already taking place on campus. As stated earlier in this chapter, it is important to consider how to use currently existing data resources while applying a masculinities lens to see the data in a new way. For example, in the Multi-Institutional Study of Leadership Survey, students are examined to understand the extent to which sociocultural conversations happen with peers (Dugan, Kodama, Correia, & Associates, 2013). These conversations are vital to the wellness of students and the institutions as a whole, and once collected they could be a great data set to explore and examine through a masculinities lens. Using existing data will help maximize time and can help uncover new or previously unknown resources.

When initiating assessment, meet with your institution's institutional review board and the research or assessment office to not only ensure that you are in compliance but also weigh the benefits and limitations of qualitative, quantitative, and mixed-methods approaches with professionals who are routinely engaged in assessment or research. Some libraries may have subscriptions to resources that can help you such as assessment-related software. Take the time to talk to and learn from your institution's offices and staff members who have unique and specialized skills in supporting your assessment agenda. Additionally, you may consider contacting faculty to see how you can support their coursework if it aligns with your program or intervention. Some faculty members may be teaching courses that require students to work with initiatives on campus, which can provide practical experience for them while also aiding you in the investigation, collection, and analysis of data.

Conclusion

Schuh (2009) argued, "Outcomes assessments are challenging to conduct, but they are essential in making the case for value that is contributed to student learning by specific programs and other student experiences" (p. 14). Indeed, college men and masculinities programs provide opportunities for student learning and development that are often complex, elusive, and therefore difficult to measure. Yet, effective assessment and evaluation of programs must be a primary component of any program or service. Assessment should be integrated into the program development process from the beginning or embedded in existing programs and services if not already. Moving through the assessment cycle supports the likelihood of having robust data to determine if intended outcomes and program goals were successful. Taking this tactful approach through the assessment cycle uses results in ways that advocate for college men and masculinities programs and services while advancing student learning, development, and success.

References

Anderson, L. W., & Krathwohl, D. R. (2001). *A taxonomy for learning, teaching, and assessing: A revision of Bloom's taxonomy of educational objectives.* New York, NY: Longman.

Angelo, T. A., & Cross, K. P. (1993). *Classroom assessment techniques: A handbook for college teachers.* San Francisco, CA: Jossey-Bass.

Bloom, B., & Krathwohl, D. (1956). *Taxonomy of educational objectives: The classification of educational goals, by a committee of college and university examiners. Handbook 1: Cognitive domain.* New York, NY: Longmans, Green.

Bresciani, M. J., Gardner, M. M., & Hickmott, J. (2009). *Demonstrating student success: A practical guide to outcomes-based assessment of learning and development in student affairs.* Sterling, VA: Stylus.

Dugan, J. P., Kodama, C., Correia, B., & Associates. (2013). *Multi-institutional study of leadership insight report: Leadership program delivery.* College Park, MD: National Clearinghouse for Leadership Programs.

Heinich, R., Molenda, M., & Russell, J. (1989). *Instructional media and the new technologies of instruction* (3rd ed.). New York, NY: Macmillan.

hooks, b. (2004). *The will to change: Men, masculinity, and love.* New York, NY: Atria Books.

Livingston, V. (2016). *Synthesizing and using results across the division.* Paper presented at the meeting of the ACPA Student Affairs Assessment Institute, Baltimore, MD.

Maki, P. L. (2004). *Assessing for learning: Building a sustainable commitment across the institution.* Sterling, VA: Stylus.

Montenegro, E., & Jankowski, N. A. (2017). *Equity and assessment: Moving towards culturally responsive assessment* (Occasional Paper No. 29). Urbana, IL: University of Illinois and Indiana University, National Institute for Learning Outcomes Assessment.

Rhodes, T. (2009). *Assessing outcomes and improving achievement: Tips and tools for using the rubrics.* Washington, DC: Association of American Colleges and Universities.

Schuh, J. H. (2009). *Assessment methods for student affairs.* San Francisco, CA: Jossey-Bass.

Schuh, J. H., Biddix, J. P., Dean, L. A., & Kinzie, J. (2016). *Assessment in student affairs* (2nd ed.). San Francisco, CA: Jossey-Bass.

Stanny, C. J. (2016). Reevaluating Bloom's taxonomy: What measurable verbs can and cannot say about student learning. *Education Sciences, 6*(37), 1–12.

Suskie, L. (2009). *Assessing student learning: A common sense guide* (2nd ed.). San Francisco, CA: Jossey-Bass.

Bloom's revised taxonomy describes increasing cognitive processes through six defined dimensions: create, evaluate, analyze, apply, understand, and remember (Anderson & Krathwohl, 2001). Corresponding verbs to each dimension includes those most frequently found in resources and publications (Stanny, 2016). Assessment is supported by using the listed verbs to describe and measure the expected behavior of student learners after participation in a program, service, or other educational activities.

Create: Put elements together to form a coherent or functional whole; reorganize elements into new pattern or structure.			
arrange	create	generate	prepare
assemble	design	invent	produce
combine	develop	modify	rate
compose	devise	organize	revise
construct	formulate	plan	write
Evaluate: Make judgments based on criteria and standards.			
appraise	conclude	evaluate	reconcile
argue	criticize	judge	set up
assess	critique	manage	synthesize
choose	defend	prepare	
compare	estimate	rearrange	
Analyze: Break material into its constituent parts and determine how the parts relate to one another and to an overall structure or purpose.			
analyze	criticize	examine	relate
appraise	diagram	infer	select
categorize	differentiate	outline	separate
classify	discriminate	point out	subdivide
compare	distinguish	question	test
contrast	divide		

Apply: Carry out or use a procedure in a given situation.			
act	demonstrate	modify	schedule
apply	dramatize	operate	show
calculate	employ	practice	sketch
choose	illustrate	prepare	solve
compute	interpret	produce	use
construct	manipulate	relate	

Understand: Construct meaning from instructional messages, including oral, written, and graphic communication.			
classify	estimate	infer	report
compare	explain	interpret	restate
convert	express	locate	review
defend	extend	paraphrase	rewrite
describe	generalize	predict	summarize
discuss	identify	recognize	translate
distinguish			

Remember: Retrieve relevant knowledge from long-term memory.			
cite	list	outline	repeat
define	locate	recite	reproduce
describe	match	recognize	select
identify	memorize	record	slate
label	name	relate	

TAKING OFF THE MASC

Healthy Masculinities Capstone Project Rubric

	Mastering 4	Proficient 3	Developing 2	Beginning 1
SLO #1: Explore how precollege experiences lead to the development of masculine identities and subsequent behaviors	In-depth reflection on personal and observed experiences, which elicits significant understanding of factors that contribute to gender identity, norms, and behavior. Aware of larger societal and community influences on one's understanding of personal masculinity while revealing new perspectives that honor a multitude of masculinity experiences and seeking to learn more.	Articulates understanding of personal and societal factors that influence the development of masculinities and related behaviors. Demonstrates a foundational understanding of how factors influence different identities for men while having a desire to learn more.	Unable to draw on larger societal factors influencing masculinity outside personal experiences. Tends to recognize their own masculinity identity as a preferred and singular experience.	Able to identify past experiences but is not able to draw conclusions on how this impacts gender. Difficulty in expressing one's own masculinity identity limiting reflection.
SLO #2: Describe how gender identity relates to power, privilege, and oppression in society and on campus	Able to articulate a clear understanding of male privilege's relationship to power structures and experiences at an individual and systemic level. Students draw strong examples where their own personal and group membership has benefited them on campus. Shows interest in learning strategies to dismantle male privilege and gender oppression.	Male privilege is primarily understood at an individual level as it relates to personal experiences before and in college. Some articulation of how male privilege shapes experiences at a systemic level.	Select examples are articulated where male privilege is recognized but lacks fully understanding of implications. Demonstrated interest and curiosity to explore how gender relates to power structures.	Shows minimal or no awareness of power structures as it relates to gender.

(Continues)

(Continued)

	Mastering 4	Proficient 3	Developing 2	Beginning 1
SLO #3: Integrate self-defined masculinities supportive of healthy behaviors into their personal and academic lives	Students self-define their masculine identity as aligned to their values and goals while acknowledging the complexity and intersections with other identities and communities. Students demonstrate a strong relationship between their masculine identity and healthy behaviors through academic and personal experiences.	Students demonstrate congruency between an expressed masculine identity and their values and goals. Some awareness of how masculinity intersects with their other identities and communities. Demonstrated relationship between how self-defined masculinity positively impacts personal and academic experiences.	Identifies cultural norms as it relates to gender but prefers those preset expectations of masculinity. Does not fully recognize intersections among other identities and surrounding communities as well lacks awareness of how masculinity influences healthy decisions and behaviors.	Unable to express an understanding of one's masculine identity or stated identity is largely based on societal expectations and predetermined gender roles. Masculine identity is not integrated due to a lack of self-awareness.

PART THREE

SPECIFIC PROGRAM CONTENT AND DELIVERY

To send nearly one million college-educated men into the world with troubled masculinities, underdeveloped gender identities, and erroneous assumptions concerning men and other men with whom they co-occupy society makes contemporary institutions of higher education one of the guiltiest culprits in the perpetual maintenance of patriarchy, sexism, and homophobia in America. (S.R. Harper & F. Harris III, Beyond the Model Gender Majority Myth: Responding Equitably to the Developmental Needs and Challenges of College Men, *San Francisco, CA: Jossey-Bass, 2010)*

6

DEVELOPING ENGAGING RETREAT EXPERIENCES FOR COLLEGE MEN

Peter Paquette and Vernon A. Wall

Learning in a retreat format is a useful tool in higher education to support students' learning, identity formation, self-esteem, and exploration of new ideas and identities in a unique and supportive environment (Hopkins & Putnam, 1993; Paquette, Brassard, Guerin, Fortin-Chevalier, & Tanguay-Beaudoin, 2014). Departing from campus to interact with fellow students to participate in activities, exploration of new concepts, mentoring, and risk-taking in a safe environment balances challenge and support and facilitates learning (McKenzie, 2003; Paquette et al., 2014). Retreats give participants an opportunity to escape their normal routine on campus to explore new aspects of who they are as individuals, the complexity of their interconnected identities, and who they wish to become (Tatum, 2013).

College men often arrive on college campuses prioritizing traditional notions of masculinity (Harris & Harper, 2015; Harris & Struve, 2009). In addition, many men have not had an opportunity prior to college to interrogate their own gender socialization and how it affects their behaviors, attitudes, and interactions (Harris & Harper, 2015). Exploring masculinity and its impact on college men in a retreat format can serve as a useful method for creating healthier men and safer campuses. Helping college men understand how their shared dominant identities affect themselves and others must be rooted in social justice and inclusion work with an understanding of shared liberation (Davis & Harper, 2012). To that end, retreats for men to explore and deconstruct masculinity should allow the deconstruction of toxic masculinity as well as identifying and celebrating healthier masculinities. In addition, an intersectional approach helps men understand how each individual has differing dominant and subordinate identities that affect themselves and others (Harper, Wardell & McGuire, 2011; Tillapaugh, Mitchell, & Soria, 2017).

Retreats in Higher Education

Colleges and universities use the retreat format for learning and development in a number of ways. At universities affiliated with a specific religion, retreat formats appear to be more common; for example, Catholic colleges and universities use retreats often, which is likely related to the culture at private Catholic high schools. Using retreats as an opportunity to better understand one's self allows students to identify who they are and who they wish to become personally, emotionally, and spiritually (Burke, 2012; Hopkins & Putnam, 1993; Paquette et al., 2014).

Retreats allow participants to step away from their day-to-day routine and identities and isolate identity issues (Burke, 2012; McKenzie, 2003; Paquette et al., 2014). Retreats can be used for several purposes including relationship building and team bonding, often used by athletic teams to build a strong team dynamic that continues onto the playing field (Baker, Horton, Robertson-Wilson & Wall, 2003). They can also be used to build leadership skills in task-oriented retreats many student organizations and leadership programs conduct to help students focus on their development as leaders and how an organization can achieve its goals (Janke, Traynor, & Sorenson, 2009). Retreats focused on social justice issues have become increasingly popular on campuses (Derman-Sparks & Phillips, 1997). Most retreats involve students from a variety of identity groups who gather to discuss such topics as intersecting identities, experiences and biases, privilege, dominance, and oppression. Some campuses offer single-identity retreats, which allow deeper discussions with students from their specific identity groups (Adams, Bell, Goodman, & Joshi, 2016). Topics include discussions on lived experiences, identity development, internalized oppression, and self-care.

Participants in retreats often return to their campuses more deeply committed to causes, their own development, or other aspects of their developmental and educational goals. Because of the success of retreat-format development, colleges and universities use it in what are commonly called extended orientation camps. Intensive or extended orientation programs demonstrate an increase in retention and affinity (Michael, Morris-Dueer, & Reichert, 2017). In these extended-format camps, the primary goal is often peer connection and campus affinity (Barr, 2010).

Participants return to campus, often before the entire first-year class has arrived, with a deep connection to peers, institutional traditions, and affinity for the place itself after being able to spend multiple days focusing only on their own development.

Supportive Environments for College Men to Unlearn Toxic Masculinity

As mentioned earlier, retreats provide participants with the opportunity to isolate their focus, attention, and commitment on a singular issue. In addition, they provide participants with the opportunity to step outside their day-to-day expectations as individuals, leaders, teammates, employees, and gendered beings, making retreats an ideal environment for college men to explore their own masculinity. The masculine norms operating in U.S. culture dictate that a man should be tough, stoic, accept homophobia, and not express pain (Arbeit, Hershberg, Rubin, DeSouza, & Lerner, 2016; Oransky & Fisher, 2009; Pascoe, 2007; Way, 2011). These same norms push boys and men away from one another and create barriers for interpersonal connection. As Burke (2012) states, retreats focused on men's development allow a break from what he and Pascoe (2007) call *fag discourse*. Men can engage and are encouraged to participate in activities that allow them to be vulnerable, which is often not allowed in their day-to-day environments where vulnerability and weakness are often acts associated with women and gay men. Burke (2012) discussed how participants were able to be vulnerable and engage with one another:

> On the retreats I attended, one boy spoke of losing his father and then his stepfather before the age of fourteen. Another talked of his older brother's death by heroin overdose; one admitted to loading a gun with suicidal thoughts in mind; still others mourned their own addictions to alcohol or other drugs; universally they lamented their lack of respect for their girlfriends and mothers. One boy spoke of his role in an almost-race-riot and the humanizing intervention of a counseling program, which brokered peace between black and white participants. The leaders cry as they talk, the audience sobs. The small groups begin to bond. It's a process of wearing down wariness at first, and from there it is almost necessary to reign in the sharing as boys pour out all of their concerns, fears, deaths, injuries, and shortcomings. (p. 87)

As this excerpt demonstrates, the shared vulnerability among participants affects them in ways their day-to-day interactions cannot replicate.

As many of the contributors to this volume state, hegemonic or toxic masculinity has a significant impact on the socialization of college men. Creating retreat spaces where men can be vulnerable and explore masculinities supports safer campuses as men most commonly perpetuate violence on campus, which often stems from unexplored feelings of pain and shame (Arbeit et al., 2016). Retreats for college men can be one opportunity to help men connect with one another and begin a new narrative for healthier masculinities. As Arbeit and colleagues (2016) noted,

> Analyzing the ways in which young men engage in interpersonal connection, and the ways in which young men's interpersonal connections are shaped by gender ideologies, has implications for promoting their health and well-being, and the health and well-being for young people of all genders. Girls and young women, too, are impacted by the ways in which masculinity ideologies shape the interpersonal behaviors of the men in their lives. (p. 94)

Deconstructing the way masculinity affects retreat participants has a positive impact on their behavior and well-being.

Connecting Healthy Masculinities With Retreat-Format Learning

The individuals in a man's life create expectations for him regarding the ways he should demonstrate his masculinity. The same men can be useful at deconstructing and writing a new narrative for masculinity. By adhering to gender norms, however, men often push themselves away from those who can help them (Arbeit et al., 2016; Oransky & Fisher, 2009; Way, 2011). Entering adulthood, college men often lose authenticity in their relationships, face barriers to seeking support, and distance themselves from peers (Arbeit et al., 2016; Chu, Porsche, & Tolman, 2005; Kimmel, 2008; Way, 2011).

Despite the documented norms and barriers, college men also value the space to express emotions and find support, often in very close relationships, as doing so in larger settings is often deemed unsafe for college men (Arbeit et al., 2016; Kimmel, 2008; Pascoe, 2007). Yet college men have the capacity and desire for greater emotional closeness with other men (Arbeit et al., 2016). Simply put, they long for an environment where they can put their guard down and be vulnerable with other men. According to Arbeit and colleagues (2016),

> We heard from participants that talking and listening in the context of relationships is particularly meaningful. Allowing specific time and a

structured space for young men to communicate in a safe and open environment could help them to reflect on and address hurt from relationships
while providing the opportunity to build new supportive relationships with
peers and with mentors. (p. 93)

In society men rarely are given the opportunity to engage in meaningful ways
like they can on a retreat. Once they learn these skills in the retreat setting,
their health and well-being are positively affected.

Coleman (2015) and Keohane and Richardson (2018) identified a connection between adherence to masculine expectations and inability to accept
failure as a likely connection between increased suicide rates among men.
Put another way, men who adhere rigidly to conservative gender norms are
at higher risk for suicide. Keohane and Richardson suggest creating spaces for
men to tackle the root of their disconnection from society and ways to build
capacity for connection. Oliffe, Robertson, Kelly, Roy, and Ogrodniczuk
(2010) noted "the same hegemonic discourses linked to socialized behavior
that make it difficult for men to ask for help might then become a driver for
extreme self-damaging behaviors, including suicide" (p. 995). Men's retreats
allow participants to explore their pain, struggles, and shortcomings in a safe
environment and may create the space for men to find alternatives to harmful
or self-destructive behaviors.

Creating an Intersectional Retreat Program

Retreat programs often involve a group of men departing campus together
to engage in and deconstruct masculinity. By design, women and trans feminine individuals are not often present on retreats. Based on this, it is vital to
create partnerships to earn the trust and respect of women's centers; lesbian,
gay, bisexual, and transgender centers; and queer studies and women's studies programs on campus. After all, the work of deconstructing and creating
healthier masculinities is rooted in feminism and shared liberation, and for
many of us engaging in this work, we have feminist scholars to thank who
labored to help us understand our masculinity (Heasley, 2013).

In addition to being rooted in feminism and shared liberation, developing programs to help men deconstruct masculinity must operate from
an intersectional perspective. According to Robbins and McGowan (2016),
gender and other social identities cannot be separated or isolated; they are
inextricably connected. Social identities, race, social class, sexual orientation, and religion have an impact on one's understanding of gender. Taking
into account that these identities are connected, retreats for men can be
successful in creating a sense of belonging (Robbins & McGowan, 2016).

Heasley (2013) said that by recognizing the established work of marginalized groups on campus, interdisciplinary and intersectional work is most effective.

In addition to attracting and meeting the needs of cisgender men on campus, retreats must be designed to meet the needs of trans students on campus. Creating a healthy masculinity is important to trans*masculine college students (Jourian, 2017). Jourian (2017) said that trans*masculine college students' lived experiences compelled them to desire authentic masculinities without the harm that comes from hegemonic masculinities. Many participants in Jourian's study sought to craft their masculinities "with intentionality and imbu[e] them with gentleness" (p. 259). Based on Jourian's research, we suggest that colleges and universities have an imperative to support trans*masculine college students to craft their masculinity in ways each student finds healthy. Designing curricula for men's retreats with input from and attentiveness to the needs of trans*masculine students is one way campuses can help support trans*masculine students.

In addition to creating a retreat rooted in feminism and shared liberation, accounting for the needs of minoritized populations, and adopting an intersectional approach, a strong retreat for men must take into account the ways it can meet the needs of international students. Masculine expectations differ, yet no man in the United States is free from hegemonic masculinity. As discussed earlier, destructive approaches to masculinity put college men at a higher risk for self-harm and suicide, which can be heightened for certain international populations on U.S. college campuses (Oliffe et al., 2010). Oliffe and colleagues (2010) stated that colleges and universities have a responsibility for engaging international men in creative ways to support their wellness: "A moral imperative exists for Western universities to actively engage international students in ways that promote men's mental health rather than relying on self-management, peer support, and/or the ability to appropriately judge when and how to access professional services" (p. 995). Retreats for college men are one concrete way colleges and university in the United States can support the success and well-being of international male students.

Creating a Retreat to Meet Campus Needs

The previous sections discuss the need for an intersectional and shared liberation perspective to creating a men's retreat, often leaving the practitioner creating a retreat uncertain how to meet the unique and varying needs of potential participants. Creating cross-campus collaborations and coalitions are essential to meeting these needs. An effective way to create a retreat and curriculum that meets the unique needs of an individual campus is to form a committee of key individuals who represent the diverse identities on campus. This group can be useful to identify the unique needs and potential ways to meet those needs.

To help those on your campus understand the need for and benefit of a retreat focused on deconstructing masculinity, it is important to use not only data and research to justify the retreat but also firsthand stories from students who have benefited from deconstructing their own masculinity. Dean's (2013) firsthand account helps portray the personal benefits of men's development programs like retreats:

> I was cut from my college basketball team in the fall of my sophomore year. In my time away from the sport I gained the reflective space necessary to comprehend the anxiety that a life of hypermasculine athletic competition had created within me. I realized that I felt trapped in a paralysis of expression and forced to perform a balancing act between who I was and what I was expected to be. I suppressed compassion and empathy for the sake of pursuing my place in a masculine pecking order. Certain emotions were restricted, trapped within, and left to boil inside; their existence only evidenced by the steaming anxiety that fogged my path to personal growth and meaningful relationships. (p. 4)

Using existing data, such as reports from campus climate studies, can be useful in articulating needs and securing funding from campus partners.

Many men's support or leadership groups have sprung up on college campuses across the United States, which often provide a useful support to participants but may not have an aspect of deconstructing hegemonic or toxic masculinity. At times these programs support participants but also offer spaces to continue to perpetuate masculinities that have a harmful impact on individuals and the campus. We suggest being clear throughout all stages of development that this will be part of what transpires in the retreat. In addition, it may be easier to create a retreat for a group or team that already exists, yet some campuses find benefit in creating retreat programs that allow men from different backgrounds, experiences, and interests to converge in a two- to three-day retreat weekend.

Finally, it is important to build a retreat with the unique mission, vision, and values of the university in mind. We recommend using common campus nomenclature. For example, a Jesuit institution using terms like *magis* or *men for others* speaks common campus language and helps build support. Using common campus vernacular and aligning with the mission and vision of the university, as well as the unit that sponsors the retreat, will help the retreat achieve overall campus goals and help garner campus acceptance or support for the project.

Curriculum Design

In designing an effective curriculum it is important to determine what the unique needs or opportunities are on the campus where the retreat will occur and what the learning outcomes for the retreat will be. Unique needs may stem from incidents where toxic masculinity garnered campus attention, and for another campus it may be an individual fraternity that has a history of celebrating and embracing diverse masculinities. In addition, student groups whose purpose and mission is to explore or deconstruct the notion of masculinity are beneficial partners in recruiting participants and obtaining campus support.

Next, create a curriculum that is engaging and inclusive. Marchesani and Adams (1992) identified four dimensions to consider when developing an inclusive curriculum: facilitator, students, content, and pedagogy. Bell, Goodman, and Ouellett (2016) stated they would add one more dimension to the mix: climate and group dynamics. The first dimension addresses who we are as facilitators. We bring our full selves into the space, including our social identities, cultural styles, preferred facilitation approaches, personalities, knowledge bases, triggers, and biases (Bell et al., 2016). The second dimension addresses getting to know the participants in the experience. Bell and colleagues stated that important factors to consider are the multiple social identities, interests, expectations, needs, prior experiences, lived realities, and learning preferences that participants bring to the experience. The third dimension addresses choices facilitators make about the content, perspectives, and voices to include in the experience. In initiatives and experiences related to social justice education, there are often three broad goals: increase personal awareness, expand knowledge, and encourage action (Bell et al., 2016). These goals can also be a helpful framework in developing content for men's retreats. The fourth dimension addresses how facilitators engage with participants, with the content, and with each other to promote learning. Bell and colleagues (2016) believe that the degree to which this is done successfully determines whether an inclusive learning environment will be created and sustained.

The previous four dimensions each affect how participants experience the learning environment. Bell and colleagues (2016) believe that climate and group dynamics are central in creating an inclusive environment for all and are shaped by the other four dimensions. More specifically, they stated,

> The better the facilitator is at creating and sustaining an inclusive climate—by designing and implementing structures and activities that enable

participants to engage honestly and thoughtfully with the curriculum and each other—the more likely participants will be open to express and explore unexamined beliefs and values and learn. (p. 67)

In the end, the goal is to provide a positive and productive learning experience for all.

To create learning outcomes, Covarrubias (2012) describes learning outcomes as the building blocks for all men and masculinity programs (see chapter 5 for additional information on crafting learning outcomes), stating,

It is important to be intentional with the wording and meaning behind the outcomes. It is important to develop learning outcomes that directly relate to the type of program(s) you will be creating. Be realistic with your learning outcomes and what can be accomplished within the scope of the program. (p. 6)

The following is a sample list of potential learning outcomes suggested by Covarrubias (2012). The list is a nice guide, yet it is not meant to be cut and pasted onto your curriculum. Learning outcomes must be written to meet unique campus needs, and we recommend creating four to six learning outcomes for a retreat.

- Participants will begin to define masculinity
- Participants will develop a personal definition of masculinity
- Participants will explore the intersections of social identities
- Participants will gain a basic understanding of male socialization
- Participants will gain a basic understanding of the concept of male privilege
- Participants will develop reflection and critical thinking skills
- Participants will develop the ability to express feelings and emotions not normally expressed by men
- Participants will gain an understanding of how male socialization can impact decision-making
- Participants will talk to other men about issues of male socialization and how to have healthier relationships
- Participants will engage in bystander intervention behaviors to prevent sexual violence and homophobia on campus and in the community (p. 6)

A sample weekend retreat schedule can be found in Appendix 6.A.

Implementation, Logistics, and Considerations

Covarrubias (2012) identified several considerations and cautions to provide an authentic and ethical experience for students. The following are questions offered by Covarrubias that the planning committee should address as the program is developed:

- How to be inclusive of the multiple identities of men (race, ability, sexual orientation, class, etc.) and honor multiple masculinities?
- How do we keep from giving the participants and facilitators the "Superman Cape" and avoid the "Pedestal Effect"?
  - Superman Cape: When participants and facilitators of men's programs are seen as the "good men" and "heroes" on campus; and as a result, are given (and expect) unearned trust and privileges.
  - Pedestal Effect: When participants and facilitators of men's programs internalize the "Superman Cape" and see themselves as above other men.
  - As a result, the participants and facilitators stop being self-reflective of their own actions and thoughts and are no longer open to being challenged on their own sexism and homophobia.
- How will the program work collaboratively with women's groups and trans' groups on campus to build a community of accountability? (p. 10)

Next, we provide a sample of potential tasks when planning for a men's retreat.

Create a Coalition to Assist With Recruitment and Curriculum

Chapter 3 offers ways to create and sustain campuswide coalitions to ensure the long-term success and growth of men's retreat programs and that of their participants.

Recruit and Invite Participants

To recruit a group of committed participants, general advertising using the usual campus methods is recommended. In addition, we have had great success in recruiting participants by direct invitations, electronically and in person. Generating a list of potential participants from well-respected members of the campus community and mentioning the name of the individual who nominated the recommended participant can also be useful in garnering participant attendance.

Identify a Retreat Location

Finding a retreat location that allows ample space for large-group interactions as well as smaller group conversations is useful. In addition, having space for recreation and time to interact informally is also helpful. Retreat locations within two hours from campus are recommended for ease of transportation. It is important to recognize that certain retreat centers are not inclusive and welcoming spaces for all potential participants, and a retreat center that has a history of exclusion of underrepresented groups is not recommended. In addition, the accessibility of the retreat grounds should be considered so that all participants can fully engage in retreat activities.

Identify Students, Faculty, and Staff as Facilitators
A four-person facilitation team of two student leaders and two faculty or staff leaders has been an effective method for us. It is useful to have a facilitation team that consists of varying social identities that demonstrate varied expressions of masculinity. Leaders who have engaged in critiquing their own masculinity in depth are useful to have on the retreat leadership team but not required of all members of the team.

Secure Funding and Sponsorships
Involving multiple offices across campus to cosponsor the retreat is helpful in securing wide acceptance and support. For example, sponsors like the athletics office or the fraternity and sorority life office may be more apt to encourage participation among the students overseen by their offices. Participants have also found great support by asking the senior student affairs officers on their campuses to directly support men's retreat initiatives.

Identify Specific Campus Needs and Learning Outcomes
Although this chapter offers sample outcomes and many ideas for a campus retreat, each campus will have different needs and goals. A retreat should cater to individual needs as well as the mission of the specific institution hosting the retreat. For example, using campus strategic plans and mission statements as guiding documents is helpful in designing objectives that meet campus needs and garner campuswide support.

Communication to Campus

Advertising for a retreat focused on healthy masculinities is as much about recruiting participants as it is securing campus support and educating the campus on what the retreat is attempting to achieve. Creating an announcement or press release for campus news sources and campus partners is useful in achieving this goal and making sure the campus has a clear understanding and expectations of the purpose of the retreat and what will occur during the experience.

Logistics and Time Line

An effective retreat should be planed three to four months in advance to find a location, determine transportation, secure funding, recruit participants, and create a detailed curriculum. Particularly in the first year of a retreat on campus, ample planning is necessary. Detailed logistics planning also includes executing a preretreat meeting for participants to create rapport if possible. In addition to large-scale items like a preretreat meeting, small details should also be addressed, from how participants will register to how they will purchase snacks and meals if not offered by the retreat site. If funding permits, creating a retreat T-shirt can be a useful item to continue group connection and raise campus awareness of the retreat after its conclusion.

Assessment

Chapter 5 discusses assessment in detail, but designing assessment tools for a retreat is important in determining the growth and development of the participants as well as their satisfaction with retreat logistics and location. Feedback from assessments is essential for closing the communication loop with campus partners who sponsored the retreat so they know what participants experienced.

Assessment is a vital part of retreat planning. A useful men's retreat assessment will gauge the learning and development that occurred as well as the participants' satisfaction with the experience itself. Chapter 5 contains discussions of what professionals might consider when developing their assessment plans for men's programming. It is common for retreat leaders to determine the success of a program by its number of attendees. We caution against this, as a retreat of 8 participants can be equally as effective in meeting its stated learning outcomes as a retreat of 24. In fact, we recommend starting small and aiming for about 12 participants in the first year of a retreat program of this nature.

After the Retreat

Retreats are useful, but participants' learning from them must not stop on the day the retreat ends. In his critique of men's retreats, Burke (2012) noted that retreats can be a useful way to unpack sexism and homophobia as they allow participants to share intense feelings and emotions in a safe place. However, those same emotions rarely have an opportunity to resurface in common campus settings. As Burke (2012) noted, retreat participants

> continually and violently cry as they reminisce and think about the ways that their mothers and fathers love them (or fail to do so). They talk about how much they care for their girlfriends, for their boy-friends. They hug

each other and hold hands. All of this, though, goes again underground upon return to the school. (p. 86)

It is important to build in a plan for bringing the learning and experience back to the campus in a safe way. This can be done by sponsoring reunions once a month or once a semester where participants can discuss and implement their learning on campus. In addition, campus engagement could be built into the retreat curriculum where participants spend time in the final stages of the retreat determining how they will share their learning with the campus. For some campuses, the energy created from a men's retreat has resulted in creating a men's campus organization to deconstruct masculinity more regularly.

Conclusion

We have the opportunity in higher education to provide opportunities for students to engage in dialogues that encourage them to be better citizens in the world. We must continue to have discussions and work to develop solutions to address unhealthy cultural norms of masculinity on campus. By offering retreats and other structured immersion experiences, college men can find healing and support through conversations on emotional labor, consent, violence, communication, empathy and vulnerability. As one student who attended a men's retreat at Denison University stated after his experience: "We should work to not put each other down, but to build each other up."

References

Adams, M., Bell, L. A., Goodman, D. J., & Joshi, K. Y. (Eds.). (2016). *Teaching for diversity and social justice: A sourcebook.* New York, NY: Routledge.

Arbeit, M. R., Hershberg, R. M., Rubin, R. O., DeSouza, L. M., & Lerner, J. V. (2016). "I'm hoping that I can have better relationships": Exploring interpersonal connection for young men. *Qualitative Psychology, 3*(1), 79–97. doi:10.1037/qup0000042

Baker, J., Horton, S., Robertson-Wilson, J., & Wall, M. (2003). Nurturing sport expertise: Factors influencing the development of elite athletes. *Journal of Sports Science & Medicine, 2*(1), 1–9.

Barr, M. J. (2010). Preface. In J. A. Ward-Roof (Ed.), *Designing successful transitions: A guide for orienting students to college* (3rd ed., pp. ix–x). Columbia: University of South Carolina, National Resource Center for the First-Year Experience and Students in Transition.

Bell, L., Goodman, D., & Ouellett, M. (2016). Design and facilitation. In M. Adams, L. A. Bell, D. J. Goodman, & K. Y. Joshi (Eds.), *Teaching for diversity and social justice* (pp. 55–93). New York, NY: Routledge.

Burke, K. J. (2012). A space apart: Kairos and masculine possibility in retreats of adolescents. *Journal of Men, Masculinities & Spirituality, 6*(2), 77–93.

Chu, J. Y., Porche, M. V., & Tolman, D. L. (2005). The adolescent masculinity ideology in relationships scale: Development and validation of a new measure for boys. *Men and Masculinities, 8*(1), 93–115. doi:10.1177/1097184X03257453

Coleman, D. (2015). Traditional masculinity as a risk factor for suicidal ideation: Cross-sectional and prospective evidence from a study of young adults. *Archives of Suicide Research, 19*, 366–384. doi:10.1080/13811118.2014.957453

Covarrubias, A. (2012). *Men's group/program development guide.* Workshop presented at the NASPA–Student Affairs Professionals in Higher Education Conference, Phoenix, AZ.

Davis, T. L., & Harper, S. R. (2012). Promoting learning and development with college men. *Journal of College & University Student Housing, 39*(1), 118–123.

Dean, D. (2013). *Healing men and restoring community: Reflection on a collegiate project for men's liberation.* Retrieved from https://www.yumpu.com/en/document/view/15658833/joint20publication202013/2

Derman-Sparks, L., & Phillips, C. B. (1997). *Teaching/learning anti-racism: A developmental approach.* New York, NY: Teachers College Press.

Harper, S. R., Wardell, C. C., & McGuire, K. M. (2011). Man of multiple identities: Complex individuality and identity intersectionality among college men. In J. Laker & T. Davis (Eds.), *Masculinities in higher education: Theoretical and practical considerations* (pp. 81–96). New York, NY: Routledge.

Harris, F. III, & Harper, S. R. (2015). Matriculating masculinity: Understanding undergraduate men's precollege gender socialization. *Journal of the First-Year Experience & Students in Transition, 27*(2), 49–65.

Harris, F. III, & Struve, L. E. (2009). Gents, jerks, and jocks: What male students learn about masculinity in college. *About Campus, 14*(3), 2–9. doi:10.1002/abc.289

Heasley, R. (2013). Twenty years and counting: The relevance of men's studies in a gendered world. *Journal of Men's Studies, 21*, 9–13. doi:10.3149/jms.2101.9

Hopkins, D., & Putnam, R. (1993). *Personal growth through adventure.* London, England: David Fulton.

Janke, K. K., Traynor, A. P., & Sorensen, T. D. (2009). Student leadership retreat focusing on a commitment to excellence. *American Journal of Pharmaceutical Education, 73*(3), 1–10.

Jourian, T. J. (2017). Trans*forming college masculinities: Carving out trans*masculine pathways through the threshold of dominance. *International Journal of Qualitative Studies in Education, 30*, 245–265. doi:10.1080/09518398.2016.1257752

Keohane, A., & Richardson, N. (2018). Negotiating gender norms to support men in psychological distress. *American Journal of Men's Health, 12*, 160–171. doi:10.1177/1557988317733093

Kimmel, M. (2008). *Guyland: The perilous world where boys become men.* New York, NY: HarperCollins.

Marchesani, L., & Adams, M. (1992). Dynamics of diversity in the teaching-learning process: A faculty development model for analysis and action. *New Directions for Teaching and Learning, 52,* 9–19.

McKenzie, M. (2003). Beyond the Outward Bound process: Rethinking student learning. *Journal of Experiential Education, 26,* 8–23.

Michael, J. M., Morris-Dueer, V., & Reichert, M. S. (2017). Differential effects of participation in an outdoor orientation program for incoming students. *Journal of Outdoor Recreation, Education & Leadership, 9*(1), 42–55.

Oliffe, J. L., Robertson, S., Kelly, M. T., Roy, P., & Ogrodniczuk, J. S. (2010). Connecting masculinity and depression among international male university students. *Qualitative Health Research, 20,* 987–998. doi:10.1177/1049732310365700

Oransky, M., & Fisher, C. (2009). The development and validation of the meanings of adolescent masculinity scale. *Psychology of Men & Masculinity, 10*(1), 57–72. doi:10.1037/a0013612

Paquette, L., Brassard, A., Guerin, A., Fortin-Chevalier, J., & Tanguay-Beaudoin, L. (2014). Effects of a developmental adventure on the self-esteem of college students. *Journal of Experiential Education, 37,* 216–23.

Pascoe, C. J. (2007). *Dude, you're a fag: Masculinity and sexuality in high school.* Berkeley, CA: University of California Press.

Robbins, C. K., & McGowan, B. L. (2016). Intersectional perspectives on gender and gender identity development. *New Directions for Student Services,* 154, 71–83.

Tatum, B. D. (2013). The complexity of identity: "Who am I?" In M. Adams, W. Blumenfeld, C. Castaneda, H. W. Hackman, M. L. Peters, & X. Zúñiga (Eds.), *Readings for diversity and social justice* (pp. 6–9). New York, NY: Routledge.

Tillapaugh, D., Mitchell, D., & Soria, K. M. (2017). Considering gender and student leadership through the lens of intersectionality. *New Directions for Student Leadership,* 154, 23–32.

Way, N. (2011). *Deep secrets: Boys' friendships and the crisis of connection.* Cambridge, MA: Harvard University Press.

MEN'S RETREAT WEEKEND SAMPLE AGENDA

Friday Night:
  4:45 p.m.   Meet on campus
  5:15 p.m.   Departure
  6:30 p.m.   Arrival/Dinner
  7:30 p.m.   Welcome/Introductions/Expectations for the weekend
  8:00 p.m.   "Cross the Line" Ice Breaker
  8:30 p.m.   What it means to be a man on campus
              (Act Like a Man Box–2 versions)
  9:30 p.m.   "You Wouldn't Like Me When I'm Angry"
              (discussion–expressing anger)
 10:30 p.m.   Hook-up culture/Dating Discussion

Saturday:
  8:30 a.m   Breakfast
  9:30 a.m   Check in
 10:00 a.m.   Soundtrack of Our Lives (music and identity)
 12:30 p.m.   Lunch
  1:30 p.m.   Putting on my man face (mask-making/identity activity)
  3:00 p.m.   Fun activity (e.g., kickball/gaga/etc.)
  6:00 p.m.   Dinner
  7:00 p.m.   Saturday Night at the Movies (*Five Friends* documentary
              screening)
  8:30 p.m.   Film Discussion/Male-male relationships/Homophobia
  9:30 p.m.   Reconciling Father/Son Relationships
              *Discussion of relationships with fathers followed by writing a letter
              to fathers*
 10:30 p.m.   Bonfire

The activities discussed here are examples from retreats held at Dickinson College and Loyola University, Maryland; these retreats were co-organized by the chapter contributor along with campus colleagues.

Sunday:
 8:30 a.m. Breakfast
 9:30 a.m. Check in
10:00 a.m. Male mentors
11:00 a.m. Affirmation Activity ("Touch Someone Who . . .")
12:30 p.m. Lunch
 1:30 p.m. Departure

Detailed Descriptions of Activities:

Ice-Breaker: "Cross the Line" Example: https://my.vanderbilt.edu/vucept/
files/2014/08/Crossing-the-Line-Activity.pdf

"Act Like a Man" Box (adapted from Paul Kivel): What do we, as boys, learn about what it means to "act like a man"? To set the tone for the retreat, participants will be challenged to think of some of the messages and expectations we have been given about what it means to be a man (e.g., who we should be, how we should act, and what we should feel and say). We will draw a box around these messages, and discuss how, as young boys, we are supposed to learn how to fit in and live inside that box. We will also talk about what characteristics fall outside of the box and what happens when boys and men try to live outside the box. In addition, we will talk about how these expectations about masculinity affect women (e.g., sexism). We will create two versions of the "Act Like a Man Box," one containing general messages, and one containing messages about what it means to be a man at your particular college or university. These boxes will be hung and displayed throughout the retreat so that we can look them over and/or add to them.

"You Wouldn't Like Me When I'm Angry": We will discuss the functions of anger and how we are taught to express it (e.g., what is viewed as acceptable/unacceptable for men), relating these messages back to the "Act Like a Man" Box. Participants will be encouraged to share their experiences of how they tend to handle anger (e.g., stoicism/restricting emotional expression), and/or times when anger has felt out of control. We will also talk about how anger can be a "cover" for other emotions, and brainstorm ideas about the role we want anger to play in our lives.

Soundtrack of Our Lives: At the preretreat meeting, each participant will be asked to bring in (or e-mail us) a song that he feels represents some aspect of his identity. Taking turns, we will play at least part of each person's song, listening closely and paying attention to the thoughts and feelings that it might evoke for us. After listening, the person who brought in the song will have a chance to talk about what the song means to them, and others can share their reactions as well. Afterward, a CD containing each person's song will be created to commemorate the retreat.

Putting on My Man Face: Each person will decorate an oaktag mask on a stick as a way of representing their identity. The front of the mask will represent the man that we show the world (i.e., "public self") and the back will represent the man that we don't always show other ("private self"). Attendees will be encouraged to discuss the significance of what they put on their mask.

Male-Male Relationships/Homophobia Discussion: Facilitator begins with a story about his own homophobia and its impact on his life and ways that it limits friendships with straight men, and so on. Others will be encouraged to share their experiences of homophobia and male-male relationships. We will tie this conversation into a discussion about the documentary.

Reconciling Father/Son Relationships: This activity involves writing a letter to our fathers and/or father figures.

Male Mentors: A discussion about elders/mentors and the importance of older men (aside from fathers) in men's lives.

Final Activity: "Touch Someone Who . . .": Sitting in a circle facing out, people will take turns touching someone who fits with a description read aloud (e.g., "someone who made me think about something differently this weekend," "someone who is a good friend," etc.). Everyone will have a chance to be the affirmer and the affirmed.

7

REIMAGINING DIALOGUE-BASED PRAXIS

Wilson Kwamogi Okello and Stephen John Quaye

How do we begin healing the *split*? The split in this chapter represents the divisions in society caused by patriarchy. Anzaldúa (1987) says the split "originates in the foundation of our lives, our culture, our language, our thoughts" (p. 80). According to Anzaldúa, those interested in healing will have to conduct a massive uprooting of dualistic thinking, that is, thinking that engenders us-versus-them and one-or-the-other logic. Although the split is deeply embedded in the sociocultural fabric of Western societies, the reverberations have threatened the lives of women, trans people, some men, and all those who do not fit the stereotypical tropes of what a man should be. It can be cleaned, disinfected, and restitched through a dialogue-based praxis. As with any deep wound, it is likely that a scar will remain following antibiotic intervention; however, the public display of an internal process (scarring) is often the only sign that mending took place.

In this chapter, we take up this wound metaphor to bring clarity to the work of men's dialogic encounters with masculinity. What does it look like to accept one's gendered position and a sustained ethical commitment to engage with and participate in what has been part of the long-time feminist agenda and discourse? A sincere awareness of the patriarchal influences that are learned and transmitted through specific cultural practices can lead to an informed exploration of feminist theory and resistance to the constructed impulses of hegemonic masculinity.

In pursuit of this consciousness, the first part of this chapter, or cleaning the wound, discusses the necessity of self-reflexivity and accountability as components of the dialogue process. Self-reflexivity foregrounds the entanglement of political power and privileges and works to situate the self in relation to these forces. Accountability takes the posture of self-reflexivity a step further and considers how the self is constituted in and through communal relations. Cautiously, however, acts of reflexivity and discursive self-renderings unintentionally, yet perhaps unavoidably, facilitate the creation of idealized versions of a unified or exemplary self that has performed or achieved a progressive masculinity, exacting our need for the second part of this chapter to theorize about the disinfecting process. Awkward (1995) believes that "in exposing the latent multiplicity and difference in the word 'me(n),' we can perhaps open up a space within the discourse of feminism where a male voice can have something to say beyond impossibilities and apologies and unresolved ire" (p. 43).

This possibility leaves us with the question: How is this to be done? The third part of this chapter considers how educators might promote the development of progressive, critical masculinities that simultaneously support racial and gender uplifting while disrupting the reproduction of sexism, racism, and homophobia (hooks, 1990). In doing so, we advance a reconceptualized notion of intergroup dialogue, rooted in Black feminism, to materialize differential possibilities and challenges to normative discourses.

Introduction to Intergroup Dialogue

Oppression is a ubiquitous experience for those with minoritized identities. Intergroup dialogue was created as a way to learn across differences and work to dismantle systems of oppression (Zúñiga, 2003). These dialogues bring together two groups that have a history of conflict to engage across dominant identities (i.e., in which one holds privilege and power) and subordinated identities (i.e., in which one is oppressed). The goal of these dialogues is to learn how these systems of oppression manifest themselves and how to reduce their impact on people with subordinated identities (Buckley & Quaye, 2016).

Facilitators of intergroup dialogues mirror the identities of the participants in the dialogue. For example, a dialogue on race is facilitated by a person of color as well as a White person, and participants include people of color and White people. These dialogues bring together facilitators and students with dominant identities and those with subordinated identities. The rationale is to mirror how identities manifest themselves in society and to represent the power differentials that exist beyond the dialogue space.

Intergroup dialogues are grounded in a critical-dialogic framework (Nagda & Maxwell, 2011). The critical part of the framework is about naming and being critical of privilege, power, and oppression, understanding how they manifest themselves on the bodies of minoritized people, the difference between individual and systemic oppression, and how structural oppression works. The dialogic component of the framework means using dialogue principles like story sharing, practicing empathy, and building alliances across differences (Nagda & Maxwell, 2011). With these principles combined, intergroup dialogue works to help participants name oppression when they witness it. In the process and practice, participants are engaged in active listening to the stories of those experiencing oppression. Additionally, they foreground and validate the reality of oppression and its deleterious consequences on the emotional, mental, and physical well-being of those with subordinated identities. Moreover, intergroup dialogues are an approach for reducing the impact of oppression on people of color; women, gay, lesbian, bisexual, and trans* people; people with disabilities; and those with other subordinated identities.

Why Intergroup Dialogue Matters to Identity

In intergroup dialogue spaces, self-reflexivity and accountability are important concepts as they tie to the identities of facilitators and participants. Self-reflexivity is about embodying a critical stance toward one's self that actively reflects on who individuals are, the assumptions they bring to the dialogue, their positionality as people, and the knowledge they have and the knowledge they do not yet have. Self-reflexivity means adopting a questioning mind-set so that a person is continuously engaged in reflecting and acting on one's world. For those with subordinated identities, it also means pausing to practice self-care when needed.

Although self-reflexivity is focused on the self and can be seen as an individual process, accountability extends beyond the self to people's impact on their community, or in the case of intergroup dialogues, others in the dialogue space. Accountability for participants with dominant identities means paying attention to how much one may speak in the dialogue, what silence means, and resisting the urge to become defensive or engage in denial. For people with subordinated identities, accountability means also paying attention to the identities that hold privilege and dominance, supporting peers, and caring for oneself in the middle of difficult dialogues. To illustrate our own self-reflexivity and accountability, we share our positionality and how our identities situate us as contributors to this volume.

Stephen's Story

I am Ghanaian African American. I was born in Ghana and was around three years old when my family immigrated to the United States. I grew up in a strict culture with traditional gendered roles, with men as the breadwinners and heads of households and women primarily engaged in caretaking and cooking responsibilities. I am also quite sensitive and resist many traditionally masculine tropes. This made growing up in a strict Ghanaian culture difficult and tiring. I frequently doubted my manliness and struggled with feeling Black enough. As the son of immigrants, I attended schools that were deemed good, meaning these schools were located in predominantly White areas. I did not have teachers who looked like me until my junior year of college, which was the first time I had a person of color as a teacher. Now as a parent myself with a son, Sebastian, I am hypersensitive to the ways I socialize him on what it means to be a man. How do I provide ample possibilities for what a man looks like? How do I even question the very notion of *being a man*? How do I provide space for Sebastian to trouble over the labels *boy* and *man* and adopt a way of being that aligns with who he(?) wants to be?

These questions form the basis for how I identify and position myself. Although I resist many toxic masculine identifications, I still identify as a Black cisgender man, which grants me privilege in my cisgender man identity. My Blackness is a subordinated identity, but I cannot rest solely on that identity as I also hold dominant gender, class, and sexual orientation identities. All of these identities make me who I am; I cannot separate them. I am accountable to readers of this chapter to name my identities so they can understand the assumptions I bring to this writing. I am also accountable to my coauthor, Wilson, as we collaborate across our shared and different dominant and subordinate identities. And yet, because Blackness is not monolithic, we situate ourselves differently, even though we share some identities.

Wilson's Story

Black men are complex. This conception is robbed of humanity, bearing with it a burden of suspicion and presumption of guilt that is impossible to shed. Yet, Black men in some situations are responsible for behaviors of dominance toward women of color and nonheteronormative people. I am part of that reverberating history. Tabling the racialization of gender conversation for a moment, my association with a masculine gender identity was present at my earliest age. From the way I dressed (or was dressed) to toys I played with and the games I was steered toward, there was no room for me to believe that I could hold anything other than the masculine identity that boys were supposed to own. Serriere's (2008) caution seemed to hold true that when an idea of masculinity is inflexible, the space of possible feelings, acts, words, and bodily behavior is restricted for boys and girls alike. I was inundated with messages of strength, valor, and provision from my family, religious affiliations, and street politics. When my public masculinity wasn't sturdy enough to withstand the perception of others, I would make adjustments with alternative expressions of masculinity that better suited their definitions.

Faced with subtle and overt modes of gender policing (Serriere, 2008) from their peers and society, boys acquire the discourse of the boy code (Pollack, 1999) to enable them to secure safety in schools. In my own life, the stage lights were always on—a constant gaze I was never able to escape and even feared leaving. I remember the obsession with hypermasculinity that my friends and I felt compelled to submit to, even if that identity was inconsistent with our core selves. We adopted a *cool pose* (hooks, 2004) to compete against outside agendas and resisted, in prayer and solidarity, the narrow interpretations of what it meant to be a Black man. It was a while longer, when I started watching my little cousins and godsons come along, that I felt compelled to speak up and out against the institution of sexism and begin identifying how masculinity was an instrument of that larger institution. The institution of sexism, as Sensoy and DiAngelo (2012) contend, sets the parameters for people to operate by producing the values, language, politics, and ideologies that culture should follow. The young people in my life, and how I dreamed of them moving through the world, moved me to make sense of the ways that masculinity posed a danger to not only themselves but also women and queer communities. Any hope for a future in which they might be able to possess transgressive capital (Pennell, 2015), that is, to proactively challenge and move beyond boundaries that limit and bind them, would first have to begin with my own deconstruction of masculinity.

Theoretically Employing Feminist Ideas: Men Within Feminism

Rethinking the procedures men use to engage or reengage in the conversation on masculinity necessitates a shift from the logics and ideas that have constrained the discussion. Guiding principles that have steered the discussion, theoretically and empirically, have been based on studies that overemphasize White, cisgender, and heterosexual. Concomitantly, the services, pedagogical approaches, and strategies constructed to work with men on college campuses have foundationally, although perhaps unintentionally, made them the subject of efforts in higher education (McGuire, Berhanu, Davis, & Harper, 2014). A reliance on scholarship that does not function to interrogate the complexity of men on college campuses as gendered, classed, racialized, and sexualized beings fails in engaging them in the type of substantive and radical discourse that could lead to the dismantling of patriarchy in all its forms.

Researchers and investigators have more recently begun to take seriously this notion of examining the intersections of men's experiences as diverse beings to provide educators with functional tools to assist men in developing healthier, nonsexist, antihomophobic, and antipatriarchal identities (Harper & Harris, 2010; McGuire et al., 2014). A progressive identity politics asks "not where we share a given position but whether we share a commitment to improve it, and whether we can commit to the pain of embarrassment and confrontation as we disagree" (Johnson, 2001, pp. 9–10). Healthier identities and tools that combat these identities may lead us toward representations of masculinity that are committed to transgressing rigid heteronormative masculinities and disrupting heterosexism, homophobia, and transphobia. To accomplish this, we argue that Black feminism may offer the critical praxis and theoretical sensibilities that begin to intentionally address the open wounds inflicted by hegemonic procedures and disinfect them in the process.

Black feminism is an expansive and critical form of knowledge production and inquiry that is rooted in and created by Black women (Collins, 1990). Giving voice to standpoints that have been perpetually marginalized (hooks, 1984, 1990), Black feminism illuminates the power of controlling images in hegemonic society while discussing the interlocking nature of oppression in the lives of women of color (Crenshaw, 1991). Demanding considerations long ignored, scholars who put into practice Black feminism make note of the consequences of an analysis that refuses to acknowledge the overlapping and compounding nature of systems of oppression. The underpinnings of Black feminism also highlight the radical and ongoing work of self-definition as a centering component of Black feminist thought (Collins, 1990; hooks, 1990). The discourse has been a metronome of critical intervention in theorization and praxis, as Black women have challenged first-wave feminist discourse to do what it was unwilling to do by acknowledging and representing the voices and lives of women as racialized beings while simultaneously critiquing Black liberation fronts of the 1960s and 1970s for their persistent failure to see them.

For the purposes of this chapter, we seek to address what men, broadly, did not do then but more recently have given attention to, that is, to deeply consider what it means for men to engage feminism. Black feminist scholars submit that subjugated or minoritized identity markers cannot and should not obfuscate the responsibility that men of color, nor men broadly, possess as it relates to our roles in combating sexism, homophobia, and misogyny against (Black) women and nonheterosexual (Black) men (hooks, 1990, 2004). Rejecting the belief that social location or biology solidifies or overdetermines what our ideological commitments might be, Black feminist scholars believe that hegemonic socialization is capable of fracture, thus leaving room for the possibility of disruption and a critical positioning in relationship to sexism, racism, and homophobia (hooks, 1990, 2004). For example, when men interrupt toxic masculinity among their friends, a fracture is possible, opening up room for alternative constructions of masculinity.

As discussed in the previous sections, self-reflexivity is a fundamental component of a feminist dialogic project, specifically reflection that takes into account the individual and personal histories and the manner in which they reveal complicities in the technologies of patriarchy. Establishing a relationship to feminism must reach into the self to revisit the lessons of masculinity taught and reinforced by the context where one was or is rooted. This process means that dialogic projects should consider how, without exploiting the labor of women, to ensure that their subjectivities, perspectives, insights are integral to the reconstitution of masculinities. Treatment with this bend opens up the possibilities for a disinfectant process to reach beyond the surface of the wound, deconstructing the bacterium that sustains the aforementioned split. Disinfectants, at their best, rid wounds of bacteria and the spread of germs. Black feminism, while powerful, may not be able to provide such a cure, not because of sterile potency but because patriarchy is an adaptive disease that rebuilds itself anew across time and context. The inheritance of this disease means that educators and students should be prepared for the ongoing hermeneutic work of deconstruction and reconstruction.

Toward an Embodied Dialogic Project

Black feminist discourse as a tool of analysis can help lead to personal and political transformation. Moving from the personal to interpersonal dialogic exchange, we return to the work of Awkward (1995) for guidance on how other men have sought to use women of color feminisms to broach interrogations of the self. McGuire and colleagues (2014), adhering to the work of Awkward, use a technique referred to as *autocritography,* a compelling method described as

> a self-reflexive, self-consciously academic act that foregrounds aspects of the genre typically dissolved into author's always strategic self portraits. Autocritography, in other words, is an account of individual, social, and institutional conditions that help to produce a scholar and, hence, his or her professional concerns. (p. 7)

Accordingly, men interested in working in feminism have used this approach to demonstrate a commitment to self-reflection and vulnerability as they confront the silences of their socialization and how those experiences have contributed to their current dispositions. The power of autocritographic writing rests in its ability to combine retelling with internal processing while maintaining a commitment to female subjectivity in the storying.

In other words, particpants in autocritographic writings bear witness to and narrate accounts of their experiences with hegemonic masculinity, patriarchy, heterosexism, and misogyny as a way to point out their transgressions, blind spots, and complicities. These reflexive examinations of gendered socialization acknowledge and give full voice to women as principal agents in understanding why a transgression was a transgression instead of relying on men to be the compass for their evolution. With autocritography, women are not silent actors; instead, readers should be able to identify women as equal partners in the disruption of gendered behavior, ideas, and development (McGuire et al., 2014) and also not rely on their labor for continued learning. Building on the work of Awkward (1995), we wonder how we might provoke transparency; demand (Black) female subjectivity; and engage the mind, spirit, and body of men. To do this, we turn back to Black feminism.

Embodied practices are fundamental to Black feminist politics and sources of knowledge from which Black women make themselves known (Brown & Kwakye, 2012). Intergroup dialogue, as it is traditionally framed, sometimes establishes a mode of civil authority that often replaces emotionality for rational, masculinist discourse and renderings. Responding to Black and women of color feminisms's call to invoke affect and the body, and building on autocritograhic writing principles that embrace vulnerability, self-reflection, and transparency, we discuss *embodied* autocritography as an intervention in dialogue-based practice. This method recognizes the body as a primary site for meaning-making and is designed to make public the lived experience of self and others (Duran & Okello, 2018). Here, the autocritographic retelling takes writing a step further and asks that we not only listen to the storying of others but also witness through the body, the experience. Embodied forms of retelling, through movement and action, help narrators reinhabit experiences that are often tucked away. Doing so forces the audience, participants, and witnesses to deal differently and directly with what they observe and feel as they view the performances. Pushing dialogic questions a step further toward embodied autocritographic methods might do the following with men in dialogue spaces. In what follows, we provide a sample procedure for using this method.

Opening questions:

Facilitators ask the following questions and ask participants to write a response:

- Could you explain an experience in which you took part in a sexist or homophobic act?
- Could you share an incident in which you witnessed a homophobic or sexist act?

The facilitator shares personal writing and performs a movement or action that corresponds with the narrative. Beforehand, the facilitator invites participants to observe and take in the full performance by asking the following: What is being said? What is the body doing during the performance? What am I feeling as I listen to and watch the reading or performance? What is not being said? Where and how do I resonate with the performance? Where is the accountability to women and nonheteronormative people?

This procedure should adhere to the aforementioned principles of intergroup dialogue praxis, which includes story sharing, practicing empathy, and building alliances across differences (Nagda & Maxwell, 2011). Additionally, presence is key. Participants must be willing to relieve themselves of distractions and give their full attention to performances and dialogues. Doing so also affirms the worthiness of peers' and participants' communications, honoring their storied expressions with their fullest investment.

Feminist Reimagination of Intergroup Dialogue

To illustrate autocritography in practice in dialogue spaces, we offer an example from our own lives. Although one cannot see our bodies in the text, we model vulnerability and emotion as a way for readers to envision what this might look like in practice with dialogue groups. Before doing this, we offer some considerations for readers. First, we encourage students and facilitators to begin with lower risk activities that help foster the trust that is essential for dialogue. Second, we urge facilitators to think about how vulnerability shows up in their work. Facilitators can begin to build this trust, which is practicing vulnerability, as a way to mitigate power imbalances between themselves and students. Third, intergroup dialogue calls for naming oppression. The following example illustrates directly addressing privilege and supporting students in naming oppression.

Stephen's Work to Address Privilege

Scene 1: The 2017 Association for the Study of Higher Education (ASHE) Conference was a space where Blackness was visible and prominent in ways I had never experienced at a conference. Everywhere I looked, I saw Black people, namely, Black men in public, powerful ways. From the way 2017 President Shaun R. Harper commanded the stage to Marc Lamont Hill, one of the keynote speakers, Black (men's) power was visible.

Scene 2: The 2018 ASHE/ACPA–American College Personnel Association presidential symposium brought together three Black presidents (Lori Patton Davis and Shaun R. Harper, of ASHE, and me, of ACPA) to discuss racism and strategies to heal from racial battle fatigue and build coalitions. Again, I noticed examples of Blackness, namely Black masculine Blackness, represented powerfully in this space.

These two scenes paint a picture of Blackness and a celebration of Blackness. Black people are often invisible even when they are hypervisible. Such bold, unabashed displays of Blackness in these two arenas disrupted the myth that Black people are underachievers. And yet, I couldn't help but wonder how Blackness intersected with gender in these spaces. For although Black men were seen, Black women and other women of color, on the other hand, were almost invisible.

As the president of ACPA, I am often invited to give talks at various places. Given my own scholarship, I also consult at various campuses. And yet, I have come to realize, sometimes begrudgingly and through my own defensiveness, that I am seen and given these opportunities in part because of my privilege as a man. I believe some of it is through how I practice vulnerability, hold space for others, model authenticity, and offer an important skill set; but so do many women who are not seen because they do not have the right institutional and degree credentials and because of sexism directed toward them. I am often the beneficiary of this sexism in that my voice is given more weight and in that I accrue financial capital from sexism. I have been complicit in this sexism when I don't honor the work of women who contributed to my ideas or when I don't acknowledge the dominant gender and sexual orientation identities I hold as a cisgender heterosexual person. I am quick to see my Blackness as salient and my main identity, and I also exist at the intersection of many dominant identities as well (i.e., gender, class, ability, sexual orientation, education).

Thus, what is my responsibility as an educator and person when I reap the benefits of sexism and heterosexism? What is my role? What do I do? We respond to these questions in the "Implications" section of this chapter.

Wilson Responds to Stephen: "What Did I Witness?"

What is not being said? I believe in stories. I believe in the vulnerability required to reveal the self on paper and in print. In no way do I want to dismiss the presentation of Stephen's narrative and the potential power of it. There are places that resonate with me in what is written or performed, but I can't help wondering if there is more beneath the surface of his testimony. Several things stand out to me about this passage and instigate my suspicion that there is more to be said. Immediately I am reminded that Stephen is a faculty member, with the influence and the credibility to match. As a respected scholar for many of the reasons he named, specifically his abilities to hold space for others, model authenticity, and offer an important skill set, I wonder if there is a subconscious need to protect this image. Said differently, could the decisions made in this story, that is, the choice of topics and tone and the carefulness with which he managed his presentation (naming the practice of vulnerability in his life, a defense of Black masculinity as celebrating Blackness, an offering of the ways in which he has been complicit in sexism as determined by his own viewing) be representative of men's desires to shield themselves from the convictions of deep scrutiny?

When I read this passage, I read the words of a scholar. For better or worse, if you spend enough time in academic circles, thinking patterns begin to organize themselves in specific ways: Provide an introduction that situates the problem, write a body that presents the main crux of the argument, offer a general discussion, move away from the self into implications for larger communities with questions for research and practice. This is not a critique of Stephen's reflection so much as a critique of the ways scholars and practitioners are able to steer readers, students, and participants in ways that do not implicate the self beyond what is necessary. In traditional dialogue-based praxis, this procedure unfolds in similar ways. Instead of diving in to the messiness of an issue, it is much simpler, and in most cases meets the intent of the exercise, to offer just enough in the name of vulnerability without having to the upend perceptions of the self. This is a safe script, and I suspect that Stephen knows it too.

As a witness, returning to the earlier questions—What is being said? What is the body doing during the performance? What am I feeling as I listen to and watch the reading or performance? What is not being said? Where and how do I resonate with the performance? Where is there accountability to women and nonheteronormative people?—my sense is that there is a reluctance to name and sit with the emotionality of these experiences and, in doing so, intellectualize his participation. To me this is the bodily performance of this text. Educational spaces do not typically validate the complete body as an affective, spiritual, and historical entity. Instead, they tend to privilege the cognitive. In this way, educators and facilitators must be diligent in recognizing how they have been trained away from themselves, that is, how they have been taught to distrust embodiment (Dillard, 2012), and how their actions instruct students in similar ways of being. I want to know what Stephen was feeling as he experienced these situations. What was the bodily response? What hesitations stuck in his throat? Where is the accountability, and how did he come to know? Honest answers to questions like these provide an opportunity for embodied testimony.

Stephen's Response and Rewrite

I felt exposed, that I was found out in my conversation with Wilson. I had chosen the safe route in my story as a means to control. Although I have my perfectly logical explanation (i.e., to protect someone else's story), my story is still safe—neat, tidy, withholding. In essence, my story is a perpetuation of privilege, of not wanting to be found out. Pushing me to dig more deeply into the emotions was scary, and yet that is exactly what is needed should cisgender men wish to confront and dismantle their dominance.

In my conversation with Wilson, I am also reminded of when I do not name the women whose patience and knowledge have benefited me, I contribute to further silencing them, erasing them, and reinforcing my privilege. My partner, Chris Linder, provided the labor for my coming to see my own cisgender privilege and the ways I reinforce sexism. She has given me the eyes to notice these things, and often without her pushing and prodding, I do not see. That is how privilege works. I am not solely responsible for the voice and space others give me by inviting me to give talks and consult. What I am wholly responsible for, however, is what I do with that space. How do I take up that space or share that space? Whose stories do I tell? How do I publicly acknowledge the women who have enabled me to start to see? With awareness comes responsibility and action, and Chris cannot be the sole person who helps me be aware. I have to take ownership of my own seeing. This means holding other men accountable for the ways we diminish women and benefit from sexism. This means having the hard conversations I don't want to have. That means not retreating.

So what do I feel? I feel uneasy. I feel this tension of knowing that systemic oppression around sexism and heterosexism are real and that these systems manifest themselves without me. I also know that even so, I am responsible for working to dismantle them. I feel stuck. I feel like making excuses for my inaction. I feel like centering my subordinated racial identity only to illustrate how my Blackness works. I feel embarrassed for the ways I still do not see and the ways my behaviors affect and harm Chris and many other White women and women of color. I feel this desire to talk about how I am a good man, even though I know better. Knowing better makes me feel stuck so often, and so I overthink, and my overthinking causes me to sit in my stuff and not act for fear of being criticized.

Wilson's Reflection on Stephen's Response and Rewrite

Stephen's rewrite highlights the potential of embodied autocritography. As mentioned previously, traditional dialogue-based praxis can sometimes promote performances that prop up idealized versions of the self. The disinfectant process, as captured by Stephen, is rife with discomfort. Feelings of being exposed and found out are not trivial verbs or loosely selected language, nor are they simply products of guilt. These sentiments give insight into an internal process of disequilibrium that is or was finding its way to the surface. Stephen's rewrite is consistent with what I observed on his body as I followed up with probing questions about his original text. There was less certainty in his voice. Apprehension. Fear. Frustration. Angst. A lack of control. Pain. A stomach eating away at itself. Rubbing of the forehead. Squinting eyes. Embodied autocritography asks us to name emotions and to sit with that turmoil for what it has to teach us. The lessons and convictions met in this disinfectant space may not show up as the same for everyone, but usefulness and a move toward healing is determined by one's authentication and honesty in the process. Given the embodied dialogue we engaged in, several implications emerged for us.

Implications

Ending this chapter where we began, how do we begin to heal the splits (Anzaldúa, 1987), or the deep divisions caused by patriarchy, that originate in the foundations of our lives? We offer the following implications to assist in creating some pathways:

- Carve out intentional space for self-reflection.
- Engage in critical dialogue (consider caucusing).
- Commit to continuous growth alongside those most affected by sexism and patriarchy.

Our first implication is the importance of providing space for cisgender men to reflect on the ways we contribute to perpetuating the very systems we critique (i.e., patriarchy). The process of Wilson engaging in dialogue with Stephen enabled Stephen to reflect more deeply on his own complicity and sit with the discomfort. Given Wilson and Stephen's previous relationship, they had built a level of trust that enabled this pushing by Wilson. We recommend that those reading find spaces that also encourage pushing and that those being pushed accept the invitation to reflect. This means resisting the urge to become defensive, our second implication. As seen in Stephen's rewrite, Stephen wanted to become defensive and resistant, as is the case so often when reflecting on one's dominant identities. And yet, we must push back against this urge, listen, reflect, and continue repeating this process.

Next, cisgender men need to engage in dialogue with other cisgender men about sexism and patriarchy, broadly, as well as the particularities of cissexism and heteropatriarchy that appeal to norms that enforce gender binaries and gender essentialism resulting in the oppression of trans* and gender-non-conforming people. Sexism is not the problem of women; as men we are complicit in reifying sexism when we do not hold ourselves and other men accountable.

Third, we must acknowledge the work of women across their intersected identities (gender, race, sexual orientation). Because of the ways men's voices are heard because of privilege and patriarchy, this means saying publicly where our ideas stem from and acknowledging the labor of women in our learning. When we do not do this, we silence women and contribute to their extra unpaid labor. Consequently, we must work alongside women in dismantling sexism. This does not mean taking over but rather learning how to step back without becoming silent and not expecting praise for our efforts. This last implication is especially tricky. When we talk about our masculinity, we recenter ourselves as cisgender men, and yet when we don't acknowledge it, we contribute to reinforcing our patriarchy. Even so, we must work in this tricky, nuanced place.

We imagine these implications informing how men show up in classroom spaces, specifically in regard to what counts as knowledge and who can be knowledge holders. Training that takes into account the ever present privileges and power of sexism and patriarchy will compel men to be mindful of the space they take up—how much air time or talk time am I taking in relation to my peers, how do I assert my perspectives, why do I believe what I believe, who has not had the opportunity to talk, share, or speak in content discussions across the curriculum. For instance, tools gained in the practice of self-reflexivity encourage one to be cognizant of how privileges are present and how they might impede the learning and processing of others with whom they are learning. We also envision cisgender men becoming true partners in the work of dismantling sexism and patriarchy. In other words, dialogue-based praxis among cisgender men is a provisional conclusion in this chapter but inadequate as a long-term strategy in isolation. The praxis should always be preparing one for working in collaboration with women, trans*, and gender-non-conforming people in various organizational and institutional efforts.

Conclusion

The work of dismantling patriarchy and hegemonic masculinity is difficult as even men engaged in this work can unwittingly perpetuate the very systems they challenge and seek to destroy. Far too long, men have relied on the labor and education of women to see what we do not see in our privileged and dominant identities. In this chapter, we discussed a process whereby men can hold each other accountable in naming patriarchy, reflecting on it, and changing our behaviors to remake societies that are more equitable. A reenvisioned intergroup dialogue process, using autocritography, is one approach for engaging in this work. It demands self-reflexivity, accountability, and embracing being pushed to dig more deeply into the wounds that we do not see so that the disinfecting process can take root.

References

Anzaldúa, G. (1987). *Borderlands/la frontera: The new mestiza*. San Francisco, CA: Aunt Lute Books.

Awkward, M. (1995). *Negotiating difference: Race, gender, and the politics of positionality*. Chicago, IL: University of Chicago Press.

Brown, R. N., & Kwakye, C. J. (2012). *Wish to live: The hip-hop feminism pedagogy reader*. New York, NY: Peter Lang.

Buckley, J. B., & Quaye, S. J. (2016). A vision of social justice in intergroup dialogue. *Race Ethnicity and Education, 19*, 1117–1139.

Collins, P. H. (1990). *Black feminist thought: Knowledge, consciousness, and the politics of empowerment*. New York, NY: Unwin Hyman.

Crenshaw, K. (1991). Mapping the margins: Intersectionality, identity politics, and violence against women of color. *Stanford Law Review, 43*, 1241–1299.

Dillard, C. B. (2012). *Learning to (re)member the things we've learned to forget: Endarkened feminisms, spirituality, & the sacred nature of research & teaching*. New York, NY: Peter Lang.

Duran, A., & Okello, W. K. (2018). An autoethnographic exploration of radical subjectivity as pedagogy. *Journal of Curriculum and Pedagogy*. Advance online publication. doi:10.1080/15505170.2018.1465495

Harper, S. R., & Harris, F. III. (2010). *College men and masculinities: Theory, research, and implications for practice*. San Francisco, CA: Jossey-Bass.

hooks, b. (1984). *Feminist theory: From margin to center*. Boston, MA: South End Press.

hooks, b. (1990). *Yearning: Race, gender, and cultural politics*. Boston, MA: South End Press.

hooks, b. (2004). *We real cool: Black men and masculinity*. Hove, UK: Psychology Press.

Johnson, E. P. (2001). "Quare" studies, or (almost) everything I know about queer studies I learned from my grandmother. *Text and Performance Quarterly, 21*(1), 1–25.

McGuire, K. M., Berhanu, J., Davis, C. H. F. III, & Harper, S. R. (2014). In search of progressive Black masculinities: Critical self-reflections on gender identity development among Black undergraduate men. *Men and Masculinities, 17,* 253–277.

Nagda, B. A., & Maxwell, K. E. (2011). Deepening the layers of understanding and connection: A critical-dialogic approach to facilitating intergroup dialogues. In K. E. Maxwell, B. A. Nagda, & M. C. Thompson, (Eds.), *Facilitating intergroup dialogues: Bridging differences, catalyzing change* (pp. 1–22). Sterling, VA: Stylus.

Pennell, S. M. (2015). Queer cultural capital: Implications for education. *Race Ethnicity and Education, 19,* 324–338.

Pollack, W. (1999). *Real boys: Rescuing our sons from the myths of boyhood.* New York, NY: Henry Holt.

Sensoy, O., & DiAngelo, R. (2012). *Is everyone really equal?: An introduction to key concepts in social justice education.* New York, NY: Teachers College Press.

Serriere, S. C. (2008). "The making of masculinity": The impact of symbolic and physical violence on students, pre-K and beyond. *Democracy and Education, 18*(1), 21–27.

Zúñiga, X. (2003). Bridging differences through dialogue. *About Campus, 7*(6), 8–16.

8

MEN'S PEER EDUCATION AND MENTORING PROGRAMS

Taj Smith, Vern Klobassa, and Cristobal Salinas Jr.

Men's peer spaces in higher education fall along a spectrum of problematic to promising. On a sociological level, peer groups are influential organizations in socialization processes that assist in regulating culturally acceptable practices of masculinity (Connell, 2005; Gilbert & Gilbert, 1998; Mac an Ghaill, 1994). Men's peer groups are primary social spaces that can produce and reinforce masculine performances influenced by cultural and social expectations (Migliaccio, 2009). Unfortunately, joining such groups often requires restrictive practices that result in some men negatively policing other men's attitudes and behaviors that do not align with hegemonic narratives of masculinity (Flood, 2007). However, peer-learning spaces in higher education have also proven to be a promising practice (Boud, Cohen, & Sampson, 2013). According to Boud and colleagues (2013),

> Students learn a great deal by explaining their ideas to others and by participating in activities in which they can learn from their peers. They develop skills in organizing and planning learning activities, working collaboratively with others, giving and receiving feedback in evaluating their own learning. (p. 3)

These intentional peer-learning spaces can also serve as sites for counternarratives that challenge hegemonic masculine norms (Davis & Klobassa, 2017). Simultaneously, taking proper advantage of these peer spaces can lead to an increase in men's success and a healthier campus. For example, Harper

(2006) found in a study of high-achieving African American men that peer support from African American men and women played a significant role in encouraging the success of these high achievers. The purpose of this chapter is to provide practitioners with an overview of the literature on and practical examples of peer education and mentoring programs that can help increase engagement with and support for men on campus. Using academic literature, websites, and interviews with program coordinators, this chapter presents a handful of men's peer education and mentoring programs that have been successful in their outreach.

Men's Peer Education Programs

Institutionally supported peer education programs on college campuses have historically been situated in health and wellness units and have addressed topics such as physical safety, sexual assault prevention, alcohol consumption, anxiety, exercise, and mental health (American College Health Association, 2007). Health and wellness peer education programs on college campuses typically "share and teach health information, attitudes, values and behaviors by members of groups who are similar in age or experience" (White, Park, Israel & Cordero, 2009, p. 497). College students, more often than professionals, are successful in delivering important social norms and modeling new practices to achieve healthier outcomes on campus (White et al., 2009). In particular, college students are more aware of and able to enter environments that have a direct influence on student culture; however, they often lack the skills, knowledge, and confidence to do so (Davies et al., 2000). Berkowitz (2011) goes on to affirm that men have shared their discomfort with some men's toxic behavior yet seek approval from those same groups of men to validate their sense of belonging as a man.

Student affairs professionals and student peer educators have begun to use the influence of men's peer groups in an attempt to challenge social norms surrounding men's health. Courtenay (1998) has long advocated for the health promotion field to address the gendered influences on health behavior that lead traditional-age college men to take more risks with their health. There is a relationship between how men are socialized to perform masculinity and risky behaviors such as excessive drinking, drug use, anxiety, depression, fatal deaths, serious injuries, and high-risk sexual activity (Courtenay, 1998, 2000). Although research has illuminated the relationship between masculine performance and high-risk behaviors, little research exists on how college men's peer education spaces can actively challenge hegemonic and toxic attitudes and behaviors. Piccigallo, Lilley, and Miller

(2012) provided an example of the potential for peer education spaces to challenge hegemonic masculine narratives. They interviewed 26 men-identified students who were involved in sexual assault prevention programs and found that because these men were in an all-men's space "their knowledge related to sexual assault, their empathy for sexual assault survivors and motivation to engage in the prevention of sexual violence increased" (Piccigallo et al., 2012, p. 508). The rationale for peer education programs geared toward engaging college men is clear, but more institutions must commit to creating and funding such programs so more research can be done to assess their effectiveness on shifting unhealthy aspects of campus culture (e.g. sexual assault, binge drinking) and positively shaping healthy representations of masculinity.

Mentoring Programs

Mentoring is another strategy that can be used to support the learning, growth, success, and engagement of men on campus. Smith (2013) said there are four primary theoretical perspectives grounding research on mentoring in higher education: involvement theory, academic and social integration, social support theory, and cognitive/developmental theory. Smith argues that the "implicit purpose of each of the four theoretical perspectives is to help students understand and successfully decode the hidden curriculum" (p. 57). Therefore, it is the role of higher education professionals to mentor students, in particular historically marginalized students, by explicitly teaching them "how to acquire institutional cultural capital and social capital" (Smith, 2013, p. 57). Mentoring programs can also improve self-confidence, resilience, academic performance, the likelihood to transfer to four-year colleges, increase graduation rates, and create a stronger sense of intersectional racialized gender identity (Curtis & Hansen-Schwoebel, 1999; Hoffman & Wallach, 2005; Whitfield & Edwards, 2011).

Much of the mentoring literature in student affairs focuses on men of color mentoring (Gardenhire, Cerna, & Ivery, 2016), including African American men (LaVant, Anderson, & Tiggs, 1997; Sutton, 2006) and Latino men (Sáenz, Ponjuan, Segovia Jr., & Del Real Viramontes, 2015; Torrens, Salinas Jr., & Floyd, 2017). This can be attributed to the desire to create smooth transitions to predominantly White institutions and to account for systematic barriers that influence the retention and success of men of color. More investment should be made to better understand the impact on mentoring low-income men, men with disabilities, and men from religious minority groups.

One of the challenges mentoring programs face is assessing the impact of structure. Harper (2012) conducted a study of 219 Black men at 42 postsecondary institutions and found that "no participant attributed even a fraction of his college achievement to a [structured] mentoring program" (p. 18). Harper attributes this outcome to students being more likely to identify campus resources, experiences, and specific people who aided them in their college success. Wood and Harris (2017) stated that mentorship for men of color needs to be driven by specific needs, be activity based instead of meeting oriented, and adapt an organic approach to the matching process. Positive outcomes can also be credited to active faculty and staff mentors and older men modeling appropriate ways of expressing masculinity that invite vulnerability (Harris, Palmer, & Struve, 2011).

Torrens, Salinas Jr., and Floyd (2017) said that more research is needed to better understand the impact of mentors and mentees. In their study, they found that most college administrators do not validate the mentoring efforts of men of color staff who organize undergraduate student men of color's mentoring programs and leadership retreats. Most men of color staff had mentors throughout their undergraduate career, and as staff members of a college or university, they are very likely to pay it forward. To advance and support mentoring programs for men at colleges and universities, Torrens and colleagues suggested that

- "university leadership should embrace and promote mentoring throughout all level of the institution" (p. 14);
- universities should "dedicate space for mentoring activities . . . [and] regular contact should be encouraged and incentivized" (p. 15);
- "mentors and mentees should set clear expectations with regard to length of the relationship, contact schedule, areas of focus, goals of the mentee, and pathways to achieve goals" (p. 15);
- funding for mentoring initiatives should reflect in the universities' priorities, goals, and strategic plans; and
- "ongoing and continuous assessment should be practiced with special attention paid to goals and outcomes outlined by mentors and mentees" (p. 15).

As research on mentorship continues to grow, mentoring should be framed as "a dyadic relationship where a senior member (mentor) guides a junior member (mentee) through formal and informal professional development experiences to help expand professional, psychosocial, political academic and resource-gathering skills" (Torrens et al., 2017, p. 1) instead of trying to *fix* young men.

Men's Peer Education and Mentoring Programs in Practice

Some student affairs professionals have used peer education and mentoring as strategies for promoting men's health (Courtenay, 2000), preventing sexual assault (Foubert & McEwen, 1998), and fostering understanding of men's gendered development (Jessup-Anger, Johnson, & Wawzynski, 2012; Klobassa, 2010; Scott, Livingston, Havice, & Cawthon, 2012).

We provide a summary of a number of men's peer education and mentoring programs from a variety of functional areas in student affairs. These programs include performance groups, peer health promotion programs, men's support groups, men of color academic and mentoring initiatives, residence life programming, and fraternity programming. We discuss the following men's peer education programs: Phallacies, Dudes Understanding Diversity and Ending Stereotypes (DUDES), Beta Theta Pi's Men of Principle (MOP), and Masculinity Dialogues and then present the following mentoring programs: Urban Male Initiative and the Motivated, Empowered and Noble (MEN).

Men's Peer Education Programs

Phallacies

Beginning its work in the summer of 2008 at the University of Massachusetts–Amherst, Phallacies was inspired by campus performances of *The Vagina Monologues* and the Women of Color Leadership Network's artistic project called *Body Politics*. Phallacies, a men's health promotion and dialogue group, serves as a support space for cisgender men (although gender-non-conforming men have participated) and a peer education group that uses performance to educate the campus on how hegemonic masculinity is harmful to making healthy choices and influences the perpetuation of gender-based violence. The performance aspect of the program educates audience members on bystander skills, new language, and multifaceted representations of manhood to interrupt traditional notions of how men perform masculinity in their daily interactions. The group holds smaller performances in classrooms throughout the year and a campuswide show once in the spring semester.

An average of 12 participants meet once a week for an entire academic year for up to 2 hours to discuss a variety of issues. Participants spend an hour in dialogue addressing a range of cis men's issues (e.g., homophobia between men, hook-up culture, risky behaviors, hegemonic masculinity) or participating in activities (e.g., body image tracing, screening a film). The second hour is dedicated to turning those conversations into performance pieces such as *Letters to Our Fathers*, *I Don't Want to Talk About*, *Hugging 101*, and *Masculinguistics*.

To assess the performance aspect of Phallacies, evaluations from audience members are collected after each show. Most respondents mention learning to recognize unhealthy aspects of hegemonic masculinity and identifying realistic bystander skills. In Smith's (2015) dissertation, Phallacies program participants explained how they became more likely to share emotions, reflect on behaviors, and integrate relationships with others. The following student comments demonstrate that impact:

> To share my emotions was great. It was also cool to see other people change as well. It might have been the one space where men didn't have to hide without the impetus of alcohol. (p. 103)

> I thought about my sophomore year of college when I took an unhealthy risk with myself by drinking a lot. The [risk-taking survey] activity got me to think about my behavior in a more serious way because before, I would joke about it, and friends would laugh. (p. 109)

DUDES

In 2011 a men's retention committee was commissioned at the University of Redlands to address the persistence of all men on campus. This committee resulted in experimenting with retreats and facilitating theory-informed conversations in residence halls to better assess men's reasons for leaving the institution. Learning that traditional college men were less likely to engage in the theoretical discussions, dialogues were established to focus on relationships, alcohol consumption, and pornography use. Many of these dialogues were informed by faculty members' research but presented in a way that was more accessible for students.

In 2014 DUDES grew out of the campus dialogues and expanded into a traveling men's resource center, or a center without a physical space, located in the Office of Campus Diversity and Inclusion at the University of Redlands. The program offerings are mobile and can be taken to various student spaces, depending on the specific program or audience. The goal of DUDES is to encourage men to be their authentic selves. It offers a wide range of programming for men, women, and trans students. Understanding that men are a diverse population, the traveling men's center approach was established to maximize outreach and capitalize on different student interests. DUDES offers a one-unit credit-bearing course on masculinity, a student-led programming week, a men's two-day outdoor retreat, a social justice advocacy student group, multiple leadership development opportunities, facilitated workshops, and a speaker series.

The coordinator of DUDES reflected that men involved in at least one aspect of the peer education program deepened their emotional intelligence and learned how to have conversations about being a man. Some young men took the initiative and have created their own informal spaces or meet throughout the semester with the coordinator during office hours to further their exploration (R. Robles, personal communication, December 11, 2017).

Beta Theta Pi's MOP
During its annual convention, the Beta Theta Pi fraternity offers the MOP track designed to educate attendees on masculinity, how it shows up in the chapter and how they can educate and influence their peers to create a positive culture in the chapters. The MOP track, named for the fraternity's mission, takes place over the course of three days and is grounded in the organization's core values: mutual assistance, intellectual growth, trust, responsible conduct, and integrity. Some of the desired learning outcomes for the track include participants being able to

- identify common issues facing men in today's college environment,
- describe gender as a continuum,
- list actions that are consistent with Beta Theta Pi's Core Values,
- identify traditionally masculine qualities that are beneficial or detrimental to leadership,
- list positive and negative elements of brotherhood,
- identify the root causes of issues within their brotherhood,
- develop strategies to recruit new members using their brotherhood as a selling point,
- describe how values relate to action, and
- prioritize their actions based on their professed values. (M. Dilling, personal communication, December 7, 2017)

The core of the curriculum for the MOP track is engaging and dialogical. After an introduction, participants engage in a game of rock, paper, scissors followed by identifying some of the behaviors the activity elicits, including rowdiness, competition, and perhaps aggression. This activity serves as a grounding for continued dialogue about what masculinity is and how it shows up in participants' experiences.

The curriculum weaves in important conceptual materials incorporating scholarship such as Kimmel (2008) and popular culture such as clips of speaker and former professional football player Joe Ehrmann. For example, facilitators use Ehrmann's argument that men seek affirmation from each other in three primary ways—the ball field, bedroom, and billfold—and add a fourth, the bar, to further connect with participants' experiences.

Participants then take part in a facilitated discussion about the content, discussing questions such as,

- Why do you think men feel they must prove their manhood?
- Do you agree that young men should have to prove their manhood in these ways? Why or why not?
- Whom do you think is behind this concept of proving your manhood? Where did it come from?
- What could be the consequences of asking young men to compete to prove their manhood? (M. Dilling, personal communication, December 7, 2017)

Facilitators also engage participants in a Man Box activity (Kivel, 2010) in which they suggest common phrases, actions, ideas, and physical characteristics that fall within traditional hegemonic masculinity and place them inside the Man Box, and they put those that don't outside the box. Following a discussion, facilitators then introduce participants to concepts of social construction and socialization.

The MOP track builds connections to participants' experiences in their fraternity chapters through activities, reflection, and dialogue. One activity involves a simulated recruitment exercise, which uncovers the challenges that arise when espoused values are not aligned with actions. Throughout this portion of the track, participants are asked to reflect on and discuss a variety of questions that connect to masculinities such as,

- Why do we as fraternity men need to understand manhood if we are going to be leaders in our chapters?
- Why is it important for you to understand your own manhood to be a leader?
- What negative group behaviors are more likely to arise in male-only groups versus other groups?
- Think about a time when you saw true brotherhood demonstrated by your chapter. Then share that experience with your partner. Describe it in full detail and explain why it was so impactful to you.
- How do core values relate to how you show up in your chapter's brotherhood?
- How do we determine what we value? (M. Dilling, personal communication, December 7, 2017)

Throughout their experience with the MOP track, participants are equipped to return to their chapters to serve as positive influences on their chapter's culture and to informally educate their peers.

Masculinity Dialogues

In a residence life context, the Masculinity Dialogues program at the University of St. Thomas offers a practical example of peer education. The purpose of the program is to engage men living in an all-men's residence hall in dialogue about masculinities. The goal is to "create an environment where men could share their experiences [related to being men] free from shame and where they could learn from others' experiences and the questions being posed" (Klobassa, 2010, p. 1).

Initiated by the hall director, the program was designed to engage the resident adviser (RA) in a peer educator role. First, the RAs participated in an educational experience of their own. They were assigned to read the third chapter from Kimmel's (2008) *Guyland: The Perilous World Where Boys Become Men*, which provides an overview "of concepts such as gender role conflict, restrictive emotionality, homophobia and femininity as emasculation tools, and discussed how these concepts are reinforced by men and women" (Klobassa, 2010, p. 1). The RAs then had group conversations about the material during staff meetings and one-on-one conversations with the hall director to reflect on the content.

RAs were then tasked with facilitating a dialogue on masculinities with their floor communities using guides that included the following sample questions to help generate dialogue:

- What does it mean to you to be a man?
- How or from whom do we learn what it means to be a man?
- What are we told about what it means to be a man/woman in our society today?
- What are the advantages and disadvantages of being a man/woman in our society?
- What can we do about the disadvantages?
- What can we do to make things in our society/communities more equitable? (Klobassa, 2010. p. 1)

To evaluate the impact of the program, the hall director asked the RAs to answer questions focused on personal takeaways, dialogue preparation, and impact on residents. Responding to the question regarding personal takeaways, one RA stated, "I was definitely impacted by the fact that residents wanted to come to my room after the meeting to further discuss the topic" (Klobassa, 2010, p. 2). Another RA said,

> It created an environment for the residents to think critically and speak their mind without having anything really holding them back. It also

helped further my relationship with them and hopefully allowed them to further become more comfortable with talking to me about anything on their mind. (Klobassa, 2010, p. 2)

Men's Mentoring Programs

Urban Male Initiative

The mission of the Urban Male Initiative at Florida Atlantic University (FAU) is to develop and motivate urban male students to successfully identify and use pathways to timely graduation and job placement. This is accomplished through interactive inclusive programming focused on mentorship, peer accountability, and academic and social-based events while developing a strong sense of purpose, self-identity, and community. Similar to other colleges and universities across the country, the initiative faces the challenge of recruitment, retention, and graduation of African American and Latino men. However, FAU administrators' situation was unique because although African American and Latino men were successfully recruited, the administrators found it often took these students six to eight years to graduate. Recognizing this challenge, the vice president for student affairs dedicated funding to create the Urban Male Initiative focused on helping men of color be retained and graduate within four years and supporting successful job placement after graduation.

The program is built on 5 key objectives: fostering a sense of community, positive mentoring relationships, identifying academic and social resources for success, plan development for academic and career achievement, and assistance with academic skill enhancement. These objectives are fulfilled through informational meetings called RAP sessions, informal mentoring dialogues, social events, and 2 annual signature events: the Urban Male Institute and the Brother's Keeper Retreat. The RAP sessions are structured 1-hour conversations where various staff members from various campus offices and departments, such as Financial Aid or Undergraduate Research, are invited to provide information to students for the first 15 minutes. The remaining 45 minutes are spent discussing topics relevant to minority men's social and academic success. The mentoring program is informal, meaning lacking a direct process, where students are assigned a particular mentor and meet a certain number of times throughout the semester. Instead the coordinators and village supporters work to build relationships organically and establish an internal process where they check on students throughout the semester without them being obligated to meet with someone on a routine basis.

The Urban Male Institute and the Brother's Keeper Retreat are signature events that focus on the social and career development of students by bringing minority male executives and business leaders to provide career readiness advice and networking opportunities to participants. The retreat is a half-day-long program where mentors and mentees engage in team building, goal development, identity development, community, and career preparation. Men of color executives who are leaders in such fields as technology, finance, and business share their life story and provide mentees with practical advice to help them navigate the job market as racially underrepresented men. The Urban Male Institute is structured around the same basis as the retreat but is two days in a more formal environment that includes keynotes, panel discussions, breakout sessions, and a career-networking mixer. The institute takes place during the fall semester and is geared toward all minority males on campus, whereas the retreat is in the spring semester and is geared toward program participants only. Although these programs are still new, data from surveys analyze from each event are collected to improve future programs.

MEN

The MEN program at Palm Beach State College is a collegewide initiative that has been tasked with involving Black and Latino men in an effort to help drive student success. The initiative's approach seeks to motivate and empower. Ideally, students will become self-driven in their pursuit of academic and social success while developing a strong sense of ethical decision-making. In the long term, it is hoped that the initiative will have a positive impact on rates of persistence, retention, and graduation.

To accomplish these goals, the program uses a two-tier curriculum design. The first tier consists of a series of half-day retreats, during which students attend workshops and experience fellowship. Topics covered during these retreats offer students a fundamental understanding of campus resources (e.g., financial aid and academic advising) as well as relevant life skills (e.g., financial literacy and wellness). The goal is to offer participants a sense of awareness and refer students to the appropriate stakeholders on campus and in the community.

The second tier of the curriculum is an individualized experience, encompassing different types of activities from a preapproved list. These activities include watching and reviewing preapproved movies, reading and reviewing books from a preapproved list, completing a goal-setting exercise, or visiting a museum. The completion of this tier is reinforced through biweekly campus meetings that allow individual participants to share their progress through the Tier 2 activities. Additionally, these meetings reinforce the sense of fellowship the program strives to achieve.

To understand the program's impact, assessment is completed at two levels. The first includes an assessment of the collegewide retreats (pre- and posttests for specific workshops and student satisfaction surveys). Second, student progress is tracked from semester to semester and includes semester grade point average, number of credits taken versus credits completed, whether students have successfully completed the current semester, and whether they registered for the following semester (fall and spring).

Implementation Considerations

Now that we have covered examples of the programmatic opportunities, the challenge is to determine the best fit for a specific campus environment. As campus practitioners work to create or enhance men's peer education and mentoring programs, we offer a list of reflection questions to determine the best program for their campus:

- What is your campus climate on hegemonic and toxic masculinity?
- How would such a program contribute to improving gender dynamics on campus?
- How would a program contribute to improving the attitudinal, behavioral, academic, and postgraduation success of college-age men?
- What campuswide issues does it help solve (e.g. increase in conduct cases, suicide ideation, sexual violence, racism)?
- What financial or human assets already exist to support this work?

In the remaining part of this chapter, we discuss the following implementation considerations: creating institutional acceptance, developing recruitment strategies, intersectionality and building solidarity, and identifying and training facilitators and mentors and program sustainability.

Creating Institutional Acceptance

To sustain this work, institutional acceptance and collaboration are crucial. There are significant voices on campus beyond young men that may question the value of such strategies. One program coordinator interviewed for this chapter was once asked, "When are you going to give up your fascination with working with men?" Based on our conversations with coordinators and our personal experiences, we feel a particular caution from some women staff and faculty. They are often concerned that a men's support group on campus could have negative outcomes that lead to greater perpetuation of patriarchy and sexism. We certainly understand those concerns, and the growing men's rights rhetoric descending on campuses contributes to these fears. However, we think it is important to note that dismantling systems of patriarchy and sexism and pursing liberation requires men to do self-work (Davis & Klobassa, 2017). We believe the kinds of programs we have discussed in this chapter can create spaces for men to examine sexism, patriarchy, and privilege in ways that work toward mutual liberation.

After spending some time reflecting on the questions we posed at the beginning of this section, we encourage folks to begin identifying possible collaborators or areas of interest convergence. Do you know who on campus might have an interest in doing this work? What functional areas make natural fits for collaboration? Once you've identified these individuals, consider inviting them to have an informal discussion. Walk them through some of your reflections on these questions and invite them to share their thoughts and ideas. They may also have ideas and know of individuals who may be interested in the work, and you can begin building a coalition of interested parties (see chapter 3 for more insights).

Following initial conversations, typical next steps often involve developing a plan or proposal. Some of the challenges in this process can be securing resources, such as finding the time to devote to implementing the program or the financial support needed to run the program. Sometimes the challenges can come from a lack of understanding of how such a program aligns with institutional priorities, and other times they can come from a lack of data to support the need. Having data available to justify financial or human resources is language that some institutional gatekeepers (often White men at predominantly White institutions) can grasp. Funding to address all men's gender development is not typically first on the list because of the historical legacy of patriarchy and sexism on campus as well as implicit and explicit fears of using funding to promote the effeminizing of men. We hope that some of the literature we have cited may help in providing some of these data, but we also recognize that you will likely need to localize your argument.

Another strategy to help you in building your case is to take advantage of the language of power on your campus. Every campus has particular codes or a language that speaks to those in power. For some campuses, this may be a mission or values statement. Others may have particular focuses on challenges campuses are facing (e.g., retention or recruitment) or in strategic directions a campus may be pursuing (e.g., language found in strategic planning documents or sometimes buzzwords that gain particular traction in campus conversations). Using language that speaks to those in power and situating proposals or plans in this language can be a particularly helpful strategy in initiating and sustaining peer education and mentoring programs for college men. Additionally, sustaining these efforts is another consideration that warrants attention early in the process.

Formative and summative assessment should be created early and distributed often to understand whether learning outcomes are being achieved. Using various assessment strategies like focus groups, end-of-semester surveys, workshop evaluations, exit interviews, or taking advantage of graduate student or faculty research interests can lead to capturing the necessary data. In addition, we suggest gathering a group of stakeholders and advocates who can be involved from the start. Before creating DUDES, the University of Redlands formed a committee to focus on men's retention. This allowed campus partners to inform their thinking with existing men and masculinities research and to connect a new initiative to institutional challenges.

Developing Recruitment Strategies

Some scholars have argued that college men are less likely to participate in cocurricular leadership opportunities, dialogic spaces, or institutionally supported men's programs (with the exception of fraternities) if they are not mandatory (Capraro, 2004; Harris & Harper, 2008). Many of the programs mentioned in this chapter struggle with recruiting young men to participate. Based on our personal experience and learning from the programs in this chapter, the following are some strategies for recruiting and engaging men:

- Meeting men in spaces they often frequent (e.g., cafeteria, recreational centers, sporting events, business school, residence halls)
- Communicating active and application-based learning to appeal to traditional masculine values on learning
- Incorporating programs into first-year experiences
- Collaborating with cultural organization and fraternities
- Working in partnership with departments and academic disciplines that focus on diversity or identity development
- Getting out of the office and being visible on campus to attract less engaged students

For Phallacies, the in-class and campuswide performances and occasional trip to the residence halls serve as the best recruiting ground. College men watching the performance are able to engage in deep reflection and value assessment as other men their own age are challenging hegemonic masculinity in a public forum, perhaps something they might have always wanted to do but felt alone in doing it. Additionally, the role of women in helping to recruit has to be validated as they play a significant role in the mentorship of men. Women staff, faculty, or students often invite or strongly encourage their men-identified peers to attend a show or workshop. At times during the program's development, women's voices came into the space, and some participants saw the limitation of not being able to apply their new learning with women in a safe and dialogic space.

Several of the facilitators and coordinators interviewed mentioned getting referrals from colleagues on campus, such as the dean of students, counseling services, or fraternities. Although this is appropriate on a small scale, we would caution against recruiting men who are sanctioned to attend versus those who voluntarily participate. Any initial attitude of contempt might hamper the involvement of other men in the group.

Peer-to-peer mentorship is important for men's peer programs and mentorship programs. Also, it is important to have faculty, staff, and administrators engaged in this type of programing to help mentor students. To recruit mentors for mentorship programs, we encourage facilitators and coordinators to find individuals who are committed to serve as mentors. All stakeholders should know about the program's purpose, outcomes, and time commitments. This information can be posted in the colleges' or universities' announcements, disseminated by e-mail, and shared during faculty and staff meetings. Additional items to consider are stressing the top five reasons for becoming a mentor or mentee, encouraging former mentees to become mentors, and asking former mentors and mentees to share their experiences in the program.

Intersectionality and Building Solidarity

Recognizing the complexity in students who identify as men is important to formalizing and assessing your strategic engagement plan. As stated by Robbins & McGowan (2016), "Gender cannot be understood in isolation from other social identities" (p. 71). Despite our shorthand, use of *college men, ethnicity, socioeconomic status, faith, geographic location, height*, and other aspects of self influence how men shape their identities and choose their bonding spaces. As they arrive on campus these identities assess whether a college environment will affirm, further develop, or place gendered assumptions on who they are (Robbins & McGowan, 2016). We would recommend for each institution to

- evaluate its gendered assumptions and initially focus on the most popular and most underrepresented intersectional men groups on their campus and
- determine whether a single men's space where multiple and intersectional identities can be discussed or multiple intersectional spaces to attract different kinds of men-identified students is of greater value.

Many of the spaces we've discussed in this chapter are geared toward working with cisgender heterosexual men and men of color specifically in the mentoring section. If an institution focuses on multiple men's groups to serve different social identities, we recommend some solidarity building between each space to push on learning edges. In other words, professionals working with these groups must ensure that participants are learning in different ways or being challenged outside of their comfort zone of how they interpret their sense of masculinity and organize a collective and holistic approach to challenging the culture of hegemonic and toxic masculinity on campus.

Identifying and Training Facilitators and Mentors

Based on our research and from interviewing program leaders, there seems to be very little formal training for facilitators or mentors. Many of the facilitators find their way to this work through previous mentoring relationships, graduate assistantships, RA responsibilities, or through research interests. In the case of a peer health education program, there is some intentionality with hiring an employee or involving a faculty member with a research interest in men's engagement.

Facilitators "must embody the very processes they are describing when they discuss the centrality of gender" because students notice the gender of their professors and if they are living their message (Kimmel, 1997, p. 191). Therefore, self-reflection and vulnerability are two skills that resonate with all facilitators and program coordinators. Cofacilitators did mention the importance of checking in with one another after each session to reflect on personal experiences, modify facilitation tactics, and to create accountability for not letting things go, such as sexism, heterosexism, racism, or hegemonic behavior. Others used professional association electronic mailing lists to conduct informal benchmarking with similar institutions and to bounce ideas off colleagues. Depending on the population of men you are trying to serve, identifying facilitators or mentors who represent similar and different fraternal affiliations, age, racial, ethnic, sexual, and gender expressive backgrounds is critical for recruitment and program effectiveness.

Summary

Our goal is to provide readers with an overview of the literature on peer education and mentoring programs that may be helpful in gaining traction on campus and to provide examples of successful programs we hope inspire ideas for programs that would meet needs on readers' campuses. We believe these peer education and mentoring programs will help your institution achieve the following outcomes:

- Improve the persistence and graduation of all men, especially marginalized men (e.g., men of color, gay men, trans-men, low-income, rural men)
- Develop emotional intelligence and the capacity to express emotions other than anger
- Become (more) comfortable with critically discussing hegemonic and toxic men and masculinities attitudes and behaviors with other men
- Build a mentoring relationship that can lead to the development of positive life and professional skills
- Prevent risky and unhealthy behavior (e.g., binge drinking, fighting, stalking, verbal abuse, sexual violence) on campus, which leads to the improved public health of a college campus

Additionally, we believe that the implementation considerations in this chapter provide a helpful starting point for individuals seeking to support and enhance the educational experiences of college men on campus.

References

American College Health Association. (2007). National college health assessment. *Journal of American College Health*, 55, 195–206.

Berkowitz, A. (2011). Using how college men feel about being men and "doing the right thing" to promote men's development. In J. Laker & T. Davis (Eds.), *Masculinities in higher education: Theoretical and practical considerations* (pp. 161–176). New York, NY: Routledge.

Boud, D., Cohen, R., & Sampson, J. (2013). *Peer learning in higher education.* New York, NY: Routledge.

Capraro, R. L. (2004). Men's studies as a foundation for student development work with college men. *New Directions for Student Services*, 107, 23–34.

Connell, R. W. (2005). *Masculinities* (2nd ed.). Cambridge, England: Polity Press.

Courtenay, W. H. (1998). College men's health: An overview and a call to action. *Journal of American College Health*, 46, 279–290.

Courtenay, W. H. (2000). Engendering health: A social constructionist examination of men's health beliefs and behaviors. *Psychology of Men and Masculinity*, 1(1), 4–15.

Curtis, T., & Hansen-Schwoebel, K. (1999). *Big Brothers Big Sisters school based mentoring: Evaluation summary of five pilot programs in Philadelphia.* Philadelphia, PA: Big Brothers Big Sisters of America.

Davies, J., McCrae, B., Frank, J., Dochnahl, A., Pickering, T., Harrison, B., . . . Wilson, K. (2000). Identifying male college students' perceived health needs, barriers to seeking help, and recommendations to help men adopt healthier lifestyles. *Journal of American College Health, 48,* 259–267.

Davis, T., & Klobassa, V. (2017). Honoring the face behind the mask: Interrogating masculine performatives as counter-hegemonic action. In P. L. Eddy, K. A. Ward, & T. Khwaja (Eds.), *Critical approaches to women and gender in higher education* (pp. 299–322). London, England: Palgrave Macmillan.

Flood, M. (2007). Involving men in gender practice and policy. *Critical Half, 5*(1), 9–14.

Foubert, J. D., & McEwen, M. K. (1998). An all-male rape prevention peer education program: Decreasing fraternity men's behavioral intent to rape. *Journal of College Student Development, 39,* 548–556.

Gardenhire, A., Cerna, O., & Ivery, A. (2016). *Boosting college success among men of color.* Retrieved from https://www.mdrc.org/publication/boosting-college-success-among-men-color

Gilbert, R., & Gilbert, P. (1998). *Masculinity goes to school.* Sydney, Australia: Allen & Unwin.

Harper, S. R. (2006). Peer support for African American college achievement: Beyond internalized racism and the burden of "acting White." *Journal of Men's Studies, 14,* 337–358.

Harper, S. R. (2012). *Black male student success in higher education: A report from the National Black Male College Achievement Study.* Philadelphia: University of Pennsylvania, Center for the Study of Race and Equity in Education.

Harris, F. III, & Harper, S. R. (2008). Masculinities go to community college: Understanding male identity socialization and gender role conflict. *New Directions for Community Colleges, 142,* 25–35.

Harris, F. III, Palmer, R., & Struve, L. (2011). Cool posing on campus: A qualitative study of masculinities and gender expression among Black men at a private research institution. *Journal of Negro Education, 80*(1), 47–62.

Hoffman, A., & Wallach, J. (2005). Effects of mentoring on community college students in transition to university. *Community College Enterprise, 11*(1), 67–78.

Jessup-Anger, J. E., Johnson, B. N., & Wawrzynski, M. R. (2012). Exploring living learning communities as a venue for men's identity construction. *Journal of College and University Student Housing, 39*(1), 162–175.

Kimmel, M. (1997). Integrating men into the curriculum. *Duke Journal of Gender Law and Policy, 4,* 181–195.

Kimmel, M. (2008). *Guyland: The perilous world where boys become men.* New York, NY: HarperCollins.

Kivel, P. (2010). *Men's work: How to stop the violence that tears our lives apart* (2nd ed.). Center City, MN: Hazelden.

Klobassa, V. (2010). *Masculinity dialogues: A theory to practice program.* Retrieved from http://www.myacpa.org/sites/default/files/SCM_Briefs_S10_Practice_Brief _2.pdf

LaVant, B. D., Anderson, J. L., & Tiggs, J. W. (1997). Retaining African American men through mentoring initiatives. *New Directions for Student Services*, 80, 43–53.

Mac an Ghaill, M. (1994). *The making of men: Masculinities, sexualities and schooling.* Buckingham, England: Open University Press.

Migliaccio, T. (2009). Men's friendships: Performances of masculinity. *Journal of Men's Studies*, *17*, 226–241.

Piccigallo, J. R., Lilley, T. G., & Miller, S. L. (2012). It's cool to care about sexual violence: Men's experiences with sexual assault prevention. *Men and Masculinities, 15*, 507–525.

Robbins, C. K., & McGowan, B. L. (2016). Intersectional perspectives on gender and gender identity development. *New Directions for Student Services*, 154, 71–83.

Sáenz, V. B., Ponjuan, L., Segovia, J. Jr., & Del Real Viramontes, J. (2015). Developing a Latino mentoring program: Project MALES (Mentoring to Achieve Latino Educational Success). *New Directions for Higher Education*, 171, 75–84.

Scott, D. A., Livingston, W. G., Havice, P. A., & Cawthon, T. W. (2012). Men's identity development: Issues and implications for residence life. *Journal of College and University Housing*, *39*(1), 200–213.

Smith, B. (2013). *Mentoring at-risk students through the hidden curriculum of higher education.* New York, NY: Lexington Books.

Smith, T. (2015). *Phallacies: Constructing a critical space and pedagogy for college men to engage across non-hegemonic masculinities* (Doctoral dissertation). Retrieved from https://scholarworks.umass.edu/cgi/viewcontent.cgi?article=1381&context=dissertations_2.

Sutton, E. M. (2006). Developmental mentoring of African American college men. In M. J. Cuyjet (Ed.), *African American college men* (pp. 95–111). San Francisco, CA: Jossey-Bass.

Torrens, O. D., Salinas Jr., C., & Floyd, D. (2017). Examining the value of mentoring and men of color staff members of a community college. *Mentoring & Tutoring: Partnership in Learning*, *25*(5), 1–20.

White, S., Park, Y., Israel, T., & Cordero, E. (2009). Longitudinal evaluation of peer health education on a college campus: Impact on health behaviors. *Journal of American College Health, 57*, 497–505.

Whitfield, K., & Edwards, C. (2011). Mentoring special populations. *Educational Gerontology, 37*, 422–443.

Wood, J. L., & Harris, F. III. (2017). *Supporting men of color in the community college: A guidebook.* San Diego, CA: Lawndale.

9

ACADEMIC CURRICULUM

Jason Laker

T his chapter is intended to provide guidance to student affairs practitioners interested in developing, teaching, and collaborating to
incorporate men and masculinities topics into credit-bearing courses
and other curricular-type experiences. These may be in the form of courses
or course modules, or they may be associated with an academic program
of study through such formats as living-learning programs (residential or
not); community-based learning, research, or service activities; internships
and Cooperative Extension programs; or other partnerships in or outside the
classroom and campus environment.

Such endeavors are likely to be attractive to student affairs because of
wide interest in gender topics (after all, identity and development are corner-
stones of our field), the belief that introducing topics of men and masculinities may address a gap or concern, and a desire among practitioners to forge
partnerships with academic colleagues or to have meaningful involvement
in academic curricula more generally. This chapter discusses motivations,
considerations, risks, and benefits associated with developing and offering
credit-bearing men and masculinities programs and content. It also addresses
knowledge, skills, and dispositions for practitioners to consider when designing curricula on these topics. The chapter concludes with ideas and examples
for program content and structure, including course and module outlines,
key course assignments, and observations about synergies between didactic
material and students' personal development and academic success. Although
the chapter offers some specific practical ideas and examples, it is primarily concerned with the pedagogical considerations associated with men and
masculinities studies and educational programs. This is intentional and arguably more important than the particular delivery format. Readers are likely
already familiar with how academic courses and programs are structured.
Whether one is planning a credit-bearing course or module in one of these

courses or creating an experiential opportunity such as study trips, internships, or living-learning programs, the most challenging aspects of developing programs focused on men and masculinities issues tend to relate to the content knowledge and dispositions of the educators involved. It should be noted that context and timing might also substantially influence such efforts, including such variables as local political and social views, and whether any recent or current situations or issues activate tensions, hesitation, or urgency. As part one of this volume shows, it is arguably the case that educators well versed in the conceptual, theoretical, and practical aspects of gender and masculine role socialization will be well prepared to customize or adjust their approach in an appropriate and beneficial manner. To support readers in their desire to offer such programs, this chapter focuses more on the underlying assumptions, tensions, content, and dispositions underwriting the applications. Gender and sexual identities are diverse, complex, and contested, and the term *men* is used in this chapter to refer to people across the variety of iterations associated with male and masculine identities.

Men and Masculinities Programs: Contexts, Considerations, and Motivations

Why Men and Masculinities Programs?

To maximize substance and impact, it is necessary to consider the rationale for overtly incorporating men and masculinities concepts—for academic credit or not—into work with college students. There are benefits, risks, and tensions associated with pursuing such initiatives, making critical reflection about motivations and goals a critical part of planning and success. For instance, such programs are often developed in reaction to a problem such as misconduct by college men. The term *toxic masculinity* is often invoked under such circumstances and has become rather common in the public sphere and certainly in collegiate student affairs circles. Douglass (2017) describes this concept as being "built on two fundamental pillars: sexual conquest and violence—qualities men regale as manly and virtuous" (para. 3). He further argues that "toxic masculinity in American culture starts with straight, white men and trickles down through marginalized groups, affecting the way they perceive themselves and behave" (para. 7). It is therefore not surprising that many programs targeting men or that deal with issues of men and masculinities are often inspired by and focused on a desire to reduce sexual violence and other misconduct by men. Indeed, some of these programs are used as disciplinary sanctions intended to remediate the thinking and behavior of the men who are referred to them. In other instances, such programs are developed for, promoted to, or required of men who are involved in activities such as fraternities and athletic teams. There is good reason for such targeting. After all, research has clearly demonstrated a link between fraternity membership and higher levels of perpetration and acceptance of sexual violence (Seabrook, Ward, & Giaccardi, 2018). As uncomfortable and provocative as it may be to state this in such stark terms, it nonetheless represents factual and problematic realities student affairs practitioners (and students) must contend with.

Student affairs practitioners tend to recognize and sometimes remark about the fact that college men are implicated in higher levels of disruptive and problematic behavior than other students without much reflection or discussion about why this is the case; it is uncritically regarded as a self-evident fact. However, examination is very important because it can interrupt reductionist perceptions, approaches, and responses associated with men. Developing material about so-called toxic masculinity or targeting men for gender-related educational efforts without thoughtful and substantive preparation can severely undermine quality and impact and risk alienating students from engaging with material and experiences of value to them. Laker (2005) examined the professional socialization of new student affairs practitioners and noted a lack of explicit content and training about masculine role socialization and gender identities in graduate preparation programs and professional training. The benefits of introducing this information to students are discussed further, but first it must be emphasized that practitioners have much to learn about the development of college men and arguably have a duty to do so. Learning and preparation among practitioners is of great importance because it not only pertains to key aspects of student development but also can lead to more nuanced, principled, and effective work with students.

Programs With and for, Rather Than at or About College Men

Returning to the earlier point about motivations, developing programs primarily to prevent or respond to the misbehavior of college men can have the effect of reinforcing a defeatist and dualistic portrayal of men and masculinities. We can be more ambitious by inviting and inspiring students of all gender and sexual identities to examine masculinity scripts in a manner that displays a rich and hopeful set of possibilities and alternatives. It is imperative to consider what we hope to use as replacements for limiting or toxic masculinities rather than rooting in a *not this* ontology in which the already impossible to achieve hegemonic models of masculinity are indicted. Students are likely to notice when masculinities topics are only discussed in situations that are compelled (e.g., disciplinary sanctions) or targeted to groups they feel strong bonds with (e.g., fraternities, athletic teams).

In addition to the content, the contexts and tone in which these subjects are raised are part of the messages given to students and significantly affect the success of the program. Time and care must be taken to demonstrate a genuine interest in students' well-being and dignity, especially when the intention is to raise critical questions about and challenges to the gendered paradigms students have been socialized in for at least 18 years before enrolling in college. The educator is also encouraged to consider seemingly defensive reactions by men as evidence of dissonance between their current worldview and the enacted gender identity and a prospective and expansive alternative. In short, rather than taking students' edgy responses personally, it is important to show appreciation for their reasons and respectfully invite further analysis in a spirit of mutual respect and curiosity.

Developing and Enacting a Gender-Informed Professional Practice With College Men

For professional educators to be effective in work with college men, it is essential to have substantive and contemporary knowledge about them. Unfortunately, as mentioned earlier in this chapter and elsewhere in this volume, student affairs practitioners rarely receive overt graduate or professional training about men's development or read and discuss scholarly and professional materials about masculinities. There are arguably two intertwined beliefs in student affairs professional circles that maintain this disconnect and merit some discussion here because they are relevant to self-awareness and preparation to be good at this work and because they can be openly discussed with students as a component of meaningful, facilitative engagement.

First, although there have been appropriate critiques of foundational student development research and theories, a "been there, done that" trope interferes with recognition that the earlier work was similarly inadequate for understanding and addressing men's development as well. As Meth and Pasik (1990) noted nearly 30 years ago,

> Although psychological writing has been androcentric, it has also been gender blind and it has assumed a male perspective but has not really explored what it means to be a man any more than what it means to be a woman. (p. vii)

Second, even as student affairs' professional values call for advancing inclusion and equity commitments, a lack of exposure to men and masculinities research and a review of its implications for practice maintain reductionist perceptions about men. It is all too easy to conflate patriarchal systems with the socialization and lived experiences of individuals. As Kaufman (1999) articulated well,

> Though men hold power and reap the privileges that come with our sex, that power is tainted. There is, in the lives of men, a strange combination of power and privilege, pain and powerlessness. Men enjoy social power, many forms of privilege, and a sense of often-unconscious entitlement by virtue of being male. But the way we have set up that world of power causes immense pain, isolation, and alienation not only for women, but also for men. This is not to equate men's pain with the systemic and systematic forms of women's oppression. Rather, it is to say that men's worldly power—as we sit in our homes or walk the street, apply ourselves at work or march through history—comes with a price for us. This combination of power and pain is the hidden story in the lives of men. It is men's contradictory experiences of power. (p. 59)

hooks's (2000) graciously titled chapter, "Men: Comrades in Struggle," made the point that

> men are not exploited or oppressed by sexism, but there are ways in which they suffer as a result of it. This suffering should not be ignored. While it in no way diminishes the seriousness of male abuse and oppression of women, or negates male responsibility for exploitative actions, the pain men experience can serve as a catalyst calling attention to the need for change. (p. 73)

The critical points raised by Kaufman (1999) and hooks (2000) have at least two key implications for professional practice:

1. Student affairs practitioners should become familiar with masculine role socialization and men's development issues before introducing students to these topics.
2. Practitioners should examine their own perceptions and dispositions regarding men to ensure their professional values and commitments animate their work with men.

Whereas our psychotherapist colleagues are trained in methods for recognizing and reducing transference, countertransference, projections, biases, and the imposition of their own values on the client, student affairs practitioners who are not therapists rarely receive such training. This is unfortunate because it interferes with achieving the richness and positive impact with students that is genuinely desired. Designing and facilitating programs, content, and discussions about something as consequential as gender and other social identities require introspection, intention, and care to be effective. It should be evident to students that practitioners' efforts and interactions with them arise from genuine care and interest in their development and success. Even when a program is related to disciplinary sanctions, a restorative lens is more likely to be effective than a punitive one. As noted earlier, readers are encouraged to share or paraphrase these passages with students. From my experience, they will likely generate meaningful conversations and key opportunities for the practitioners' and students' mutual benefit.

Addressing and Transforming the Male Elephant in the Room

One of the common tensions undermining practitioners' effectiveness with college men arises from past negative experiences associated with dominant masculinity scripts. In short, many of us are mistrustful or have negative views of male students, even those of us who identify as male, that are connected to our own past observations and interactions with male students. For example, practitioners' personal experiences or observations of sexist, racist, homophobic, and other biased conduct by male-identified people in general and by students specifically deserve acknowledgment and supportive responses. The process of reconciling and healing should be supported while avoiding working it out at the expense of our students and ourselves. This is a conundrum for practitioners whose own identities may involve disproportionate costs and challenges when working with students. We can and should adhere to the complexity of a both-and framework in which the constraints and costs of hegemonic masculine scripts and structures are interrogated and addressed while we compassionately and intentionally support the development, encouragement, and success of men. Wagner (2011) noted, "Patriarchy can exist even without men in the room" and "we all contribute to the socialization of gender" (p. 221). She frames her work with college men as feminist while affirming the importance of self-awareness to determine when it is necessary to take a break or to ask colleagues to step in, which, as mentioned earlier, is something therapists are trained and encouraged to do.

Hence, readers are encouraged to critically reflect on their own fluency and relationships with the subject matter and beliefs and feelings about men as part of their own preparation to offer programs to students. This can begin with personally or collaboratively asking some basic questions such as,

- What do I currently know about men and masculinities issues?
- How do I feel about these issues and college men?

- In terms of my own relationship with these topics, am I holding residual pain or unfinished business?
- How is it evident to students who are men that I value and understand them?
- What is it like to identify as a college man at this institution, and how does that vary by race, sexuality, and other intersecting identities?
- In terms of tone and content, how are men and masculinities topics discussed on campus with and between students and practitioners?

Strategies for Building Curricula

Meeting Students Where They Are, Not Just Where We Are

As has been discussed throughout this book and elsewhere, societal notions of gender primarily remain binary, equating masculine with (cisgender) men and feminine with (cisgender) women. Many in student affairs circles have developed more expansive perspectives and have experiences of gender that incorporate fluidity, queerness, or trans, among other nonbinary and agendered experiences and identities. Many practitioners are eager to engage students by either introducing them to such diversity if they are unfamiliar and acknowledging and supporting students whose own identities do not comport with the hegemonic binary arrangements and ideas of gender. These commitments are squarely aligned with the professional values associated with student affairs practice. Often students enroll in college already having more experience and knowledge about social identities and diversity than many of the staff and faculty. Nonetheless, it is still quite common, and mostly the case in some places, for students to arrive at college with more traditional and binary gendered experiences and beliefs, whether overtly in their awareness or uncritically present in their thinking and interactions. One example of an accessible and inclusive approach to introducing gender concepts is illustrated by the Masculine Identity Map exercise (Ashlee & Cash, 2017).

As stated in the assignment's instructions (see Box 9.1), students have an opportunity to reflect on their gendered experiences from early childhood to the present and produce a visual representation with physical materials (e.g., construction paper) or conceptually using programs or software (e.g., PowerPoint, Prezi). This assignment doesn't require students to be familiar with the vocabularies and concepts they will learn in the course nor any artistic or technical capabilities. Rather, it invites reflection on students' gender socialization using the common reference of their own lifespan.

In their eagerness to interrupt limiting perceptions and educate students about such matters, practitioners sometimes forget to heed the oft-repeated advice to meet students where they are, which is illustrated well by the Masculine Identity Map exercise, by introducing the topic either through accusatory and correcting phrasing or speaking about it as if students were already familiar with the jargon and concepts being discussed. Using accusatory or correcting phrasing may be in the form of a response to student behavior such as aggression, property damage, or biased remarks, particularly by cisgender men, which the practitioner consciously or unconsciously views as typical of these students. Laker (2005) describes such an approach as *bad dogging* students by diminishing them in a manner that provokes hurt and mistrust and is more likely to rigidify rather than change their views and behavior. Practitioners who use jargon or concepts incorporate technical social science terms associated with gender theories and studies into their vocabularies without first determining if students are familiar with the terms and if they experience discomfort or show resistance to them. In such interchanges, an impromptu kinship often develops between the speaker and those students present who are nodding and otherwise expressing affirming nonverbal gestures or overt remarks. Although a feeling of mutual support may arise between the practitioner and the like-minded students or students whose gender performances are nonbinary, it is exclusionary and limiting to those students who are not accustomed to the phrasing or who experience dissonance because of differences in values and

BOX 9.1
Masculinity Identity Map

> Students will create a visual representation of their life from the perspective of gender. Beginning with the day they were born (or earlier if they would like to discuss other members of their family), students should describe the story of their lives in relation to their gender. Paying particular attention to critical incidents or moments of heightened awareness, students should highlight at least five moments in their life. These moments might include earliest memories related to their gender, happy or humorous experiences related to their gender, painful or stressful experiences related to their gender, main lessons they learned about gender growing up, and where those lessons were learned. This map can be created using any medium (construction paper, poster paper, PowerPoint, Prezi, etc.). Students should strive for creativity and personal expression over perfection. All students will present their Identity Map during the week of [due date].

Note. From *WGS370N: Exploring masculinities* [Course syllabus], by K. Ashlee & B. Cash, 2017, Oxford, OH: Miami University Women's, Gender and Sexuality Studies Program. Used with permission.

beliefs. Both of these approaches are problematic and undermine professional values and effectiveness.

Hence, when developing curricula, whether for academic degree credit or not, it is critical to begin at the beginning so to speak. In addition to the guidance discussed earlier, we must construct the content in a manner that will orient newcomers to the subject matter and vocabularies associated with it, introducing material in a progressive manner arranged from foundational to more advanced. The Masculinity Photo Assignment (Ashlee & Cash, 2017) is a versatile example because it can be used in undergraduate and graduate courses or in cocurricular program (see Box 9.2).

Requirements such as whether an assignment will be completed individually or in groups, length of papers, whether and how theoretical and conceptual vocabularies and citations are needed, and so forth can be modified as appropriate to the course and context. Ideally, entire courses on the topic of men and masculinities would be commonplace in student affairs graduate preparation programs. Because students in such programs come from a variety of undergraduate majors, one should not assume prior knowledge of gender and sexuality material, perhaps even more in regard to men and masculinities research given its continued limited use in higher education. Table 9.1 provides an example of a graduate course I developed and taught in a graduate preparation program.

The course included readings, personal reflections, discussions, films, and in-class exercises intended to familiarize emerging practitioners with masculine role socialization topics, men's psychosocial development, and

BOX 9.2
Masculinity Photo Assignment

Students will take 5 photographs which represent different aspects and issues related to masculinity. The images must be the student's own original work, capturing masculinity in their everyday environment. The photographs should be compiled into a word document with a 50 to 100 word caption for each image, describing the aspect or issue of masculinity being addressed in the photo. This collection of photographs will be shared with the class. While students have the freedom to choose the content of the photos for the assignment, they should be mindful of the impact that graphic content can have on others in the class. To complete the assignment, students must upload their collection of photographs to the class's learning management system by [due date].

Note. From *WGS370N: Exploring masculinities* [Course syllabus], by K. Ashlee & B. Cash, 2017, Oxford, OH: Miami University Women's, Gender and Sexuality Studies Program. Used with permission.

TABLE 9.1
Graduate Preparation Course: Gender and the Male Student

Session	Topic
1	Welcome and Introductions: Your Own Gender Role Journey
2	Masculine Role Socialization
3	Psychology of Men and Masculinities: Gender Role Conflict
4	Men in Higher Education
5	Inviting and Inspiring Men to Learn
6	Masculinities, Multiple and Intersectional Identities
7	Sexual Identities and Orientations
8	Socioeconomic Statuses and Work Identities
9	Masculinities, Bodies, and (Dis)Abilities
10	Men in Groups
11	Living, Being, and Doing Manhood
12	Men, Health, and Well-Being
13	Masculinities, "Being Bad," and Disciplinary Issues
14	Committing to Better Ways of Being

their relationships with men's diverse and intersectional identities. Course assignments included activities such as viewing and analyzing popular media depictions of men (see Box 9.3), a team project examining the situation of a subpopulation of men and making recommendations for advancing their development and academic success, and conducting three interviews, including one with a male peer, a younger adult man, and the participants' father or a man of similar age (accommodations are made if the father has passed away or is estranged, or the requirement is unworkable for other reasons).

Attracting Men to Men and Masculinities Studies

Harry Brod (2002), a pioneering men and masculinities studies scholar credited as the first to pluralize *masculinity*, recalled a comment he attributed to another prominent scholar, sociologist Michael Kimmel, who noted ironically that *"real men don't study gender"* (p. 161). This adage recognizes that critical examination of men and masculinities, even using the plural in this regard, is transgressive. The dualistic model of who and what defines men and being masculine is a pernicious and powerful force of identity and social relations. The professional values of the student affairs field are more expressive

BOX 9.3
Masculinity Media Assignment

For this assignment you are being asked to look at, listen to, or otherwise experience media with a critical view rather than simply "taking it in" for entertainment or information.

Identify a media source that you ROUTINELY experience (e.g., a favorite show, movie, radio station). Watch or listen to it in the same increment you normally would (an episode, the whole movie, driving to/ from somewhere, etc.), but THIS TIME, document the gendered messages in this media item.

Write a paper of approximately two pages in which you discuss the following items:

- What were your assumptions before working on this assignment about whether and to what extent gender messages exist in this media item?
- How did these assumptions get affirmed or challenged during your work on this assignment?
- What specific gender messages were contained in the media item? (cite examples)
- What are the implications of these gender messages? In other words, what might be the consequences (positive, negative, not sure) of these messages alone or in conjunction with similar messages in other media?
- Tell one other person, not enrolled in this course, about this assignment and your findings. What is that person's reaction?

Do not simply cover these questions in order. Take time to analyze and reflect on the media item, your assumptions, and gender messages contained therein. Give thoughtful discussion that incorporates the things asked about here.

If possible, you are encouraged to bring in a sample (e.g., a tape, picture, cut-out, print-out from a related website) to discuss in class.

and nurturing, and the majority of its practitioners might possibly be so as well, an aspect worthy of critical reflection and deliberation but beyond the scope of this chapter. Nonetheless, many, if not most, of our students arrive at college well-saturated in the binary gender and sex scripts and at least initially disinclined to consider or discuss them. Frankly, this is normal and to be expected, although our professional discourse treats it as a problem to be solved rather than the business condition that it is. It is no surprise then that programs labeled with terms such as *men's issues, toxic masculinity*, and the like are either poorly attended or low in enrollment numbers or attract students who represent the proverbial choir.

The implications of this situation are that students must either be compelled to participate, such as in disciplinary meetings, orientation programs, and required events for fraternity members and athletes, or the approach and content must be adjusted to be attractive. Be assured that it is possible to engage rank-and-file or particular groups of men students in a compelling and effective way without compromising the integrity of the course, program, or its goals. This might begin with simply naming and describing the opportunity in a manner that resonates with the dominant paradigm, or it might require a more elaborate effort so that the structure and promoted content do so.

For example, I developed an honors course for the women's studies department titled Guy Things: Men and Masculinities in America at a public predominantly White institution in the upper Midwest. During the initial offering, the course enrollment was 50% each of men and women and was the first time that more than a couple of men had enrolled in courses offered by the women's studies department. This was of benefit to the department and to the students, and the content of the course itself didn't require modification to maintain the men's interest. This resonates with a colleague who serves as the director of a university's theater arts program, who said that getting men to the theater the first time is hard, but once they attend, they keep coming. Experience has demonstrated this to be true with gender lessons as well, assuming care is taken to provide a proper invitation and introduction to the material. When contemplating how to get men to willingly attend events or enroll in academic courses or programs, it can be useful to begin with considering why they would avoid doing so. One such reason pertains to Kimmel's (2002) observation mentioned earlier, suggesting there is something personally threatening or embarrassing associated with attending or enrolling in these types of activities and programs.

This informed the reason for the title of the course Guy Things, which was humorous and disarming and avoided the use of the term *gender*, which often conveys women (i.e., not for men). This rhetorical strategy also had the effect of implying that the men who might enroll already have some expertise in the topic based on their lived experience, which also circumvented the common, often secretly held, insecurity among many men that they might face personal attacks or be made to feel stupid. As Berila observed in her reflections, "Because of widespread misperceptions, men are often 'scared away' from Women's Studies, while women are often afraid that the inclusion of men will shift attention away from women's issues" (Berila, Keller, Krone, Laker, & Mayers, 2005, p. 35). Student affairs practitioners interested in teaching gender and men and masculinities issues likely appreciate this dilemma. Feminist teacher Berila and four colleagues (including myself) discussed the implications of including men and masculinities studies in women's studies curricula (Berila et al., 2005). In a nod to the feminist context, each of the contributors offered their views on the topic. Berila pointed out that

> Women's Studies classrooms are often presumed to be safe spaces that must be protected from encroachment, but I am deeply skeptical of the notion that women-only spaces are inherently safe spaces or are necessarily safer spaces than ones that include men. (Berila et al., p. 35)

Berila's observation also alleviated my insecurities about ensuring an ethical entry as a cisgender male teaching women's and gender studies subjects to students of various identities. She further mentioned the stakes that women who hold intersecting, marginalized identities (e.g., queer, Jewish, of color, with disabilities, etc.) have in maintaining bonds with men who share their subaltern identities, pointing to the critical importance of intentional design, pedagogy, and dialogue facilitation for increasing the likelihood of success with these curricula. In the case of the Guy Things course, these considerations yielded positive results, and the pilot course was continued the next term. Although there are many excellent undergraduate textbooks (my course used a popular one by Kimmel & Messner, 2012), many instructors choose another good option, which is assembling a course reader with their preferred materials customized to accommodate the course's focus, context, and student population. See Table 9.2 for the weekly topics in Guy Things.

Promoting Men and Masculinities Topics in Other Academic Programs

Although courses about men and masculinities have a lot of value, it is not workable to rely primarily on this format. Such courses might not fit in many students' academic programs, or they might require a larger commitment than a student is ready and willing to make. Given the pervasiveness and primacy of gender in organizing identity and social relations, inclusion of a module in a broader general education or required major or minor course can be a valuable approach as well. It is already commonplace for student affairs practitioners to advertise their availability to speak with students in academic courses. For instance, health and wellness practitioners routinely offer to visit

TABLE 9.2
Guy Things: Men and Masculinities in America

Session	Topic
1	Welcome and Introductions: Masculinity Awareness Worksheet
2	What's All Men's Studies Stuff About, Anyway?
3	Perspectives on Masculinity I: Images
4	Perspectives on Masculinity II: Cross-Cultural Voices
5	Boyhood
6	Collegiate Masculinities
7	Men and Rape
8	Men and Work
9	Men and Health: Body and Mind
10	Men in Relationships
11	Male Sexualities I
12	Male Sexualities II
13	Men in Families
14	Men, Movements, and Future

courses to discuss campus resources relating to stress management, nutrition, and other issues that affect students' performance. Career center staff often visit classes to discuss employer recruitment or internships in the field associated with the particular course. Here again, readers are likely already familiar with such collaborations and offerings and how to elicit faculty interest in visiting classes. By extension, these same strategies can be used to collaborate with faculty or in any case to introduce men and masculinities topics to students in similar fashion.

Student affairs units and practitioners offering programs, services, and information about men and masculinities can begin with approaching more obvious academic departments and faculty such as those who teach classes about gender and other social identities to request opportunities to present or coteach relevant modules. It is just as workable to identify departments where men are the majority of enrolled students, such as engineering or computer science, and to arrange a visit to introduce students to men and masculinities issues by either presenting and discussing why men are overrepresented in those majors or to speak about the stresses men face in college and offer invitations to continue the dialogue or partake in program offerings.

Just as with other types of programs, novel incentives such as giveaways and food can be helpful. Bringing along like-minded men who graduated from the program or who work in that professional field to share how they bene- fited from reflecting on gender and masculinity can be a compelling strategy. The oft-repeated joke that professors are people too (e.g., references to the shock of encountering them in grocery stores and restaurants) provide great potential for encouraging faculty to share their reflections on gender as part of a discussion during or outside class meetings. Student affairs practitioners can be good peer mentors for their faculty colleagues to provide this powerful experience for students.

Other Forms of Credit-Bearing Masculinity Curricula

In preparing this chapter, a good colleague named Nick Bilich, who serves as coordinator of men and masculinity programs at California Polytechnic State University in San Luis Obispo, told me about an internship associated with his university's programs. According to the recruitment marketing materials for prospective interns, the "program exists to promote and cultivate healthy models of masculinity at Cal Poly" (N. Bilich, personal communication, February 12, 2018). Once selected, interns work in one of the specialty areas or partnerships such as Greek life or the marketing or assessment areas in the Student Affairs Division. Interns initiate discussions about issues of mas- culinity, plan programs and events related to these topics, and attend staff meetings alongside professional colleagues. Most important, they receive professional development training focused on understanding masculine role socialization and strategies for incorporating such concepts into their assigned areas. The internships are also considerate of the incumbents' career and academic goals, making them especially beneficial and supportive experi- ences for those serving in these roles. This model provides academic credit and relevant experience, making it instrumentally attractive to students and offers an opportunity to bring in interns from any major, which can be stra- tegically useful when directing efforts toward a particular department, col- lege, or subpopulation. This concept offers particularly robust potential for increasing academic engagement, retention, and graduation rates in partner- ship with academic deans and department chairs.

Community service-learning is a recognized high-impact practice with multiple benefits for students, academic programs, community partners, and social benefits more generally. Coordination of such projects are time inten- sive, and so a willingness to take on such tasks as establishing and main- taining relationships with community partners and tracking student hours can be greatly appreciated by faculty whose skills and obligations might not be suited to these tasks but are commonplace among student affairs practitioners. It is critical to remember that learning is scaffolded through reflections and connections. Hence, when employing experiential techniques such as community service-learning, it is essential that beyond the logistical elements discussed here, debriefing and processing experiences are incorporated into the design. One should not assume that assigning or participating in the tasks and projects, no matter how well planned, will achieve the learning and development goals intended. It is all too easy to focus on the instrumental requirements of the assignment and lose or diminish the substance. It is recommended that learning and development goals and the supporting literature (e.g., articles about masculine role socialization, college men's development, impact of experiential and service-learning) are transparent and overtly discussed before, during, and after the experience. There are many community service-learning projects that can focus on, incorporate, or relate to men and masculinities issues. These can include something as simple as having students provide subject-matter tutoring or even reading to boys. More focused efforts such as working on violence prevention programs might be appropriate as well. With that said, some projects can be transformational for men without being about them. Just about any task that transcends stereotypical limitations of masculinity by encouraging sensitivity, expression, and kindness can be transformational for students generally and for men in particular. This expands possibilities for partnerships that mutually advance the aims of faculty and academic programs, student affairs colleagues and programs, and students themselves. The following are a few examples to illustrate how men's issues can be implicated in a variety of activities in more or less obvious ways:

- Providing tutoring, homework support, or recreational activities to children in neighborhood community centers or living in domestic violence shelters
- Engineering students offering ergonomic assessments for people with disabilities to ease difficulties with certain necessary tasks
- Math- and statistics-related majors offering research and assessment support to human service organizations
- Developing and assisting with marketing campaigns and educational materials for antiviolence programs
- Providing blood pressure checks and other basic health program outreach targeting men to increase their self-care habits

Finally, much of what was discussed in terms of a lack of attention to men and masculinities issues in student affairs graduate preparation programs applies similarly to undergraduate peer education courses. The variety of credit-bearing courses offered to, or required of, prospective and selected resident assistants, teaching assistants, and other peer leaders can similarly benefit from incorporation of gender and masculinities issues. The merits and impact of peer education need not be revisited here. Rather, the point can be made that well-prepared peer leaders are in a particularly key position to speak about these issues with substantial credibility. They may also be well positioned to challenge fellow students in ways that are difficult for professional staff simply because of peer leaders' in-group status. Resident advisers obviously share living quarters with fellow residential students and are more likely than professional staff to be ready, willing, and available to have a powerful and transformative conversation in the middle of the night or on slow weekends when many men students' psychic armor is temporarily discarded. After all, how many readers' decisions to enter student affairs are rooted in such moments during their own undergraduate experience?

Conclusion

As indicated at the beginning of this chapter, there are many important considerations associated with designing and offering men and masculinities programs, whether for academic credit or not. Incorporating these issues into academic courses and programs involves additional opportunities and challenges that are worth the effort. Regardless, one's own preparation in the form of developing the knowledge, skills, and dispositions to credibly and ethically discuss these issues with students is much more consequential than a particular assignment, exercise, or format of delivery. The chapter discusses a variety of conceptual and philosophical dimensions associated with this work and offers some examples of course outlines, program elements, and ideas for implementation. Appendix 9.A provides a short list of online resources and sample assignments to support colleagues reading this chapter in engaging students in the project of elevating and expanding possibilities for men's gender identities and expression and those of all people as a result.

References

Ashlee, K., & Cash, B. (2017). *WGS370N: Exploring masculinities* [Course syllabus]. Oxford, OH: Miami University Women's, Gender and Sexuality Studies Program.

Berila, B., Keller, J., Krone, C., Laker, J., & Mayers, O. (2005). His story/her story: A dialogue about including men and masculinities in the women's studies curriculum. *Feminist Teacher, 16*(1), 34–52.

Brod, H. (2002). Studying masculinities as superordinate studies. In J. Gardiner (Ed.), *Masculinity studies and feminist theory* (pp. 161–175). New York, NY: Columbia University Press.

Douglass, R. (2017, August 4). More men should learn the difference between masculinity and toxic masculinity. *The Huffington Post*. Retrieved from https://www.huffingtonpost.com/entry/the-difference-between-masculinity-and-toxic-masculinity_us_59842e3ce4b0f2c7d93f54ce

hooks, b. (2000). *Feminism: From margin to center* (2nd ed.). Cambridge, UK: South End Press.

Kaufman, M. (1999). Men, feminism, and men's contradictory experiences of power. In J. A. Kuypers (Ed.), *Men and Power* (pp. 59–83). Halifax, Nova Scotia, Canada: Fernwood Books.

Kimmel, M. S., & Messner, M. A. (2012). *Men's lives* (9th ed.). New York, NY: Pearson.

Laker, J. (2005). *Beyond bad dogs: Toward a pedagogy of engagement of male students* (Doctoral dissertation). Retrieved from https://repository.arizona.edu/handle/10150/193751

Laker, J. (2015). *EDCO 289: Gender and the male student* [Syllabus]. San José, CA: Department of Counselor Education, San José State University.

Meth, R., & Pasick, R. (1990). *Men in therapy: The challenge of change*. New York, NY: Guilford Press.

Seabrook, R. C., Ward, L. M., & Giaccardi, S. (2018). Why is fraternity membership associated with sexual assault? Exploring the roles of conformity to masculine norms, pressure to uphold masculinity, and objectification of women. *Psychology of Men & Masculinity, 19*(1), 3–13. doi:10.1037/men0000076

Wagner, R. (2011). Embracing liberatory practice: Promoting men's development as a feminist act. In J. Laker & T. Davis (Eds.), *Masculinities in higher education* (pp. 210–223). New York, NY: Routledge.

ONLINE RESOURCES

Searching the Internet using the phrase *men's studies syllabus* will yield numerous samples that can be modified to fit a particular course.

> American Men's Studies Association, http://mensstudies.org/
>
> Michigan State University: Changing Men Collection, https://lib.msu .edu/spc/collections/changingmen/
>
> Society for the Psychological Study of Men and Masculinity: Division 51, http://division51.net/
>
> Stony Brook University: Center for the Study of Men and Masculinities, www.stonybrook.edu/commcms/csmm/
>
> Teaching Psychology of Men Web Resource Page, https://sites.google .com/site/teachingthepsychologyofmen/
>
> Voice Male, https://voicemalemagazine.org/
>
> XY Men, Masculinities and Gender Politics: The Latest Blogs, www .xyonline.net/
>
> XY Men, Masculinities and Gender Politics: An XY Collection, www .xyonline.net/content/curricula-men-and-masculinities-xy-collection

COMPREHENSIVE INITIATIVES AND PROGRAMS FOR COLLEGE MEN

Cameron C. Beatty, Jonathan A. McElderry, and Jason J. Dorsette

Historically, the importance of connecting men to curricular and cocurricular programs in higher education is important when considering outcomes and student success, specifically for men of marginalized identities (Davis & Laker, 2004). In the context of higher education, gender socialization appears to be viewed as an instructive theory of gender difference in achievement, degree attainment, and success—success being relative. Socialization tends to sculpt young boys into a "rigid, sexist, or restricted gender role" that often leads to many unhealthy choices by college-age men (Davis & Laker, 2004, p. 50). Despite the attention that many practitioners have given to the impact that socialization can have on people's understanding of their gender identity, not much direct attention has been given to focusing on the negative impact that social expectations have on young men and their self-perceptions of masculine gender norms. This chapter discusses the history of comprehensive cocurricular programs targeted at college men, how these programs are structured and implemented, and how these programs can affect the success of college men with historically marginalized identities.

Historical Intersections of Gender, Race, and Identity in Higher Education

Research on men's development has helped to raise awareness of the ways unhealthy hegemonic masculinity affects college men's lives (Davis & Laker,

2004; Harper, 2014; Harper & Harris, 2010; Pollack, 2001). Particular attention has been paid to college men who have historically marginalized identities and their experiences while navigating through postsecondary education. Scholars and practitioners have called attention to a deeper exploration of the ways marginalized college men experience their masculinity on college campuses, the ways curricular and cocurricular programs can support men's success, and strategies for developing comprehensive programs to achieve this success (Davis & Laker, 2004; Harper, 2014; Harper & Harris, 2010; Pollack, 2001). Both of the program examples we provide later in this chapter, from the University of Missouri and Oregon State University, center marginalized men and also offer a space for college men to critique Whiteness and masculinity and explore how masculinity is racialized. Marginalized college men include individuals from racially minoritized, sexual minority, and trans* communities. The following section provides some historical context related to the evolving understandings of men's identities and the intersections of gender, race, and sexual identity in higher education.

Black Boys

During their K–12 schooling, many young Black boys are exposed to false images of hypermasculinity that trade brutish intimidation for confidence and humility; thus Black students are socialized to not ask for help or seek academic support (Harrington, 2013). In a speech given at the Ohio State University in 2013, Terrell Strayhorn noted that some Black young men often finish high school unprepared for college because of their social, economic, and political roots (Harrington, 2013). Strayhorn explained that these learned behaviors have a negative impact on the retention, persistence, and graduation rates of Black men in college (Harrington, 2013).

American social psychologist Roger Brown (1965) argues that an example of hegemonic masculinity claims real boys are stiff, sexist, or restricted in gender roles that are developed during elementary school. The saying "boys are just being boys" reflects these role archetypes, defining a *boy* as one who fights, can vocally hold his own, and not cry. Ferguson (2000), who conducted participation observation research for three years at an elementary school, noted the disproportionate number of young Black boys being suspended from school or being labeled as "trouble makers" (p. 176). This ethnographic study centered the voices of young Black boys and allowed them to speak about how it feels to be labeled as deviant, delinquent, and unsalvageable by their teachers versus than being viewed as "boys being boys" (Ferguson, 2000, p. 96).

By middle school age, expectations for boys include participating in as many sports as they possibly can, competing for attention from girls, and demonstrating their strength by fighting or being disruptive (Edwards & Jones, 2009; Pascoe, 2005). During middle school, young boys of color in particular begin to realize that branding themselves as an aggressive, hard, verbal performer (i.e., using extreme profanity in the presence of teachers, verbally harassing women and queer folk) becomes a salient way for them to establish a dominant status and name for themselves and to achieve a high level of cultural capital and gain (Ferguson, 2000).

During high school, boys make the transition into young men; experience an increased amount of maturity by way of assuming more personal and social responsibility; and are expected to be antiacademic, promiscuous, and full of sexual experimentation and activity with woman as well as testing drugs and alcohol (Edwards & Jones, 2009). Morris (2012) refers to this approach to school as the "contrive[d] carelessness" (p. 54) phase when boys become more likely to be tardy or skip school, make light of or joke about how unprepared they are for a test or quiz, and adopt this "too cool for school" (p. 49) attitude. In particular, when Black men approach their second to third year of high school, they enter a realm of *Black men's privilege*, which is a concept defined as "aspects of Black men's lives [they] take for granted, men privileges that come at the expense of women in general and African American women in particular" (Woods, 2010, p. 28).

Sexual and Gender Minority Men

Similar to the emergent work on men of color and their masculinity, recent studies investigating the experiences of sexual and gender minority men and their masculinities have been explored (Catalano, 2014; Tillapaugh, 2015). Engagement in cocurricular programs and initiatives for sexual minority men became salient for students' making meaning of their multiple identities (Tillapaugh, 2015). Findings from Tillapaugh's (2015) research revealed that a greater exposure to social justice education led to an increased understanding of how power and privilege play out in sexual minority men's daily lives. Tillapaugh concluded that for sexual minority college men, developing a holistic sense of self, rooted in honesty to one's self and others, is a key aspect of a person's growth and learning. As noted later in the chapter, a holistic sense of self is becoming a common learning outcome for comprehensive men's programs.

In his research on transgender men in college, Catalano (2014) found some transgender college men were more engaged through leadership with their transgender identity, which included serving on panels on gender identity and engaging in positional leadership roles in lesbian, gay, bisexual, and trans* student organizations. However, some participants experienced increased burnout from their involvement. Others encountered difficulties with the tensions among subgroups of students (i.e., lesbian, gay, or bisexual students versus transgender students) or a reinforcement of the gender binary in student organizations (Catalano, 2014). Nicolazzo (2016) provided key implications for how educators understand and work in collegiate environments steeped in binary understandings of gender. For example, rather than situating trans* students as problems requiring accommodation, Nicolazzo problematizes the college environment and frames trans* students as resilient individuals capable of participating in supportive communities and kinship networks and of developing strategies to promote their own success. Nicolazzo stressed the need for trans* students to feel centered and have a community to process transphobia and oppression as a significant part of the liberation process. Although there are comprehensive men's programs that include some conversations on sexuality and gender performance in the curriculum and learning outcomes for the programs, very few center sexuality. As noted later, exploring the intersections of sexuality, gender identity, and race broadly are all topics and learning outcomes that practitioners should consider when thinking about developing comprehensive men's programs.

Developing Curricular and Cocurricular Programs

Davis and Laker (2004) proposed a framework for designing student services and programs for college men, guided by three fundamental questions:

1. Are they consistent with what we know about developmental theory and the socially constructed contours that shape men's development?
2. Do they recognize important differences among men and masculinities?
3. Do they balance challenge and support? (p. 49)

These questions are an excellent start to providing a framework for intentionally developing services to support college men. But we propose the following additional questions to consider when designing programmatic initiatives for marginalized college men:

4. Are college men from marginalized identities engaged from the beginning in the development of programs that are meant to serve them?
5. Do these programs and initiatives challenge hegemonic masculinity, White supremacy, sexism, and transphobia?

6. Do these curricular and cocurricular programs meet the equitable academic and social needs of the student subpopulation they are intending to serve?

The MDRC (2016) analyzed 82 support programs and initiatives and categorized their most common components: (a) academic advising and counseling, (b) academic and study skills training, (c) leadership training, (d) mentoring, and (e) special events. Academic advising and counseling includes help from professional advisers and counselors to create course-specific, sequenced pathways for earning a degree or certificate; navigate academic and social hurdles; and access available campus resources to support student success. Academic and study skills training primarily includes tutoring and study halls. Leadership training encompasses opportunities for students to demonstrate leadership in planning events and activities, community service, and managing or coordinating group meetings. Mentoring includes peer-to-peer and adult-to-peer mentoring relationships that foster a sense of inclusion, support students, and provide them with advice or guidance on how to resolve academic or personal issues. Special events encompass guest speakers, special presentations, conferences, and meetings on topics related to identity and student success (MDRC, 2016).

Although some comprehensive initiatives and programs have been designed to support men of color in college, even fewer support sexual minority men specifically. These programs have highlighted key outcomes and some of the failures of the programs focused on success. For example, since the early part of the twenty-first century with the evolution of the Black men's success movement, many books, articles, and initiatives were created to improve the status of Black men collegians (Harper, 2014). However, despite these efforts, this movement has failed to achieve its goals, which can be attributed to a lack of direction and strategy (Harper, 2014). There are several reasons that may explain the failure of the success movement. The homogenization of Black undergraduate men, misplaced onus for student success, amplification of deficits, and the creation of programs based on incomplete data can all be cited as key weaknesses of the movement (Harper, 2014). These failures to create successful movements can be seen in other minoritized college men subpopulations. Next, we offer two institutional examples of thriving comprehensive cocurricular men's programs and initiatives to provide key implications for practice and praxis in relation to serving Black and Latino community college men.

Mizzou Black Men's Initiative

The University of Missouri is historically White with an undergraduate enrollment of 25,898 students, 796 of whom identify as Black men

(University of Missouri, 2014). In 2009 the Mizzou Black Men's Initiative (MBMI) was created to address low graduation and retention rates among Black men on campus and was revamped in 2013 to provide course credit and focus specifically on the first years. The MBMI is a leadership development program of the Gaines/Oldham Black Culture Center at the University of Missouri. Taking into account the challenges associated with leaving home, the purpose of the program is to assist in the successful transition of Black first-year men to the collegiate environment.

Using a theory-to-practice model, the MBMI program is guided by Black identity development (Cross & Fhagen-Smith, 2001) and sense of belonging (Strayhorn, 2012) theories. The program operates under three pillars: support, development, and involvement. At the start of the academic year, student support is in the form of a needs assessment, development of short- and long-term goals, and regular office hours for staff to monitor students' academic and social progress. Development occurs through the mandatory first-year seminar Student Success Course 1150. In an effort to develop the skills necessary to emerge as a leader on campus, students participate in several required leadership and service-oriented activities on and off campus. Finally, students are encouraged to become involved through lectures from campus faculty and administrators and to use campus resources and engage in cocurricular activities.

There are many key elements to successfully implementing a Black men's initiative program. It is important for campus administrators to determine a need by looking at the campus climate and researching institutional and national data on these specific populations. Using a relevant theory- or research-to-practice model to design the program ensures acceptance from senior administrators, faculty, staff, and students. The MBMI program secured financial support by working with Mizzou's University Advancement to involve alumni; applying for local grants and seeking institutional funding from senior leadership can assist administrators in starting a program on their campus. Annual assessment can be used to tell the story of the program and its impact on the increased sense of belonging, high levels of campus involvement, improved grade point averages, and an overall positive experience in the program. The challenges to creating a program can be securing enough resources, the inability to engage all men in the population on the campus, and not seeing immediate results while the students are enrolled in the program. During the course of its existence, the MBMI has seen areas for improvement and many successes. By using a theory-to-practice model, the program sets a foundation and eases the entrance into a new environment by focusing on Black men's academic success, sense of mattering, and self-awareness.

Oregon State University Distinguished Scholars Initiative

Oregon State University (OSU) is a historically White public land-grant university and offers more than 200 undergraduate degree programs and 80 graduate degree programs. Furthermore, OSU is 1 of 2 sea-, space-, sun-, and land-grant universities in the United States. Similar to many other colleges and universities in the nation, OSU's underrepresented racial minority men (African American, Native and Alaskan Native, South East Asian, Pacific Islander, and Latino) have persistently lower degree attainment rates than their women counterparts and the overall OSU undergraduate population. In 2013 OSU enrolled 27,925 students with 52.8% (14,745 students) of them identifying as men and 1,881 of the male students identifying as Latino (OSU, 2018). To that end, in fall of 2016, after a series of institutional transitions, OSU decided to embark on a bold initiative to address the retention and graduation rates of men-identified students of color by creating the Distinguished Scholars Initiative (DSI). Initially, DSI was funded by an external grant focused on well-being from the American Association of Colleges & Universities' Bringing Theory to Practice program. These funds were then matched by OSU's Office of the Vice Provost for Student Affairs. The grant was awarded to OSU and 16 other colleges and universities with the intent to foster a collaborative learning community, encourage practices and development of policies that demonstrate institutional commitment, and promote transformative learning opportunities for higher education students. As of August of 2018, DSI became fully funded at OSU.

The mission of DSI is to academically, socially, and emotionally stimulate the ambitions of historically underrepresented men at OSU to ensure their success in the academy, community, and in their personal and professional lives. The four largest underrepresented men's ethnic groups at OSU at the time DSI was created were Latino, Asian, African American, and Native students (OSU, 2018). Hence, given the campus demographics, DSI participants are mostly Latino men followed by African American men. Furthermore, we initially refer to the student participants of DSI as *scholars* to reaffirm that they matter, they are intellectuals, and they are positive contributors to the academy and our greater society.

Using a hybrid of theoretical frameworks and approaches, DSI incorporates the model of Hispanic identity development (Torres, 2003), Black identity development (Cross & Fhagen-Smith, 2001), and sense of belonging (Strayhorn, 2012) and respectfully and appropriately draws from Black feminist legal scholar Kimberlé Crenshaw's (2011) intersectionality theory.

DSI is a cohort-based program with 25 scholars who meet biweekly in one of OSU's cultural resource centers (Asian & Pacific Cultural Center,

Lonnie B. Harris Black Cultural Center, Native American Longhouse Eena Haws, Centro Cultural César Chávez, Ettihad Cultural Center, Pride Center, and Women & Gender Center) and then individually and informally connect biweekly with an assigned OSU staff or faculty member. The collective cohort biweekly meetings are referred to as *general body* meetings, and the individual meeting with OSU staff or faculty members is called a *scholar DSI academic success coach meeting.* The general body meetings begin with an icebreaker or team building exercise followed by an interactive open dialogue or activity facilitated by guest speakers (mostly OSU faculty, administrators of color, or alumni of color) to address current academic social issues affecting men of color on campus. During this meeting we draw from Arao & Clemens's (2013) work, which discusses creating a brave space framework. Creating brave spaces is a strategic way to specifically encourage taking risks in discussions focused on broad social justice and diversity topics (Arao & Clemens, 2013). Constructing brave spaces is beneficial because they center genuine dialogue regarding challenging and controversial topics.

Scholars are also encouraged to participate in monthly reflection opportunities and respond to prompts on self-efficacy, academic success, relationships with faculty, and belonging, to name a few, through our DSI Canvas site. Canvas is the Oregon State University's Web-based learning management system platform that is used for course materials and all activities related to teaching, learning, and instruction. Finally, scholars participate in at least one civic and service-learning project per year and one out-of-state academic and cultural excursion. Similar to the MBMI program, securing resources to serve more students in a larger capacity continues to be a struggle for growing and sustaining the program over time. Considering funding sources but also continuing to be creative with cross-campus collaborations in academic affairs and students affairs helps address the concern of limited resources. Participating in campus collaborations, especially with supporting the service-learning project, is also an ongoing initiative to provide more men with the opportunity to engage with the each other and achieve the learning outcomes of the program.

Conclusion and Key Considerations

Many young men aspire to attend and succeed in college. However, postsecondary educational institutions around the country continue to struggle with how to best enroll, support, and graduate marginalized students. The need for evidence-based approaches that support men of color throughout the educational pipeline is evident, especially at the postsecondary level, where so many men of color and other men on the margins are so close to reaching their goals and fulfilling their potential as college graduates. Curricular and cocurricular comprehensive initiatives and programs in postsecondary education targeted to serve men, specifically marginalized men, can have specific contributions to men's success if designed and implemented with intentionality. Finally, we offer some key considerations when developing comprehensive men's programs, specifically those intended to serve and support marginalized men:

1. Using a relevant theory- or research-to-practice model to design comprehensive programs will ensure acceptance from senior administrators, faculty, staff, and students.
2. As noted in the MMBI example, securing financial support through working with the advancement office to engage alumni, applying for local grants, and seeking institutional funding from senior leadership can assist administrators in starting a program on their campus.
3. Remember to conduct regular assessment of learning and overall program outcomes. Annual assessments are great tools of evidence to tell the story of the program and its impact on the increased sense of belonging, high levels of campus involvement, improved academic performance, and an overall positive experience in the program for college men.
4. Be critical of who is really welcome in the space that is created for college men. People with what marginalized identities feel safe in the space? People with what identities feel unsafe? What is causing them to feel this way? Are all forms of masculinity acknowledged and celebrated, or is the comprehensive men's program privileging some masculinities over others?

References

Arao, B., & Clemens, K. (2013). From safe spaces to brave spaces. In L. M. Landreman (Ed.), *The art of effective facilitation: Reflections from social justice educators* (pp. 135–150). Sterling, VA: Stylus.

Brown, R. (1965). *Social psychology*. New York, NY: The Free Press.

Catalano, D. C. J. (2014). *Welcome to guyland: Experiences of trans* men in college* (Doctoral dissertation). Retrieved from https://scholarworks.umass.edu/cgi/viewcontent.cgi?article=1014&context=dissertations_2

Crenshaw, K. W. (2011). Twenty years of critical race theory: Looking back to move forward. *Connect Law Review, 43*, 1253–1353.

Cross, W. E., & Fhagen-Smith, P. (2001). In C. L. Wijeyesinghe & B. W. Jackson III. (Eds.), *New perspectives on racial identity development* (pp. 243–268). New York, NY: New York University Press.

Davis, T. L., & Laker, J. (2004). Connecting men to academic and student affairs programs and services. *New Directions for Student Services, 107*, 47–57.

Edwards, K., & Jones, S. R. (2009). "Putting my man face on": A grounded theory of college men's gender identity development. *Journal of College Student Development, 50,* 210–227.

Ferguson, A. (2000). *Bad boys: Public schools in the making of Black masculinity.* Ann Arbor: University of Michigan Press.

Harper, S. R. (2014). (Re)setting the agenda for college men of color: Lessons learned from a 15-year movement to improve Black men student success. In R. A. Williams (Ed.), *Men of color in higher education: New foundations for developing models for success* (pp. 116–143). Sterling, VA: Stylus.

Harper, S. R., & Harris, F. III. (2010). *College men and masculinities: Theory, research, and implications for practice.* San Francisco, CA: Jossey-Bass.

Harrington, S. (2013, January). Some black men face difficulty in college, Ohio State professor says. *The Lantern.* Retrieved from https://www.thelantern .com/2013/01/some-black-men-face-difficulty-in-college-ohio-state-professor- says/

MDRC. (2016). *Boosting college success among men of color: Promising approaches and next steps.* Retrieved from http://www.mdrc.org/publication/boosting-college- success-among-men-color

Morris, E. W. (2012). *Learning the hard way: Masculinity, place, and the gender gap in education.* New Brunswick, NJ: Rutgers University Press.

Nicolazzo, Z. (2016). *Trans* in college: Transgender students' strategies for navigating campus life and the institutional politics of inclusion.* Sterling, VA: Stylus.

Oregon State University. (2018). *Institutional research: Retention/degree/graduation reports.* Retrieved from http://institutionalresearch.oregonstate.edu/retentionde greegraduation-reports

Pascoe, C. J. (2005). "Dude, you're a fag": Adolescent masculinity and the fag discourse. *Sexualities, 8,* 329–346.

Pollack, W. S. (2001). *Real boys workbook: The definitive guide to understanding and interacting with boys of all ages.* New York, NY: Villard.

Strayhorn, T. L. (2012). *College students' sense of belonging: A key to educational success for all students.* New York, NY: Routledge.

Tillapaugh, D. (2015). Critical influences on sexual minority college men's meaning making of their multiple identities. *Journal of Student Affairs Research and Practice, 52,* 64–75.

Torres, V. (2003). Influences on ethnic identity development of Latino college students in the first two years of college. *Journal of College Student Development, 44,* 532–547.

University of Missouri. (2014). *Fall 2014 enrollment summary report.* Retrieved from https://musis2.missouri.edu/enrollment_sum_report/enrollment_summary _reports.cfm

Woods, J. (2010). Black men privileges checklist. In M. S. Kimmel & A. Ferber (Eds.), *Privilege: A reader* (2nd ed., pp. 27–37). Boulder, CO: Westview Press.

II

CONTEMPORARY ISSUES FOR COLLEGE MEN AND MASCULINITIES

Z Nicolazzo

He who has a why to live for can bear with almost any how.
(Nietzsche as cited in Frankl, 2006, p. 76)

Over the span of my career, I've had a unique relationship with the topic of college men and masculinities. Much of my time as a master's degree student at Western Illinois University and my professional experience in student affairs was invested in exploring notions of college *men and masculinities* (more on the italics later). However, I made an intentional decision to move away from this work when I pursued my doctorate at Miami University and in many ways have never looked back, or at least not for long—until now. Temporally speaking, my shift away from men and masculinities synced with—but was not because of—my coming out as trans*. The more I learned about myself and my trans* communities, the more I realized how notions of college men worked to erase trans* peoples' experiences. Furthermore, I realized how I, as someone who had previously understood herself to be a highly effeminate, queer cisgender man had reified normative (read ciscentric) notions of masculinity I now understood to be intensely limiting. So, yes, my move away from men and masculinities work was somewhat about my discomfort with my own complicity in propping up ciscentric understandings of gendered ways of being; however, it was also a self-preservation tactic and a way to learn about and be with my communities, which were erased, overshadowed, unknown, and—when we were discussed—exoticized throughout higher education research.

Over the past year and a half, I have been called back to men and masculinities work by some of the only people who could ever entice me to do so (and all of whom are a part of this book). Beyond providing scathing critiques on how scholars and scholarship on men and masculinities have mucked up understandings of trans* people—hence my use of the italics—my peers have asked for me to go back to my *why* regarding my research agenda, which centers on cultural discourses of gender and how these discourses mediate life chances for trans* people in postsecondary education. Although I am unapologetic about my centering trans* people in my work, I know that a part of my why must also be about how to "work the weakness of the norm" (Butler, 2011, p. 181) of gender, requiring an affirmative engagement with scholars and scholarship on college men and masculinities. In this chapter, I draw on what the other contributors to this volume have written to cultivate a call to action for college student educators on contemporary issues that are affecting the lives of college men, a category I embrace at its most capacious. In so doing, I propose a set of key considerations for student affairs professionals and faculty members to find their whys regarding gender-based educational praxis, because as Frankl and Nietzsche remind us in the epigraph to this chapter, if one has one's why, one can get through almost any how.

For Your Consideration

Pursuant to chapter 1 in this volume, I do not intend for what I write to be a dogmatic list of things educators must, should, or ought to do. Instead, I propose some ideas for the reader's consideration. In so doing, I invite readers to explore ways to think and do college men and masculinities work with more depth and prudence.

Consideration 1: Embrace Disembodied Notions of Men and Masculinities

One of the well-placed critiques of college *men and masculinities* work is that it often focuses on how the labels of *men* and *masculinity* stick to one's body in normative ways (Admin, 2017). Put another way, much of the previous research conflates the ways certain sexed bodies (e.g., those bodies that have a penis) are always already tethered to certain gendered realities (e.g., these bodies are masculine bodies and are presumed to be men). However, what is incredibly clear through some of the emerging research on college men, and the ongoing theorizing and research about gender beyond the field of higher education, is this is a false equivalency. Just as some bodies assigned male at birth don't align with masculine-gendered realities, many bodies *not* assigned male at birth *do*. Moreover, to suppose there are only two gendered possibilities (i.e., man and woman), and that they are dichotomous, is disingenuous at best, and dangerous at worst. For example, when we as educators negate the realities of female masculinity (e.g., Halberstam, 1998), how are we actively limiting life chances for people whose masculinity may not be written on their bodies in ways we have been socialized to believe they ought? Additionally, when we deny the ethereal and shifting nature of one's gendered experiences, how are we participating in reifying environments that also deny one's humanity? I invite readers to think beyond bodies in ways that recognize masculinity in various identities, expressions, and embodiments. I also invite readers to openly question why and how certain primary and secondary sex characteristics, attitudes, and behaviors even came to be known as masculine through U.S. cultural discourse. For example, men are not the only people who wear facial hair, and yet these people are often thought of as normatively masculine. This is a dangerous precedent to set, and one that limits who we think of when we do *men and masculinities* work.

Consideration 2: Embrace the Discomfort of Unlearning Cissexism

Look, I get it—admitting you continue to invest in cissexist ways of thinking is not a comfortable thing. It never feels good to openly admit when we hurt others, especially for those of us who pride ourselves on believing in equity- and justice-based work. However, I would counter that by *not* exploring, owning, and unlearning how we have *all* continued to engage in the propping up of cissexism, we are only furthering cissexism. Furthermore, as I often talk with students about, we need to think about our unlearning of oppressive ideologies as a both-and proposition. In other words, we need to recognize how we maintain systems of oppression (e.g., cissexism) and, at the very same time, are working to dismantle these systems. In this sense, either-or paradigms oversimplify our complex actions and provide normative judgments about ourselves linked to our behavior (e.g., we are good if we dismantle cissexism, whereas we are bad if we prop it up). As the character Harvey stated in the film *American Splendor*, "Ordinary life is pretty complex stuff" (Hope, Bergman, & Pulcini, 2003), and we need to embrace these complex realities, including that we can and do disinvest in systemic oppression at the same time.

So what do we do with this? We talk about it. We keep a journal about it. We move past the guilt associated with it. We find other people with similar identities and experiences to ours to hold us accountable, especially those of us with privileged identities. We go back to chapter 4 in this volume to recognize how our various identities mediate our experiences with gender.

We recognize that "social justice is both a process and a goal" (Bell, 2016, p. 3) and never stop unlearning how cissexism seeps into our lives, work, and research. We do all of this not to present visions of our own enlightenment but because this sort of vulnerable and intense personal exploration and sensemaking is itself an important part of the work of liberation (see also chapter 7 of this volume).

Consideration 3: Know Your Epistemological Leanings

I rather adore that Tillapaugh and McGowan structured this text to start with a chapter that highlights how one's epistemology serves as a foundation for educational practice (see chapter 1). In so doing, readers are invited to do some backward thinking (Tillapaugh & Nicolazzo, 2014) and recognize that how we come to know (e.g., our epistemologies) influences what we come to know and, by extension, how we put what we know into action. What Tillapaugh, Catalano, and Davis do in chapter 1 is quite smart in that it elucidates for readers what various epistemologies sound, feel, and look like in practice. In a field that is erroneously desirous of being results driven, however, we are not always (or often) encouraged to think about how we come to know (i.e., our epistemologies) shaping what it is we know and do. Therefore, our epistemologies are tucked away from view and framed as not mattering in relation to our work. This is a gross misstep, which I invite readers to reconsider and challenge. I invite readers to gather in groups and ask each other how they came to know what they know. I also would invite readers to recognize the linkages between one's epistemology and educational practice, as well as the potential possibilities and limitations therein. For example, if we come to know gender through constructivist leanings, how might this proliferate and restrict possibilities for gendered futures on our campuses? Moreover, if our epistemologies differ from those of our colleagues (e.g., those whom we may report to, such as senior student affairs officers), how can we speak and work with these colleagues in ways that center liberatory praxis for those students most on the margins? Sometimes moving backward is important to forward progress; I would offer this is one of those times.

Consideration 4: Move Beyond Mere Words

In forwarding this consideration, I have two things in mind. First, as I have written about elsewhere (Nicolazzo, 2016c), I have grown increasingly skeptical of people who continue to claim they want to do better in relation to issues of gender. When, I wonder, will they actually stop saying they want to do better and actually just do better? Second, I find the overreliance on merely shifting one's language (e.g., asking for people's pronouns, and sharing one's own in return; no longer using pejorative terms for queer and trans* people) as a signal of their forwarding progressive practice to be disingenuous. Yes, language matters, and we really do need to attend to the ways language mediates campus climates; however, if we are solely focused on language, we miss all the other ways gender negatively mediates college environments (Nicolazzo, 2017). Chapters 6 and 7 signal how educators can move beyond mere words to create better environments on college campuses. In addition to these authors' provocative considerations, I would invite readers to think about how they may use the notion of doing better as a way to not do further learning about gender. In other words, how do you share your desire of doing better *as a way to not actually do better?*

I also propose for readers to consider how words can and do cause actual harm, regardless of one's intentions. Although some words and phrases may seem innocuous to some, long histories and entrenched realities accompany some that are not easily forgotten. Moreover, some words are often used in particular groups—often in marginalized groups as a form of reclamation—that have quite a different ring, force, and impact when used by those who do not identify or experience the world in similar ways. Thus, although I invite readers to move beyond mere words, I also encourage readers to understand how the harmful impact of the words we use is much more important than—and regularly supersedes—their intentions.

Consideration 5: Take a Break From Higher Education Texts

It's perhaps ironic to suggest in a higher education text to take a break from reading higher education texts. It's all the more ironic because I myself write—you guessed it—higher education texts. However, there are two truths about higher education as a discipline: It is very young and, as a result, very behind in relation to expansive understandings of gender. Although this volume and various other books, articles, think pieces, commentaries, and gray literature are attempting to help the field of higher education catch up regarding gender analyses, the fact remains that there is an incredibly rich pantheon of work across fields and disciplines, as well as in and beyond the academy. I invite readers to engage with work, thinking, and activism in gender studies, disability studies, English, philosophy, race studies, ethnic studies, and art. I invite readers to watch shows like *Pose* (Murphy, Falchuk, & Canals, 2018), *Her Story* (Freeland, Richards, & Zak, 2015), and *My House* (Jonze, 2018) and think about how these shows push against notions of masculinity as affixed (or not) to particular bodies (i.e., Consideration 1). I invite readers to watch films like *Tangerine* (Baker, 2015) and read books like *Butch*

Queens Up in Pumps (Bailey, 2013) to think about how race and class mediate notions of gender and masculinity. I invite readers to follow the work of Black trans* activist and archivist Tourmaline (www.reinagossett.com) to disentangle how bodies are misunderstood, and how that misunderstanding is itself a result of patriarchal notions of normative gender. Although I do not advise we scrap the work being done in higher education—after all, I think books like this one and the work of my colleagues are quite rich—I do think taking a break and getting lost in some other fields, disciplines, and venues may not be the worst idea.

Consideration 6: Embrace a Trickle-Up Approach to Educational Praxis

As Ashlee and Wagner discuss in chapter 4, it is important to continually center those who are most on the margins. When thinking about college men and masculinities, then, this means centering the experiences of queer and trans* men, disabled men, men of color, and lower-class men, among others (and including those men with multiple marginalized identities). Beyond just centering these men's experiences, however, I have written previously about the need to embrace a *trickle up* approach to educational praxis (Nicolazzo, 2017). In other words, we as educators must guide our practice by those who are most on the margins, as any access or rights we gain for those who are most vulnerable will benefit—or at the least, not harm—those with more privilege. In terms of working alongside college men, I would invite readers to consider how centering those who are most on the margins is a way to disrupt normative notions of masculinity and, as a result, move beyond mere words (Consideration 4). I would also invite readers to think about what they need to do, individually and with their staff groups, to reframe their work through a trickle up approach. Once readers do this, my next question would be: What is holding you back from now putting this approach into practice?

Consideration 7: Move Beyond Best Practices

Readers who have engaged with my scholarship previously are likely aware of my disillusionment with best practices (Nicolazzo, 2016a, 2017). In brief, I find best practices to offer a false promise in that they suggest one-size-fits-all solutions devoid of institutional context and history. They also do not take into account how institutional memory or actors influence what occurs on any given campus and the differences between and among campuses. Although this book offers provocative perspectives and desperately needed epistemological and empirical shifts in relation to college men and masculinities, I feel compelled to caution readers to not view this text as a set of best practices. In fact, I would invite readers to consider any list of best practices, or promising practices or whatever new language shifts folks may be using of late, with more than a little skepticism. Are these practices actually worth considering for your campus context? Do they make sense for the populations you work alongside? What about them may (or may not) adequately transfer to your particular thinking, work, or practice? Rather than accepting these lists wholesale, as they are often understood, ask questions about the epistemologies, methodologies, and findings implied through these lists. Finally, I would offer that in seeking our whys, we are doing the work of eschewing best practices. In other words, we are finding our own purposes for our work rather than relying on some staid list of what we must, should, ought do, which is an investment in our particular locations, histories, and future possibilities.

Consideration 8: Disagree With Me

My last consideration for readers is quite simple: Do not take it from me. Just like I find best practices dubious, I never want to create the impression that I know everything in relation to contemporary understandings of gender. I am equally ambivalent about writers, consultants, and speakers who propose to fix or solve problems merely through their writing, consulting, and speaking. So I would invite readers to disagree with me, to push back on what I have written, and to not take my word for it. I caution readers, however, not to just disagree with me because you find what I have shared to be uncomfortable or rubs up against your previous practices and ways of thinking. Instead, disagree with me because there is a flaw in my argument or because it does not make sense for your institutional context. Disagree with me because I missed something or because you can extend my analysis but not because I have elucidated some previously unthought realities you prefer not to confront. All in all, I invite readers to disagree with me but to be careful about why, when, and how they do the disagreeing.

Conclusion

As Gossett, Stanley, and Burton (2017) have stated, visibility is a double-edged sword. Many of the contributors to this volume, myself included, have taken great efforts to increase awareness and visibility of previously invisible people for whom the category of college men and masculinities resonates. However, while we are deconstructing normative notions of gender, and specifically masculinity, we are also *re*constructing new normativities. As I have written about before (Nicolazzo, 2016b), the politics of visibility often lead to what I term the *hegemony of visibility*, or the idea that what is visible is real, true, and good. So although it is important to make visible those people who and populations that have always been shrouded from view, it is equally important to recognize that such a focus on visibility is mediated through interlocking systems of privilege and power and that relying solely or heavily on what or whom we see is in and of itself a limiting reality.

I share this as the conclusion to my chapter not to intentionally confuse or obfuscate what I have written but to suggest that what we know about any given topic (e.g., college men and masculinities) is not as simple, straight-forward, or easy as we may hope it to be. Just as we come to know new pos-sibilities and realities regarding the notion of college men and masculinities, we must contend with the new normativities these possibilities and realities may create. This, then, reminds me of the cyclical nature of the pursuit of social justice discussed earlier and should—I hope—evoke a response in you as a reader to never stop but always seek liberation and justice for the most vulnerable, whether we see them on college campuses or not.

References

Admin. (2017, September 6). Dear cis "gender" researchers: Stop erasing trans* people (part 1). [Web log post]. Retrieved from http://writewhereithurts .net/2017/09/06/dear-cis-gender-researchers-stop-erasing-trans-people-part-1/

Bailey, M. M. (2013). *Butch queens up in pumps: Gender, performance, and ballroom culture in Detroit*. Ann Arbor, MI: University of Michigan Press.

Baker, S. (Director and Producer). (2015). *Tangerine* [Motion picture]. United States: Duplass Brothers Productions.

Bell, L. A. (2016). Theoretical foundations for social justice education. In M. Adams, L. A. Bell, D. J. Goodman, & K. Y. Joshi (Eds.), *Teaching for diversity and social justice* (3rd ed.) (pp. 3–26). New York, NY: Routledge.

Butler, J. (2011). *Bodies that matter: On the discursive limits of "sex."* New York, NY: Routledge.

Frankl, V. E. (2006). *Man's search for meaning*. Boston, MA: Beacon Press.

Freeland, S. (Director), Richards, J. (Coexecutive Producer), & Zak, L. (Coexecutive Producer). (2015). *Her Story* [Television series]. San Bruno, CA: YouTube.

Gossett, R., Stanley, E. A., & Burton, J. (2017). Known unknowns: An introduc-tion to Trap Door. In R. Gossett, E. A. Stanley, & J. Burton (Eds.), *Trap door: Trans cultural production and the politics of visibility* (pp. xv–xxvi). Cambridge, MA: MIT Press.

Halberstam, J. (1998). *Female masculinity*. Durham, NC: Duke University Press.

Hope, T. (Producer), Bergman, S. S. (Director), & Pulcini, R. (Director). (2003). *American splendor* [Motion picture]. United States: Good Machine & Dark Horse Entertainment.

Jonze, S. (Executive Producer). (2018). *My house* [Television series]. New York, NY: Vice Media.

Murphy, R., Falchuk, B., & Canals, S. (Cocreators). (2018). *Pose* [Television series]. Los Angeles, CA: FX Networks.

Nicolazzo, Z. (2016a). "Just go in looking good": The resilience, resistance, and kinship-building of trans* college students. *Journal of College Student Development, 57*, 538–556. doi:10.1353/csd.2016.0057

Nicolazzo, Z. (2016b, September 25). Mirror, mirror on the wall: Why seeing isn't always believing in higher education (Pecha Kucha Session) [Web log post]. Retrieved from https://znicolazzo.weebly.com/trans-resilience-blog/mirror-mirror-on-the-wall-why-seeing-isnt-always-believing-in-higher-education-pecha-kucha-session

Nicolazzo, Z. (2016c, February 11). My exhaustion with the "do better" illogic [Web log post]. Retrieved from https://znicolazzo.weebly.com/trans-resilience-blog/-my-exhaustion-with-the-do-better-illogic

Nicolazzo, Z. (2017). *Trans* in college: Transgender students' strategies for navigating campus life and the institutional politics of inclusion.* Sterling, VA: Stylus.

Tillapaugh, D., & Nicolazzo, Z. (2014). Backward thinking: Exploring the relationship among intersectionality, epistemology, and research design. In D. Mitchell Jr., C. Y. Simmons, & L. A. Greyerbiehl (Eds.), *Intersectionality & higher education: Theory, research, & praxis* (pp. 111–122). New York, NY: Peter Lang.

AFTERWORD

I remember writing a literature review in graduate school and struggling to find research in the field of higher education and student affairs on men and masculinities. It motivated me to write my master's thesis and doctoral dissertation and begin my scholarly career focusing on topics related to gender and masculinities. *Men and Masculinities: Theoretical Foundations and Promising Practices for Supporting College Men's Development* illustrates how much has changed in the past 25 years. Rather than translating seminal work on men and masculinities from other fields (primarily psychology, sociology, and women's studies) into the context of student affairs in postsecondary education, this book demonstrates the ways evolving theories can be used to guide practices and programs that support and challenge college men's development. Although not dismissing earlier conceptual models—after all, science evolves through a series of experimental discoveries—Tillapaugh and McGowan situate this book's practice focus in the latest poststructural and critical frameworks. Moreover, instead of delivering a menu of prepackaged interventions as best practices, it engages student affairs practitioners with important questions like the following:

- What are the specific intended outcomes of a particular program, and what are the best ways to assess it?
- What are the sociopolitical implications of focusing on men and masculinities on your campus?
- How can coalitions be built to more effectively address multiple masculinities and forge the kind of alliances on campus that foreground mutual liberation?
- How do educators provide support for and compel accountability in college men?
- How can we model being with each other and learning in the highly contentious discussions involving identity politics so that we move together toward liberation rather than maintaining the stifling status quo?

Most centrally, the contributors to this volume grapple insightfully with pragmatic issues that influence the effectiveness of professional student affairs programming and practices related to college men. In fact, Tillapaugh and McGowan thoughtfully gathered some of the leading thinkers in the field to expand professionals' conceptualization of men and masculinities to include critical contemporary complexities. More than any other book I've read on men and masculinities, this text illustrates quite clearly and specifically the program frameworks and key considerations for actually doing theory—the nexus where theory becomes educational practice.

The preceding chapters show how much more we now know and need to know about the multifaceted identity dimensions of college men, their lived experiences in shifting historical-cultural contexts, and the often hidden but all too real ways that systems coalesce to subjugate and advantage. Although the complex critical theoretical frameworks are not fully elucidated, each chapter of this book is consistent with and illuminating in up-to-date sophisticated conceptual thinking. Moreover, the main purpose of this book isn't to articulate theory but to fill the immense void in translating what we know into practical efforts to promote growth and development in college men. Such efforts are needed for all students to improve learning, increase retention, and deliver the outcomes that society expects of higher education.

In addition to the questions raised earlier, several themes emerged that deserve additional dialogue, critical inquiry, and empirical attention. First, although intersectionality and critical and post-structural theories are thoughtfully described in this text, our practices lag far behind our philosophical frameworks. Readers are provided with clear markers for moving theory to practice. However, to effectively affect change, professionals will need to develop a praxis where theory is practice. It's worth spending time reflecting and unpacking the rich meanings associated with praxis so that theories become more than tools and professionals become more than technicians following blueprints and instructions. Praxis is the process by which theory becomes embodied. For me, it also represents the space between my epistemological assumptions, lived experiences, conceptual knowledge and a student with whom I am subjectively interacting. If I hold on too tightly to my own theoretical understandings, I force someone else's lived experiences into that box. If I listen deeply to someone without connecting to my own positionality, epistemology, and various theoretical lenses, I become just another traveler on the life path rather than a professional educator. According to Freire (1970), praxis is "reflection and action directed at the structures to be transformed" (p. 125). It requires one to read the word (theory) and read the world (critical awareness of one's own condition). For the current text to be more than a useful guide and to narrow the gap between theory and practice, student affairs professionals need to integrate the excellent insights offered in this book by asking critical questions, testing them, and assessing the conditions under which they work and are ineffective, hopefully resulting in a disposition reflective of mindful praxis.

The effectiveness gap that serves to prevent substantive challenge to the status quo regarding men and masculinities is crafted, in part, through dualistic and hierarchical thinking. The artificial distinctions we create, for example, between mind and body, self and other, and theory and practice need to be dissolved by practitioners. The resulting integrity that emerges can move us toward a professional disposition where interventions are not just universally applied but thoughtfully contextualized in a manner that honors students' full selves and particular subjectivities. For example, rather than simply using gender role conflict (O'Neil, 2015) to understand how men negotiate hegemonic masculinity, a discerning professional mindfully considers and asks questions about how disability, social class, and other important dimensions of identity repositions a particular person in a manner that might dramatically affect an intervention's effectiveness. Considerations of context, timing, political climate, developmental readiness, cultural nuances, and so forth also are part of a professional's radar screen for individual, programmatic, and policy interventions. Research needs to continue to expand, and new programs should be developed that reflect the lived experiences of college men who are still understudied and undertheorized in the literature, like trans* men, men of color, and religiously marginalized men. At the same time, our practice needs to balance our similarities with our differences. We should remember that although institutional oppression emphasizes how we are different, we essentially have common ground to build a foundation of understanding. As my close friend and colleague JQ Adams often articulates in his multicultural presentations, if you have a belly button, we have a shared humanity to build relationships toward realizing social justice.

Second, mindful praxis also pushes professionals to remember that they themselves are also multifaceted individuals who are idiosyncratically positioned in a complex culture of power. Such awareness shows up in practice as empathy for how systematic domination obscures unearned advantages and materially injures those targeted for subordination. That is, practitioners should expect denial of privilege or, on the other hand, anger related to past injuries resulting from oppression. Chapters 1 and 7 provide compelling clues for moving epistemological frameworks from abstraction to enacting practice and using self-reflexivity as a practical strategy for developing a professional disposition that is mindful, highly nuanced, growth inducing, and an embodied model of the changes we seek. Again, however, the space between theory and practice needs to be reduced and mindfully negotiated so that we engage students and others with balanced attention to conceptual content and pedagogical sophistication. Understanding how sexism operates and shows up, for example, does little to challenge the status quo unless professionals pay careful attention to learning processes that engage, invite reflection, and avoid shaming. Investigations into how professionals develop such a mindful disposition are sorely needed.

A third theme that materialized in the book relates to the dynamic balance between meeting college men where they are and providing sufficient support on the one hand and challenging hegemonic masculinity and reducing the negative consequences of patriarchal subordination on the other hand. Some chapters reflect a tone that disrupts the centering of men and masculinities, whereas others focus directly on college men, particularly those who are cisgender. Readers are encouraged to avoid the call to take sides and instead engage with the tension that arises from troubling the narratives that are being delivered. Learning in general and discussing topics that are rooted in the complexities surrounding identity politics in particular require a willingness to see some biases and limits in one's own perspective and the truths and cogency in another's viewpoint. According to hooks (2006), when we are more energized by taking someone's inventory and blaming than we are by promoting transformative learning, we are not relieving our own frustrations, we are actually creating an environment that reifies the status quo. I've written elsewhere about the dangers and ineffectiveness of using conceptual criticality without empathy and compassion (Davis, 2015; Davis & Moody, 2018). Again, there are significant insights in this text that will challenge readers to reflexively engage their blind spots, dogmas, and pain and frustrations that can lead to transference or other inappropriate and ineffective practices. The conceptualizing will, however, remain impotent unless we develop a clear understanding of how to employ what we know in practice. Research on curricular and cocurricular interventions that focus on helping practitioners develop effective pedagogical practices, like those offered throughout this book, need to be expanded. The current text is a powerful step in this direction and can serve as a resource for those seeking topics for future research, content for professional development workshops, and ideas for appropriate programmatic interventions.

Finally, the importance of student affairs professionals understanding history and context rise to the surface in this book. Conceptualizing college men's identity and how systematic oppression operates does little to improve practices congruent with equity, inclusion, and social justice if we fail to place ourselves and our interventions in historical and cultural contexts. Expecting an 18-year-old college student to immediately apply post-structural concepts like Butler's (1990) disembodiment of gender and focus on performativities belies the current context of high school education that often whitewashes

ethnic histories, conceals colonial legacies, and rejects gender-inclusive policies. Student affairs professionals practice in a very particular moment in
time and in distinctive social, political, cultural contexts. Developmental
interventions need to reflect awareness of the past and how it shapes the present. Someone unfamiliar with the Federal Housing Administration's redlin-
ing practices or systematic colonization implemented throughout the history
of this country, for example, will be less inclined to acknowledge the present
impact of historical racism. In addition, contextual factors like those offered
throughout the book, but particularly noted in chapters 2, 5, 7, and 9, can
offer scholars a career's worth of research evaluating college men's program
effectiveness, for example, given varying environmental factors like institutional mission, human demographics, macro-level policy shifts, and current
climates like the #MeToo movement. As mentioned earlier and elucidated in
chapter 10, the impact of context has very pragmatic implications in terms
of uprooting best practices that may be successful in one setting and quite
possibly ineffective or even harmful in other locations when key cultural
background factors are different.

Moving forward, scholars and practitioners are well advised to engage
with, disagree with, and raise questions about the insights offered in this
book, much like the vulnerability and growth-inducing process described by
Okello and Quaye's use of embodied autocritography in chapter 7. Rather
than outlining areas for future research or program development, I challenge
student affairs professionals to engage with the process of interrogating this
text, including my views here, to develop their own ideas about what needs
to be done. Such a challenge, if authentically encountered, will be unsettling,
invoke humility, and contain the possibilities of promoting real change. I
experienced all of these when I read the book from start to finish. I realized
how truly unfinished I am. Although I have added a critical theory praxis
to my work with college men, I realized how much more I needed to learn
about not only the lived experiences of trans* men, for example, but also
how to practice in ways that align with my values of balancing critical theory
with compassionate pedagogy, which I have previously termed *mindful masculinities*. Tillapaugh and McGowan have gathered an impressive group of
contributors and have put together a volume of scholarship. Student affairs
professionals can no longer complain that there is nothing available to assist
them with designing and evaluating effective programs and practices regarding college men and masculinities. My dear colleague and friend Rachel
Wagner asked me a decade ago to imagine what liberation looks like. Today,
I imagine it looks a lot like the process of honestly engaging with the challenging and insightful scholarship contained in the contributors' chapters
and implementing the programs and practices offered here with mindful

attention to important contextual, developmental, political, and historical nuances.

Tracy Davis
Professor and College Student Personnel
Higher Education Leadership Coordinator
Higher Education Leadership Track
Western Illinois University

References

Butler, J. (1990). *Gender trouble: Feminism and the subversion of identity*. New York, NY: Routledge.

Davis, T. (2015, September 5). Using tonglen in anti-oppression pedagogy to encourage "being in it" rather than "getting it" [Web log post]. Retrieved from http://www.contemplativepracticesforantioppressionpedagogy.com/blog/using-tonglen-in-anti-oppression-pedagogy-to-encourage-being-in-it-rather-than-getting-it-by-tracy-l-davis-phd?rq=davis

Davis, T., & Moody, B. (2018). Practices for promoting mindful masculinities. *New Directions in Student Services*, 164, 95–104.

Freire, P. (1970). *Pedagogy of the oppressed* (M. B. Ramos, Trans.). New York, NY: Continuum.

hooks, b. (2006, March). *Mind, body and soul*. Keynote address at the meeting of the Women of Color 11th Annual Conference, University of Oregon, Eugene.

O'Neil, J. (2015). *Men's gender role conflict: Psychological costs, consequences, and an agenda for change*. Washington, DC: American Psychological Association.

EDITORS AND CONTRIBUTORS

Editors

Daniel Tillapaugh, PhD, is assistant professor and chair in the Department of Counselor Education at California Lutheran University, where he primarily teaches in the Counseling and College Student Personnel Program. A graduate of the University of San Diego with a PhD in leadership studies, the University of Maryland with a MEd in counseling and personnel services, and Ithaca College with a MusB in music with an outside field of sociology, he worked as a student affairs administrator for 10 years before becoming a full-time faculty member. His research interests include intersectionality and student development in higher education, college men and masculinities, and college student leadership development and education. From 2012 to 2016, he served as the chair for the Coalition on Men and Masculinities, an entity group of ACPA–College Student Educators International, which focuses on the dissemination of research and practice on college men and masculinities. He has been recognized by ACPA as an Emerging Scholar Designee from 2016 to 2018 for his research on college student development. He is the coeditor of *Critical Perspectives on Gender and Student Leadership* (*New Directions for Student Leadership*, 154, 2017).

Brian L. McGowan, PhD, is assistant professor in the Department of Teacher Education and Higher Education and an affiliated faculty of African American and African diaspora studies at the University of North Carolina at Greensboro. He earned a PhD in higher education administration from Indiana University, an MA in higher education and student affairs from the Ohio State University, and a BM in music education from Old Dominion University. His research seeks to illuminate the lived realities of underrepresented students in college using college student development theories and critical frameworks. More specifically, his research primarily focuses on Black men's achievement, identity development, and interpersonal relationships. He served as scholar in residence for ACPA–College Student Educators International's Coalition on Men and Masculinities and is an invited scholar for Research, Integration, Strategies, and Evaluation for Boys and Men of Color, a national field advancement initiative. His research has been praised through awards and honors including the Tracy L. Davis Outstanding Emerging Research Award from ACPA's Coalition on Men and Masculinities and University of North Carolina at Greensboro's School of Education Distinguished Research Scholar Award. He is coeditor of *Black Men in the Academy: Narratives of Resiliency, Achievement, and Success* (Palgrave Macmillan, 2016).

Contributors

Kyle C. Ashlee is a doctoral candidate in the Student Affairs in Higher Education Program at Miami University where his research interests include critical approaches to student affairs graduate preparation, critical Whiteness studies in higher education, and critical perspectives on college men and masculinities. His career in student affairs features experience in housing and residence life, new student orientation, leadership programs, health promotion, and gender centers, both in the United States and abroad. In addition to contributing to the field of student affairs through his professional involvement in ACPA–College Student Educators International and NASPA–Student Affairs Professionals in Higher Education men and masculinities groups, Ashlee is the founder of the Ohio Consortium on Men and Masculinities in Higher Education. He has created award-winning college men's programming as well as innovative academic courses on men and masculinities. Ashlee was awarded the 2016 Social Justice Educator of the Year award and the 2018 Harry Canon Outstanding Professional award in interest groups of the ACPA.

Ryan P. Barone, PhD, is the assistant vice president for student success at Colorado State University, reporting dually to academic and student affairs, where he is also an affiliated faculty member in the student affairs in higher education and higher education leadership graduate programs. Barone received his BS from State University of New York, Fredonia; his MS from Colorado State University; and his PhD from the University of Denver in higher education with a specialization in diversity and higher learning. Barone has published or copublished book chapters, peer-reviewed journal articles, and presented sessions and delivered keynote addresses at regional and national conferences on topics related to social justice, men and masculinities, interpersonal violence prevention, and closing achievement gaps.

Cameron C. Beatty, PhD, is an assistant professor in the Department of Educational Leadership and Policy Studies at Florida State University, where he teaches in the Leadership Studies Program. His research explores the leadership identity development of students of color at historically White institutions and how student leaders navigate racial battle fatigue. He has presented and published on topics such as exploring and understanding the intersections of race, gender, and sexual orientation and redefining masculinity in higher education learning environments.

D. Chase J. Catalano, EdD, is an assistant professor at Western Illinois University in the College Student Personnel Program. Prior to his current role, he worked in student affairs in residence life, and most recently as the director of the LGBT Resource Center at Syracuse University. His research interest focuses on gender liberation, with specific attention to transmasculinities and trans student inclusion. He is coeditor of the fourth edition of *Readings for Diversity and Social Justice* (Routledge, 2018). ACPA–College Student Educators International selected him as an Emerging Scholar Designee for 2018–2020. Catalano received his BA in American studies and his MEd in higher education administration from Dickinson College and his EdD in social justice education from University of Massachusetts Amherst.

Tracy Davis, PhD, is a professor in the Department of Educational Studies at Western Illinois University where he also coordinates the higher education leadership track of the College Student Personnel Program. He has published widely regarding men's development, sexual assault prevention, and social justice, including his most recent book, *Advancing Social Justice: Tools, Pedagogies, and Strategies to Transform Your Campus* (Jossey-Bass, 2013). His research has won numerous awards including the ACPA–College Student Educators International and National Association of Student Personnel Administrators dissertation awards, and he served as an ACPA senior scholar in 2018. Most important, he remains wildly unfinished.

Jason J. Dorsette is a PhD student in the Language, Educational Policy, and Equity Program at Oregon State University, where his research interest includes issues of access and equity in the context of higher education informed by race, gender, and the interconnectedness of other social identities. He serves as the director for advancing academic equity for student success at Oregon State University and is a faculty member in the College Student Service Administration graduate program at Oregon State University. Dorsette received his BA in history and education and MS in public policy and administration from North Carolina Central University, a historically Black college. With more than a decade of experience in higher education, Dorsette has served in leadership capacities regionally and nationally in a number of professional associations. He was the recipient in 2013 of the ACPA's Standing Committee on Men and Masculinities Outstanding Men's Program of the Year award.

Keith E. Edwards, PhD, is a speaker, researcher, and author on sexual violence prevention, men's identity, social justice education, and curricular approaches to student learning beyond the classroom. His work has received national awards and recognition including ACPA–College Student Educators International's Doctoral Research Award and was named as an ACPA Diamond Honoree. Edwards earned his PhD from the College Student Personnel Program at the University of Maryland, where he completed his dissertation in 2007, titled *"Putting My Man Face On": A Grounded Theory of College Men's Gender Identity Development*. He has continued this research project through 5-year and 10-year follow-up interviews. He regularly works with campuses on professional development for faculty and staff on college men's gender identity and programs for college men. He is coeditor of *Addressing Sexual Violence in Higher Education* (Jossey-Bass, 2018). His TEDx Talk, *Ending Rape*, has been viewed around the world.

Zak Foste, PhD, is an assistant professor of higher education administration at the University of Kansas. His research focuses on how colleges and universities can create educational contexts that prompt students with dominant social identities to think more critically about their own social location in relation to systems of power, privilege, and the marginalization of others. His latest scholarship examined how White college student leaders construct and give meaning to whiteness on campus, desires for racial innocence among White undergraduates, and the gendered experiences of college men in service-learning programs. Foste received his PhD in higher education and student affairs from the Ohio State University.

Frank Harris III, PhD, is a professor of postsecondary education and codirector of the Community College Equity Assessment Lab at San Diego State University. He is best known for his expertise in racial inequity in postsecondary education and has made important contributions to knowledge about college student development and the social construction of gender and race in college contexts. His work prioritizes populations that have been historically underrepresented and underserved in education. Harris's scholarship has been published in leading journals for higher education and student affairs research and practice. Before joining the faculty at San Diego State, Harris worked as a student affairs educator and college administrator in a variety of functional areas. He earned a BA in communication studies at Loyola

Marymount University, an MA in speech communication at California State University Northridge, and a PhD in higher education from the Rossier School of Education at the University of Southern California.

Vern Klobassa, EdD, is the director of communication and staff development for the Division of Student Affairs at the University of St. Thomas. He completed his doctoral studies in educational leadership with a concentration in critical pedagogy. He is the past chair of the ACPA–College Student Educators International Coalition on Men and Masculinities and teaches in the Leadership in Student Affairs Program at the University of St. Thomas.

Brian Lackman serves as a leadership and social justice educator at Duke University. He earned his MA in higher education administration from Oklahoma State University. Lackman has experience in the development, implementation, and assessment of programming focused on the multiple dimensions of masculinities. His research focuses on social justice issues on college campuses.

Jason Laker, PhD, is a professor in the Department of Counselor Education (and former vice president for student affairs) at San Jose State University. He previously served as associate vice principal and dean of student affairs, as a fellow in the Centre for the Study of Democracy, and on the gender studies faculty at Queen's University in Canada. He holds a PhD in higher education administration and organization from the University of Arizona and an MA in community counseling from Adams State University. His international activities include board member, visiting faculty, consultant, or speaker, particularly in Europe. His scholarly work includes four edited texts in the United States and Canada regarding gender and men's development and two on citizenship and democratic education. His current research with Erica Boas focuses on sexual consent among college students. Laker has received several awards for his scholarship and leadership on men's and masculinities issues.

Jonathan A. McElderry, PhD, serves as the assistant dean of students and director of the Intercultural Center at Wake Forest University. His experience in higher education has focused on enhancing diversity, equity, and inclusion on college campuses. Additionally, his research has sought to raise awareness of the experiences of underrepresented students at predominantly White institutions and provide strategies to increase their academic and social success. He has presented nationally and internationally, held leadership positions in ACPA–College Student Educators International, and has received several awards for his work in higher education. McElderry earned a PhD in educational leadership and policy analysis with an emphasis in higher education from the University of Missouri, an MEd in college student personnel from Ohio University, and a BS in administration of justice from George Mason University.

Z Nicolazzo, PhD, is an assistant professor of trans* studies in education in the Center for the Study of Higher Education at the University of Arizona. Her research focuses on discourses of gender in higher education, with a specific focus on affirmative and resilience-based studies alongside transgender students and educators in postsecondary education contexts. She also has written about trans*-centered epistemologies and methodologies in educational research. Nicolazzo received her BA in philosophy from Roger Williams University, her MS in college student personnel from Western Illinois University, and her PhD in student affairs in higher education from Miami University. Nicolazzo has five years' full-time student affairs experience and is the author of *Trans* in College: Transgender Students' Strategies for Navigating Campus Life and the Institutional Politics of Inclusion*, (Stylus, 2017).

Wilson Kwamogi Okello, PhD, is a visiting assistant professor of Black World Studies in the Department of Global and Intercultural Studies at Miami University. His research is an intervention against schooling as an overarching system of thinking that functions through curricular and conditioning strategies to reproduce the status quo. Bridging the scholar-artist divide, he employs Black feminisms and aesthetics to critique and advance meaning-making theory and pedagogical praxis. Theorizing with Black feminism has allowed him to interrogate epistemological and ontological frames that serve to reproduce rationality, (self-)destructive behaviors, and social inequality. His work has appeared in the *Journal of College Student Development*, *Africology: The Journal of Pan African Studies*, and the *International Journal of Qualitative Studies in Education*.

Peter Paquette, PhD, serves as the dean of students at Coastal Carolina University. His current research focuses on college student resiliency and persistence and the experiences of first-generation college students and first-generation higher education executives. He has done extensive research and program development on the experiences of men and masculinities in college, and he has implemented numerous programs for college men to deconstruct masculinity and the role it plays in their lives. He has more than a dozen years' experience as a higher education administrator. Prior to his post at Coastal Carolina University, he served in administrative roles at Emory University, Georgia Institute of Technology, Dickinson College, North Central College, and Loyola University-Maryland. He holds a BS in graphic design and communication studies from Edgewood College, an MA in higher education and student affairs administration from the Ohio State University, and a PhD in counseling and student personnel services from University of Georgia.

Stephen John Quaye, PhD, is an associate professor in the Student Affairs in Higher Education Program at Miami University and past president of ACPA–College Student Educators International. He values the power of dialogue and activism as vehicles to promote change in society and is currently studying the strategies Black student affairs educators use to heal from racial battle fatigue. His work is published in different venues, including the *Journal of College Student Development*, the *Journal of Diversity in Higher Education*, and *Teachers College Record*. He is also coeditor of *Student Engagement in Higher Education: Theoretical and Practical Approaches for Diverse Populations* (Routledge, 2015) and coauthor of the latest edition of *Student Development in College* (Jossey-Bass, 2016). His PhD is from Penn State University, his MA is from Miami University, and he holds a BA from James Madison University.

Cristobal Salinas Jr., PhD, is an assistant professor in the Department of Educational Leadership and Research Methodology at Florida Atlantic University. His research promotes access and equality in higher education and explores the social and political context of education opportunities for historically marginalized communities. His research reflects the lived experiences of and is in partnership with historically marginalized communities that are oppressed at the institutional, cultural, and individual level. At the institutional level he studies community colleges, hazing and language at the cultural level, and at the individual level he focuses on the experiences of men of color in educational settings. He is founder and manager editor of the *Journal Committed to Social Change on Race and Ethnicity*.

Lucas Schalewski serves as the associate director of assessment, research, and grant development in the University of Arizona's Division of Student Affairs, Enrollment Management, Academic Initiatives, and Student Success. In this role, he provides consultation and data analysis support on assessment to more than 45 units in the division. Schalewski is currently pursuing a PhD at the University of Arizona's Center for the Study of Higher Education. He holds an MS in college student services administration from Oregon State University and a BS from the University of Wisconsin–Whitewater.

Taj Smith, EdD, is the director of the Center for Diversity and Inclusion at Xavier University. He completed his doctoral studies in education with a concentration in social justice education at the University of Massachusetts Amherst. His dissertation assessed the participant impact of Phallacies, a men's health promotion and dialogue program.

Chris Taylor, PhD, has been a student affairs practitioner for more than 25 years, serving in residence life and student conduct positions at public and private institutions, and is the current director of community standards at Wright State University. He is the former cochair of the Masculinities Committee at Miami University, where received his PhD in student affairs in higher education. His research interests include college-age men and hegemonic masculinity, and his dissertation focused on adherence to masculine role norms in fraternity men.

Jamie Utt is a doctoral student in the Department of Teaching, Learning, and Sociocultural Studies at the University of Arizona, where he studies critical mixed methodologies and the intersections of race and schooling. He also has worked for a decade in the field of sexual violence prevention through the lens of engaging men to understand their role and investment in ending gender-based violence. In this capacity, Utt has consulted with colleges and universities throughout the United States and Canada on effective, research-driven strategies for sexual violence prevention and interrupting hegemonic masculinity.

Rachel Wagner, EdD, is an assistant professor in higher education and student affairs in the Department of Educational and Organizational Leadership at Clemson University. The goal of her research is to understand how postsecondary environments can support human flourishing. Specifically, her scholarship centers critical and emancipatory perspectives of equity and social justice in higher education through two primary areas of inquiry: gender-aware and expansive practice in higher education and social justice approaches to student affairs practice.

Vernon A. Wall has accumulated more than 30 years of professional student affairs experience at Iowa State University, the University of Georgia, University of North Carolina at Charlotte, and University of North Carolina at Chapel Hill and has experience in Greek life, new student orientation, student activities, leadership development, global education, and university housing. Wall currently lives in Washington DC, and is the director for business development at LeaderShape and also president and founder of One Better World, a consulting firm specializing in engaging others in courageous social justice and equity conversations. With degrees from North Carolina State University and Indiana University, he is the consummate scholar-practitioner. He has received several awards for his contributions to the quality of student life, is a nationally known speaker in the areas of social justice and leadership, and is one of the founders and facilitators of Social Justice Training Institute.

INDEX

Abes, E. S., 78
accountability, 34, 70–71, 84, 131–35
ACPA. *See* American College Personnel Association
Adams, J. Q., 207
Adams, M., 120
African Americans, 8, 42, 76, 133, 147–49, 156, 191
American Association of Colleges & Universities' Bringing Theory to Practice program, 191
American College Personnel Association (ACPA), 9–10, 11, 140
American Men's Studies Association, 10, 11
American Personnel and Guidance Association, 9
American Psychological Association, 10, 11
Anderson, K., 38
Anzaldúa, G., 131
Arao, B., 192
Arbeit, M. R., 116–17
ASHE. *See* Association for the Study of Higher Education
Ashlee, Kyle C., 13, 200
Asian Americans, 42, 44, 46–47, 191
assessment framework, outcome-based, 124, 150, 157–58, 160, 190
  assessment cycles use in, 89–90
  assessment methods design in, 93, 95–96
  challenges in, 103
  as culturally mindful, 102
  data collection and analysis in, 97–98
  definition of, 89

  equity and student populations in, 102
  findings communication in, 98–99
  goal identification and alignment in, 90
  guiding theoretical framework in, 101–2
  human capacity resource in, 103
  implementation of, 90
  institutional review board and research office meeting for, 103
  intersectional feminist perspectives in, 102
  learning and program outcome development in, 91–93, 94
  Multi-Institutional Study of Leadership Survey use in, 103
  program development integration in, 104
  refine and change phase in, 99–101
  Schuh on, 103–4
  Taking Off the Masc as, 90–91, 93, 101–2, 108–10
assessment methods design
  direct and indirect measures in, 93, 96
  intended outcomes measuring in, 93
  mixed-methods approaches in, 95
  qualitative method examples and advantage in, 93, 95
  quantitative method examples and advantage in, 95
  rubrics use and benefits in, 93, 95–96
  student learning and program outcomes in, 96

self understanding in, 33
three main steps in, 25
gender role conflict, 41–42, 47, 155,
175, 207
Gerschick, T. J., 49
Goodman, D., 120
Gossett, R., 201
Greer, K. R., 50
Guido, F. M., 5
*Guyland: The Perilous World Where Boys
Become Men* (Kimmel), 3–4, 155

Harper, Shaun R., 2, 8, 12–13, 39–45,
140, 147, 150
Harris, Frank, III, 2, 8, 12–13, 39–45,
47 150
Harris, J. C., 7
Heasley, R., 117–18
hegemonic masculinity, 48, 59, 76,
137–38, 144, 147, 149
dangers of, x
gender socialization and
interpersonal violence workshop
attempt in, ix–x
#MeToo movement against, x–xi
negative impact of, ix
racism intersection with, x
resisting impacts of, x–xi
Rodger on, x
soul murder and, ix
Hickmott, J., 89
Hill, Marc Lamont, 140
hooks, b., 170, 208
Howes, L., 38

Identity Map Sharing, 82
I-MMDI. *See* intersectional model of
multiple dimensions of identity
Innes, R. A., 38
intergroup dialogue, 145
active listening in, 133
Black feminism in, 136–37
critical-dialogic framework of,
132–33
dialogue principles for, 133

dominant and subordinated
identities in, 132, 133
facilitators example in, 132
goal of, 132
logics and ideas constraint in, 135
oppression impact reduction in, 133
oppression systems dismantling in,
132
principles of, 139
progressive identity politics in, 136
questioning mind-set adoption in,
133
scholarship reliance error in, 135
self-reflexivity and accountability in,
133
Stephen's self-reflexivity and
accountability in, 133–34
Wilson's self-reflexivity and
accountability in, 134–35
intergroup dialogue, feminist
reimagination of
autocritography in practice for, 139
privilege and oppression naming in,
139–40
Stephen's privilege addressing
example in, 139–40
Stephen's response and rewrite
example in, 142
vulnerability and emotion in, 139
Wilson's reflection on Stephen's
response example in, 143
Wilson's response example in,
140–42
intersectionality theory, xii, 4–5, 32,
75, 102, 161
I-MMDI and, 77, 79–80, 86
original creation of, 79
retreats use of, 113–14, 117–18
student development use of, 43, 50
as theoretical tool, 79
intersectional model of multiple
dimensions of identity (I-MMDI),
80, 86
context importance and example in,
78

For Product Safety Concerns and Information please contact our EU
representative GPSR@taylorandfrancis.com
Taylor & Francis Verlag GmbH, Kaufingerstraße 24, 80331 München, Germany

www.ingramcontent.com/pod-product-compliance
Lightning Source LLC
Chambersburg PA
CBHW050349270326
41926CB00016B/3661

* 9 7 8 1 6 2 0 3 6 9 3 1 9 *